About the Author

Serge Latouche is one of France's most eminent development economists. In recent years, a succession of books has added further lustre to his reputation as a highly original – not to say controversial – theoretician and critic. These include: *La Planète des naufragés: essai sur l'après-développement* (1991 – *In the Wake of the Affluent Society* is the English title of this book); *L'Occidentalisation du monde: essai sur la signification, la portée et les limites de l'uniformisation planétaire* (1989 – already translated into Italian, Arabic, Turkish and Farsi); and *Faut-il refuser le développement?* (1986). Altogether he is the author of nine works published by the French houses Presses Universitaires de France, Anthropos and La Decouverte. In addition, he serves on the editorial boards of *La Revue du MAUSS* and *L'Homme et la société*.

Professor Latouche began his career teaching Economics, first in Zaire, and subsequently in Laos, before joining the staff of the University of Science and Technology at Lille. He does a lot of consultancy work in Third World countries and is a member of the international South/North Cultures and Development Network. Since 1991 he has been Professor of Economics at the University of Paris XI.

From reviews of the French edition:

'He moves the debate on to the terrain of a critique of the basic utilitarian principles of the discourse of political economy ... . He charts the contradictions and perverse results produced by the very idea of development and criticises a developmentalist ideology postulated on the essentially Western notion that competition will automatically bring material prosperity for all.'
Economic Alternatives, January 1992

'Serge Latouche writes essentially about the failures of development ... . He should be thanked for having written a book which will perhaps prevent liberals from falling asleep on their laurels.'
Michel Lutfalla, *La Nouvel Economiste*, 29 November 1991

'Serge Latouche overthrows systematically the basic myths of development.'
Jeune Afrique Economie, December 1991

'With each successive book, Serge Latouche's denunciation of the mainstream society is gaining in vitality and rigour ... . His pages devoted in this work to the informal economy, appropriate technology and self-sufficiency are precise and original.'
Jean Chesnaux, *Le Monde Diplomatique*, November 1991

'A hard book because the author makes Westerners, so proud of their modernity, confront the global consequences ... . He does not underestimate the immense progress afforded humanity by the advances of the industrial world but he places them in context ... . He invites us to resist our ethnocentrism and suggests we should believe in a society very different from the one we inhabit, a society where the standard of living is not as important as the quality of life and where a reduction in the welfare of so many people is seen as an absurdity ... . A courageous analysis.'
Pierre Drouin, *Le Monde*, September 1991

In the Wake of
the Affluent Society

An exploration of post-development

Serge Latouche

Introduced and translated by

Martin O'Connor and Rosemary Arnoux

Zed Books Ltd

London & New Jersey

In the Wake of the Affluent Society was first published by
Zed Books Ltd, 7 Cynthia Street, London N1 9JF , UK
and 165 First Avenue, Atlantic Highlands, New Jersey,
07716, USA, in 1993. The French-language edition was first published as
La Planète des naufragés: essai sur l'après-développement by
Editions La Découverte, 1 Place Paul-Painlevé, 75005 Paris in 1991

Copyright © Editions La Découverte, 1991
Translation Copyright © Zed Books Ltd, 1993

Cover designed by Andrew Corbett

Typeset by Ray Davies
Printed and bound in the United Kingdom by
Biddles Ltd, Guildford and King's Lynn

The right of Serge Latouche, the author of
this work, has been asserted by him in
accordance with the Copyright, Designs and
Patents Act 1988.

A catalogue record for this book is available
from the British Library

US CIP is available from the Library of Congress

ISBN 1 85649 171 4 Hb
ISBN 1 85649 172 2 Pb

It is only a matter of time before what Westerners would call a 'major catastrophe of global proportions' takes place. It will be the job of the Amerindian peoples, of all the 'natural' populations, to survive.

Russel Means, of the Lakota Oglala tribe in North America, in 'Toujours la même rengaine,' *Revue du MAUSS* no. 7, 1990, p. 71

Contents

Part II   The Island Refuge

Translators' Introduction

This book has two themes, which are two sides of a coin. First, the coming apart at the seams of the Western dream of a modern, affluent, 'liberal' (and liberated) world community of nations – *the foundering of the 'grand society'*, the collapse of the *development* myth. Second, the flowering within the cracks and chasms of this modernity, within fragmenting nation-states and between the lines of transnational market society, of new social forms – *the informal* – which herald possible ways out of the impasses of modernity.

Both these theses – the disrepair of the Western *projet de société*, and the emergence of the informal as an undergrowth of novel solutions to problems of survival – are controversial. How can one doubt the Western model of society, at a time when 'the market' has unprecedented ascendancy in the West as in the East, and when democratisation of political forms is enunciated as an irreversible progressive trend? Third World economic development has had its setbacks, but surely it is still only a matter of time, and political will?

In this book, as in several previous ones, Serge Latouche sets out to question this Western vision. His work as a whole is an unremitting critique of 'development', its theory and practice, considered as an Occidental artifact miscarried into the Third World. The progressions of the market and of Western political forms across the world are a matter of historical fact. But, he argues, it is only by a selective reading of the facts, a filtration of events through the *Western 'social imaginary'*,* that one sees Progress where, from other points of view, there is none. In this Introduction we try to give an overview of the main themes and preoccupations of this book showing how it builds upon his earlier work, and thus giving a feel for the evolution of his thought.

*

* Here, as throughout the book, we use the term 'social imaginary' along the enlarged lines of the French *l'imaginaire* – the symbolic domains of social myth, ideology, common sense through which people live, communicate, and define the meanings and significance (*significations*) in a society.

Serge Latouche is currently Professor of Political Economy at the Faculty of Law, Université de Paris XI (Sud), and for several years previously held a chair in political economy in the Law School at the Université de Lille II, in north-east France. At the same time he is a research director at the Institut d'Etude du Développement Economique et Social (IEDES) of the Panthéon-Sorbonne, Université de Paris I. His two main fields of work are the epistemology of the social sciences and underdevelopment in the Third World.

In the course of his doctoral studies on worldwide pauperisation many years earlier, he taught for some time in the 1960s in Central Africa, and then in Laos. In 1967 he returned to live in Paris. Apart from his early teaching posts in the Third World, he has travelled extensively in Africa and in Western and Eastern Europe. Along with his several books, he has published numerous articles in political philosophy, critical social theory and on underdevelopment. He has also been a central figure in the Paris-based network Mouvement Anti-Utilitariste dans les Sciences Sociales (MAUSS) and in the management of its journal, the *Revue du MAUSS* (published by La Découverte, Paris) which, since its inception in 1982, has become an important forum for critiques of the hegemony of utilitarian reasoning in modern societies. Some of his books and numerous papers have also been translated into Spanish, Italian and Portuguese; but to date very little in English.

*

The theme of Part I of this book is the *'naufrage de la grande société'* – the shipwreck of the grand society, or what Latouche believes is the foundering of the Western myth of unlimited affluence and progress. This 'grand society' is simultaneously many things. Latouche's original term, *la grande société*, is the French rendering of Friedrich Hayek's 'great society' made up of free and freedom-loving individuals. Western society is *great* according to Hayek, not only because it is tending to extend itself on a planetary scale, but also because of its vocation of welcoming the whole of humanity within it, permitting to each and every person the greatest self-realisation possible. This is also Karl Popper's 'open society' characterised by emancipation through democratic debate and scientific progress. It is the 'affluent society' of mass consumption, notably critiqued by John Kenneth Galbraith. And, more prosaically, it is the 'world marketplace' brought about through the generalisation of economic development and international trade.

Retranslating from the French, we have preferred to keep the adjective '*grand*'. This makes it clear, first, that Latouche is not bound only to Hayek's concept. It also allows for the slightly archaic connotation of grandeur – the grandeur of a dream, of an ideal. This is particularly appropriate given the sense of tragedy which Latouche seeks to evoke, with his theme of *naufrage* – the foundering of the Western dream of unlimited affluence. It is also appropriate given his second theme, in Part II of the book, of *la nouvelle vie* – the new ways of life within the 'informal' sectors of society being improvised by development's castaways, who are abandoning modernity's myths in the face of a modernity that has abandoned them.

In Chapter 1 of this book, and then at more length in Part II, Latouche describes the dereliction which is the other face of modernity, the lived reality of the 'outcasts from the consumer society's banquet'. This is the 'planet of the outcasts' designated by the book's original title: *La Planète des naufragés* – the homeland of development's castaways, shipwrecked on the inhospitable shores of modernity. These are the 'have-nots' of riot-torn Los Angeles, as much as of Somalia in its disintegration or the Rio de Janeiro shantytowns, the inhabitants of the real global village who have not found a place at the great banquet table of the consumer society. Some three or four billion people round the globe get to share only the crumbs and leftovers from the feast: 'Interned or refugees, neglected in the countryside or uprooted in the towns, unemployed, without work or protection, this vast company of people live in a sort of enchanted – or disenchanted – limbo, outside the law, concealed within the global village.' In effect, Latouche asks: If this is the scale of 'underdevelopment', are we justified in concluding that development, the Western model, is the solution to humanity's miseries, or is it rather part of the problem?

*

In the Preface to this book, Latouche insists on 'the primacy of a theoretical dimension' to his work. He is primarily concerned with the *interpretation* of socio-economic change in Third World societies. Still, his book is evocative in style rather than being systematically theorised, and it is very much an empirically grounded study. First, because of the detailed use he makes of others' empirical work, especially from African sources. But also as an intimate scrutiny of what we might call the development industry – that vast buzz of activity, both intellectual and material, of government, corporate and charitable enterprise in the West itself.

To understand this book fully, it has to be seen in the context of debates in the Francophone world involving academics, researchers, non-governmental organisations (NGOs) and activist groups of all sorts. Inevitably some of the nuances of the debate will be lost on readers not familiar with the French scene. Conversely, the reader is introduced to some of the distinctive elements of development debates within the Francophone world. Latouche's own studies in the 'Third World' – the 'South', or 'Periphery', or whatever other problematical name we might choose – began with his doctoral thesis entitled *La Paupérisation à l'échelle mondiale* (Pauperisation on a World Scale) (1966) based on studies in Francophone Africa. This amounted to a transposition onto the North–South axis, of the old Marxian thesis of impoverishment of the working class through capitalist exploitation. The corresponding political agenda implied by this, resolutely *tiers-mondiste*, was for planned development in the interests of Periphery countries, based on (socialist) reforms or revolution within nations and far-reaching reformation of the international economic order. In the ensuing years Latouche has proceeded to turn this established Marxist line of argument on its head. Along the way he has developed his own distinctive analysis of the splendour and tragedy of Western 'liberal' society – its myths and ideologies, and political economic realities.

From his early work rooted in a Marxian perspective,[1] he has preserved the view that the issues of development and underdevelopment need to be analysed in terms of the asymmetric coupling of Centre and Periphery (or North and South, or First, Second and Third Worlds) as a single world system. But, in a break with Marxism, he gives a much more fundamental role to *culture* and to the *imaginary dimension* in society. In effect, he inverts the traditional Marxian view of culture as social superstructure and of the economic dimension (forces and relations of production) as primary determinant of a society's historical trajectory, and argues that 'the economic' must itself be understood in terms of culture. This critique and reformulation is seen clearly in two of Latouche's cycle of books on development themes: *Critique de l'impérialisme: une analyse marxiste non-léniniste de l'impérialisme* (1979); and *Faut-il refuser le développement?* (1986).[2] Underdevelopment for Latouche is not the simple fact of a backwardness in the forces or relations of production. Nor is the appalling destitution apparent in the Third World the simple result of centuries of exploitation – colonial plunder followed up by further appropriation of surplus value through a market dynamic of unequal exchange between Centre and Periphery, as the Marxist-Leninist view has it. Prior to and alongside material exploitation, there is *cultural* domination; and this for Latouche is primary.

Latouche's position on the primacy of culture is in many respects comparable to that of Cornélius Castoriadis, with his notion of *l'institution imaginaire de la société*.[3] According to Castoriadis, each society furnishes its own 'construction' of the world, indeed creates its own world in the sense that it invests 'what is' with its distinctive signification. Each society establishes a mode of existence, a distinctive way of understanding itself, its activity, its history and the world it inhabits, specific to it and all-embracing in its compass.

Alongside this primacy accorded to culture, Latouche puts a particular view of social science, as methodologically and epistemologically distinct from natural science, being in the first instance the study of the inter-subjective grounds of human action. This may be understood as a *critical hermeneutic* epistemological stance, with primary focus on the subjectively felt and known, and socially shared and instituted, meanings through which people live.[4] In particular, Latouche insists on the *polysemy* of history (its many meanings, its possibilities, ambiguities), and the *inachievement* or uncompletedness of social life. By this he means that each situation, each moment of history, each element of the complex texture of social life, is always open to a plurality of reasonable interpretations, differing by reason of cultural or individual context. For a given individual, and more especially between individuals or between social groups, a given event or action may, therefore, 'find sense in several ensembles and take a place within several trajectories'.[5]

On the one hand, the plurality of social worlds, the multiplicity of meanings, and the indeterminateness of situations, are sources of the very richness and diversity of social life. Culture is nothing other than the totality of 'the response given by each human group to the problem of social existence'.[6] An indefinite plurality of cultures is thus possible. At the same time, from this incommensurateness and plurality, it follows that conflicts are very real. Within social groups, the tissue of social life is traversed by contradictions; even more so for interactions between cultures. A medieval European world lived in terms of realities of salvation, excommunication and damnation, chivalry and honourable poverty, is *incommensurate* with the modernity characterised by the norms of technological mastery of nature, individual rights and democracy, consumer sovereignty in the marketplace, and the gadgetry of instant (and narcissist) gratification. The chasms between the symbolic universe of the Stone Age people of the New Guinea Highlands, or the Egypt of the Pharaohs, and the New York Stock Exchange, are correspondingly greater.

*

These propositions lie at the heart of the following assertions: (1) that development is a specifically Western cultural concern; (2) that it has transplanted badly in the societies now known as the Third World; (3) that underdevelopment stems from the collision of *very different cultural universes* with the expansionary West; and (4) that, within these imperfectly Westernised societies, the *informal* can be understood as the budding, under highly ambiguous circumstances, of qualitatively new social forms which are not 'alternative paths' of development but *alternatives to development* being invented by social groups confronted with the impasses of both modernity and underdevelopment.

Western orthodoxy considers socio-economic activity as geared, in instrumental terms, to goals of material accumulation allowing the satisfaction of individual and collective 'needs'. Technology is a simple instrument in this quest. From this point of view, the desirability of 'development', that is the development of a society's abilities to meet unlimited consumption needs, seems to go without saying. Underdevelopment has, in this logic, usually been analysed as a backwardness or blockage in productive potentials. The urgent problems of material survival in the impoverished societies of the Third World seem, self-evidently, to cry out for technical progress and a science of the efficient allocation of scarce means to desirable ends. The pertinence of what we might call the 'economic logic' for diagnostic analysis and design of remedies, thus appears self-evident. But, argues Latouche, this is not due to the universal validity of the development goals – GDP growth or basic needs, as the case may be – nor of the 'economic logic' used in their pursuit. Rather it betrays the historical fact of Occidental domination of Third World societies. The evidence of this Western ethnocentrism is simply obscured, as the economic logic first of all submerges, and then is increasingly taken on board by, the dominated cultures.

For Latouche, a human group's practice, considered in its properly *human (and hence social)* dimensions, is first of all symbolic; it is through the symbolic (or imaginary) dimension that the material problems of life receive distinctive definition and terms of resolution. Underdevelopment is not primarily a condition of material poverty, nor does it derive from a mere 'absence' of productive potentials. Neither is it a transitionary phase, a stage in a society's ineluctable upward ascent to some fully developed state. Instead, the development ideal, and the practices in pursuit of this goal, are products of a particular time and place; they are inventions of Western culture. This ideal, and the vision of the human individual and the world that goes with it, may be offered to other societies – or, as historically has been the case, forcibly implanted on them. Yet it may not be generalisable to all. In fact, as a cultural experiment, it may not even be viable for the West itself in the long term as both mounting environmental problems and increasing manifestations of human alienation are demonstrating.

*

What would prevent the North's 'development' from being transferred successfully to all peoples and all parts of the globe? First, the simple fact that some peoples may find it meaningless or undesirable. As Gilbert Rist has written, the word 'development' has no equivalent in many languages, which leads to revealing results when societies attempt to bridge the cultural gap:[7]

> The Bubi of Equatorial Guinea use a word which means both to grow and to die, while the Rwandi people construct a translation for development on the basis of a verb which means to walk or move about, without any directionality being included in the notion. This absence of equivalents should not be surprising; it simply indicates that other societies do not consider that their reproduction depends on a continuous accumulation of knowhow and of goods supposed to make the future better than the past.

For such societies to 'become developed', and even more to seek to 'develop themselves', may be synonymous with their annihilation as distinct cultures.

A second reason for doubting that development can be generalised round the globe is that, historically, its achievement by some societies has been premised on the negation of others. It is by no means clear, argues Latouche, that this asymmetry can be overcome.

The route for the development of industrial capitalism (and its socialist offshoots) was paved by a long history of European imperialism in the 'New' Worlds, destined to become the Third World.[8] The presence of a colonisable exterior was a necessary source of economic riches (first through plunder and trade, later in natural resources and cheap labour). Perhaps more importantly, the influxes of wealth and the awakening to possibilities of trade and expenditures (colonial adventuring as much as strictly commercial investment) in the new territories, brought large-scale and irreversible social transformations to Europe itself.

The success of the modern North – material affluence, industrial prowess, now held out invitingly to the South – had its basis in these historical, geographical and cultural conjunctures. The proposed 'development' of the Third World is not, and cannot be, a repeat of the North's history. Rather, the Third World's underdevelopment is the inverse or negative face of the West's own development process. For a start, it has primarily been impelled *from the outside*, rather than being a transformation from the inside as, in first approximation, occurred in Western Europe. The Third World countries are *following* the West's industrialisation model, and (whatever the local nuances) this gives the process a very different *sense* from what it had in the pioneering nineteenth-century West. Secondly, the Third World countries do not, on the whole, have the same opportunities to exploit 'Peripheral' territories for fuelling their own expansion. The asymmetries along cultural historical, geographical and political control axes are thus irreducible.

In high-level international forums, free trade is presented as the mechanism allowing economic development to be a win-win (or non-zero-sum) game. The nation-states of the world each plot their futures around hopes of annual GDP growth and increases in exports. However, contradictions abound. Examination of the obvious 'miracle' cases, such as Japan, Singapore and Taiwan, suggests that they have benefited from privileged circumstances and cultural features that permitted them to appropriate capitalist modes of activity as their own. Moreover, they are succeeding in economic terms, partly through their own colonisation of less 'advanced' territories as sources of raw materials and cheap labour. By contrast, the poorest African countries are almost irrelevant to world trade. The Indonesian authorities, seeking to join the Four Tigers as a winner in the East, propose to underpin multinational investment through (among other things) massive construction of nuclear power generation facilities. Meanwhile, plutonium-laden ships from Japan sail the high seas like oversized suicide capsules. Countries such as Brazil and Malaysia hurtle each year several percentage points closer to complete denudation of their tropical forest stocks (and their tribal peoples along with them). In both Asian and Latin American countries, much trade and GDP growth merely revolves around economic enclaves of mining, cash crop plantations and manufacturing industry, exploiting cheap labour and tightly controlled by already privileged local interests and international capital. The condition of underdevelopment signifies, for a large number of societies, a double powerlessness: the *impossibility* of their becoming developed, that is, of effecting an accumulation of capital large enough to generate a high material standard of living for the whole population; and their *impotence* to search out alternative ways of solution to their situations of misery and subjugation.

*

Exposure of Third World societies to both the ideal of development and the very real coercion to develop, implies the fact and process of their *acculturation* to Occidental values and discourse. This gain of a new culture has been accompanied by a loss at least equally radical – the widespread disintegration of the coherence of the so-called traditional social structures.

While in no way denying material domination, Latouche's analysis in terms of a 'cultural logic' locates the unequal exchange between Centre and Periphery primarily at a different level: that of symbolic domination. The vitality of a culture resides, in this view, in its capacity to *give* (both symbolically and materially). Receipt of the gift (whether this be willing, inadvertent, or forced) is prima facie evidence of its valorisation by the recipient. The gift, and the capacity to give (and to have the gift received), signifies the existence and potency of the donor as an active agent in the world. By this view, the West's imperialism with regard to the Third World resides only secondarily in its having taken over most of its material wealth. The West's primary domination lies in the monopolisation of the very terms by which value is conceived, and in its domination of the basic institutions that codify social life.

Application of the label 'underdeveloped' already signifies that these 'backward' societies are being evaluated by the standards of the dominant culture (for whom GDP per capita is the leading indicator). The *deculturation* of the dominated societies is shown by the fact that, increasingly, they exclusively voice their predicaments and aspirations in terms of the 'developmentalist' categories of the invading culture. Western culture has imposed the *obligation of acceptance* on the invaded cultures. This entails, at the limit, the asphyxiation of the recipient culture, the loss of vitality and coherence of the indigenous cultural forms. Transfers in the direction Centre → Periphery of fundamental political, economic, moral and scientific ideologies and institutions infinitely outweigh the flows in the other direction. The Third World societies have, under these conditions, little or nothing they are able to give in return. This is the most basic 'unequal exchange' in the Centre–Periphery relation, and is the fundamental logic behind their description as poor and backward, irrational, etc. The devaluation of non-Occidental societies in this way is actually the price and pre-condition of their entry onto the path of economic development.[9]

*

In sum, underdevelopment is a process of real deculturation without the material (and symbolic) benefits of the complementary acculturation. It signifies the cruel inscription of entire societies to a nominal salvation that seems increasingly uncertain. To this, one can add the increasing concern for ecological limits to growth, raising the prospect that the West's quest for material affluence grounded in the mastery of nature through technology may itself be something of a mirage.[10] This crisis of development has been widely discussed in academic and political circles, with an ever-growing number of reformulations of what constitutes good or appropriate development, along with new recipes for successful implementation. Thus, for example, we now have 'autocentric development', 'meeting basic needs', 'ecodevelopment','ethno-development', 'spontaneous development' in the informal sector, 'sustainable development', and so on.

Latouche wants to break with all this. He wants to let the indisputable *real* impasse of non-development become a motivation for questioning the rationality of adherence to the *ideal* itself. In doing this, he commits a sort of heresy. How can one doubt development? The legitimacy of Western expansion certainly did not become an issue within the West when the crusades, the conquistadors, the colonists were roaming the world. First the Christian faith, and then the conviction that they were the bearers of Enlightenment's Reason, pushed the empire-builders onwards, duty-bound in their civilising mission:

> The bloody orgy and predatory rapaciousness were unfortunate incidents along the triumphant march of the chariot, the crushing of some innocent flowers. Honest men deplored the excesses but nowhere contested the rightfulness of the Occidental expansion.[11]

Not much has changed today amongst the zealots of the market and free trade. So what is it that allows doubts to be raised about the morality of this civilising zeal, and the global uniformisation it impels? Partly, suggests Latouche, because it seems to have reached such devastating and inhuman proportions, without quite delivering the goods. And this nourishes further doubts, even within the West itself, as to whether the promised lifestyle is really as 'great' as its proponents have made out.

The West, represented indifferently by corporate capital, arms dealers, Coca-Cola and cable TV, has become, says Latouche, 'an impersonal machine, devoid of spirit and thereby without a master, which has put humanity to its service'.[12] What is from one point of view the dynamism of the market society of the West, is in other respects an awful force of deculturation. The notion that development can be varied in its form, or reformed so as to accommodate authentic cultural differences is, suggests Latouche, naive if not sinister. It amounts to 'trying to define development by its opposite'.[13] There is no doubting the sincerity of those promoting 'alternative development' paths. Yet the 'respect for difference' espoused so loudly has, up until the present, amounted largely to respects paid *post mortem*. In the end, alternative development reduces to alternative ways of becoming the same: modernised and dead.

For their own survival, says Latouche, Third World societies must resist and somehow subvert this homogenising movement. They must change their terms of reference so as to escape the disempowerment inherent in the limbo-like condition of underdevelopment, and to escape the straitjacket of the impossible model of development with its 'imaginary' dependency on the West.

*

The 'grand society' holds out the promise of affluence and liberty for all, an unlimited horizon of knowledge and technological progress. The thing that renders individualism irresistible, says Latouche in *L'Occidentalisation du monde*, 'is that to each individual it appears as a liberation'.[14] Modernity opens up a seductive infinity of possibilities, and frees the individual from the shackles of 'traditional' societies with their ties of convention and solidarity.

However, these possibilities are, like film-star, sports champion or millionaire status, achievable only for minorities, while the price in terms of destruction of real solidarities and economic security of the 'traditional' clans and tribal collectivities, is paid by all. Westernisation means denuding individuals ultimately of any sense of value or self-identity other than that obtained through participation in the global marketplace. The cumulative result is a *deterritorialisation* of economic activity, epitomised in export-led growth, in the world play of financial markets, and in the growth of transnational corporations whose circuits of capital swamp all but the largest nations' GNPs. In this game of buying and selling, and capital accumulation, not everyone starts with an equal chance of winning, and *some lose absolutely* (death or definitive exclusion from the game). A small number obtain the satisfactions that power, wealth and notoriety can bring. But the so-called sovereignty of choice of the worker/voter/consumer in the affluent society is a hollow farce – replayed endlessly as entertainment in the sit-coms sandwiched between *Dallas* and the latest news on Somalia's famine crisis or the Gulf War aftermath. In practice, development is a dynamic that universalises 'the loss of sense and the society of the void'.[15]

The accomplishments of the West in science, politics and technological capability are truly remarkable. But Western civilisation is now also confronted with the dark side of its Progress: the perception that power to create is also power to destroy; that power over nature is often more imagined than real; that market autonomy is often also an awful desolation, insecurity and simple nullity – numbness in front of the TV, or Lotto, walkman, glue-sniffing, or some other virtual reality. What, in human life, is truly richness and progress? Progress of real significance today, proposes Latouche, may be through a devaluing of the paradigm of development – to dethrone it, reverse its paramount status and leave it behind in pursuit of radically alternative visions of social life.[16] What the societies of the Third World once esteemed in concrete solidarities, notions of honour, ecstasies and intimate knowledges, is now denied, devalued; yet they are excluded from the material and symbolic benefits of the Western notion of the grand society. So it is in all their interests to invent, if they can, other 'games' – and to ' "remake" themselves to become *nouveaux riches* in other ways'.[17]

*

Frequently, so-called traditional customs and social structures have been interpreted as holding up the development process. Latouche argues for an alternative vision of their roles. The vestiges of the past are, in the first place, a brake on and resistance to the real deculturation process taking place. But more than that, tradition along with the crazy cults and improvisations which from the developmentalist point of view may seem irrational, introverted and irksome, are also the latent bases for invention by the peoples involved of novel and radical ways out of the mess of underdevelopment.

This thesis is not a romanticisation of traditional societies; rather it is a valorisation in principle while admitting the ambiguities in fact. Latouche's view throughout is that there exist, and may come to exist, an indefinite *plurality* of social forms, each of which establishes its own norms of richness and adequacy. On this basis it becomes possible to grasp the phenomena of resistance to the Westernisation process as evidence of the vitality of cultural modes contrary to (and brutally contradicted by) those valorised by dominant Western institutions. What from one point of view looks like impasse and chronic crisis, is, from another, the hothouse for a flowering of new social worlds, of new civilisations that circumvent the imperatives of development and establish their own meaningfulness. As he writes in *L'Occidentalisation du monde*, these different projects being searched out through make-shift improvisation, 'may well give birth to monsters, or be recuperated by the machine; but they in any case nurse the hope that the blockage of the machine will not be the end of the world, but the dawn of a new epoch which enjoys many different humanities.'[18]

A 'return to the past' is neither possible nor – in many cases – particularly desirable. Throughout the present book he refers to the 'synthesis' that the castaways must attempt, between their twin heritages of modernity denied and lost tradition. How might Third World social groups, he asks, torn between their non-access to the benefits of modernity, and the impossibility of retrieving lost traditional social worlds, search out solutions to their predicaments? For hints of an answer, he looks at those bastard creations as they concretely appear in embryonic form, in the informal.

What is 'the informal' in Third World societies? It is, says Latouche in this book's opening chapter, 'an enormous nebula which expresses the seething chaos of human life in all its dimensions, with its horrors and its marvels'. Most tangibly, it is the 'informal economy', that bastard category lumping together subsistence (non-monetised) food harvesting activities, craftspeople of all sorts, drug-dealing, organised crime, and all sorts of buying and selling that eludes the taxman's net. The variety is extraordinary, ranging from household refuse collection to hawking kitsch souvenirs to tourists, from elaborate workshops to electronic repairs, to specialised courier and entertainment services. But the informal is not merely a shady and obscure economic reality. More fundamentally it is:

> a society which is unreadable and delicately placed in relation to modernity, being neither legal nor illegal, literally *elsewhere*, outside the terms of reference and normative imperatives of the dominant society.[19]

Employment within the informal is estimated by official studies to furnish between 60% and 80% of urban jobs in most Third World cities. As the informal connects also with the countryside, and as the monetised informal sectors have their own multiplier effects on activity in the formal economies, the whole informal nebula involves literally several billion human beings. The strictly economic activity within the informal is underpinned, given sense and impetus, by a seething variety of 'imaginary' creations – religious cults, local political activism, communitarian movements, revolutionary ideologies, and so on. The role of these movements is to *make sense of and give sense to* the situations and actions in which the people are involved. Complex networks of solidarity are established – often with tribal, clan or familial structures, along traditional or syncretic lines – which assure for their members a belonging and a minimum of economic security within the vast shantytowns. Without closing our eyes and painting too rosy a picture, Latouche suggests, it is legitimate to see in much of this activity an ongoing effort at rebuilding social bonds, even in the heart of modernity's dereliction.

*

Behind this valorisation of the informal, and the *choice* to see it as perhaps heralding novel social forms,[20] is an ethical stance. Concluding *L'Occidentalisation du monde*,[21] Latouche insisted on the possibility of an 'authentic dialogue between cultures' that could mean also an authentic coexistence of different cultures. Yet antagonisms may be irreducible:

> We share the conviction that each culture has much to learn from the others, can enrich itself with numerous carryovers. It is not certain, for all that, that each can play at this reciprocity, that is, can renounce concretely its own 'barbary' in order to have the other renounce his own, so as to permit the two to enjoy the pleasure of reciprocal exchanges. But as there is no hope of founding anything durable on the short-change of a pseudo-universality imposed by violence and perpetuated by the negation of the other, the venture is warranted that there is a common space of fraternal coexistence yet to discover and construct.

Tolerance of radical difference in the sense of goodwill and openness to the existence of the other *qua* other, is a risky affair. It means willingness to tolerate contradiction, to act generously in situations of unresolved antagonism. This, says Latouche, is the gauntlet that must be run. Over the past two hundred years, the West has taken a monopoly over the very definition of the problems of existence of all societies in the world. In its most recent forms: Vive the market! and Pax Americana.

The crucial challenge for those in the West wishing to afford genuine respect to those 'other' than themselves would be to relinquish this monopoly, and listen more openly to the discordant messages of silenced populations. There is something to be learned, Latouche seems to suggest, from the notions of reciprocity, solidarity and hospitality found in many non-industrial cultures, and in the heart of the modern 'informal'. There is something to be learned from the many sub-cultures within the West itself, including the poor, Blacks and women, whose understanding of the brash charades of modernity and of the impasses of poverty – both cultural and material – have frequently been held in disdain. In 1986, he wrote:

> As for new civilisations whose emergence we think to be ineluctable, mushrooming up from the ruins of murdered societies, we can specify only certain negative aspects: for example, rupture with the paradigm of development, exit from the world economy, invention of an original social form through reappropriating knowledge of real problems and bringing to these appropriate solutions. ... Our role here is fulfilled in the encouragement to go counter-current to history, inasmuch as the latter has been monopolised by the Occident which pretends to master, by terror, every signification.[22]

Might one not riposte that this is still a Western voice, and speaking still from a position of unique privilege? In some ways this is true. How does one avoid the cynicisms allowed by a privileged position on the one hand, and the bad faith of White man's guilt on the other? While it is cynical (or perhaps, in certain contexts, naive) to suppose that true respect for the other can come at no cost to oneself, is it *a priori* true that martyrdom through self-destitution or armed revolutionary zeal is a more meaningful gesture?

Latouche is mainly concerned with discarding corrupt solutions. This means divesting ourselves of a heritage of brash confidences and pieties which, in his view, serve us all rather badly. The founding political myth of liberal society, going hand in hand with the conquest of nature, is that self-interested pursuit of profits and satisfactions can, through the miracle of market exchange, be a win-win game. The proposition is that people can relate to each other exclusively as means to their own ends while still respecting each others' rights. The real result is a pillage of the natural world and a downright cynical disregard for the dereliction and ennui imposed on so much of humanity. So his suggestion is that we reconsider the quality of social relations and the realities of human suffering in 'post-modern' market society. Is the impoverishment of spirit, which is so much a symptom of the modern world, a lesser degradation than the material poverty distributed through the Third World? These are old questions, and this book is not the last time they will be asked.

The search for reciprocity – of a 'space of fraternal coexistence' – is itself an ethical choice which carries some real implications. It implies an affirming of the richness of the other, even in their poverty. If it is a matter of quality and not quantity of life, all helping is reciprocal, just as all learning can be reciprocal. 'Development assistance' provided to another based on a patronising mentality of 'us helping the needy' is liable to be corrupt, degrading of all concerned. Respect of the other – other persons, other life forms, future life – implies acceptance of dissension, of loss, and of death. Acceptance of death or loss can be a gift given to another. Even when people do live, and meet, in true generosity, there will remain situations of reversal (accidents, sickness, unrequited love), of material discomfort, of pain and dissension, where difficult choices must be made, not easily resolved. What it means to be tolerant in adversity, we leave – as Serge Latouche leaves it – as an open question.

*

Our emphasis in the translation of this book has been on rendering clearly the argument, while preserving the flavour of the original. In a few passages the original French text was amplified or rearranged so as to make the argument clearer to the Anglo-Saxon reader; but the substance of the argument is unchanged. Events taking place in 1990-91, when the French edition was written, have been placed in the past. A few references have been added, and others updated, especially where the original reference was to a manuscript or semi-published form. Some errors in citations have been corrected; our notes and references are therefore definitive.

In structure, there are some modifications compared with the French edition. First, for the convenience of the reader, the English edition has a full bibliography of works cited and a subject index. Secondly, the notes have been placed at the end of each chapter, rather than at the foot of the page. Thirdly, we have split the original Chapter 6, titled 'La société des naufragés' (The Castaways' Society); the two halves titled 'Niveau de vie' (Standard of Living) and 'La nouvelle vie (The New Life) in the original, become respectively the new Chapter 6: The Standard of Living, and the new Chapter 7: The New Society of the Castaways.

Our policy with citations has been as follows. Where the work cited by Latouche has an English original we have, wherever possible, found a published English form. (The very small number of cases where this has proved impossible are noted.) In the case of French language originals, unless explicitly indicated, we give our own translation from the French original. However, we have indicated English language editions where possible, at the same time listing a French edition. This policy reflects the role of French as source language and tradition for Latouche. For works originally in other languages, we have improvised. Where possible we have indicated English editions and used them for textual citations; but where this was inappropriate or impossible, we have resorted to our own translation via the French.

Numerous thanks are due for the collective effort of translation. First, to Elizabeth O'Connor for help with parts of the translation, and to Serge Latouche for his willingness to peruse the entire manuscript and provide good-natured assistance on many of the mysteries of French language and literary tradition. Thanks also to Susana Berestovoy, Judithe Bizot, and again Serge, for moral and practical support to Martin on his visits to Paris. Robert Molteno at Zed Books provided excellent editorial support; Mark Brooks scoured libraries to search out references and English language citations; and Jeanne Lee helped a lot with the typing.

Martin O'Connor and Rosemary Arnoux
Te Whare Waananga o Taamaki-Makaurau
(University of Auckland)
Aotearoa (New Zealand)

Notes

1. In addition to his doctoral thesis, see in particular *Le Projet marxiste: analyse économique et matérialisme historique*, Presses Universitaires de France, Paris, 1975; and *Epistémologie et économie: essai sur une anthropologie sociale freudo-marxiste*, Editions Anthropos, Paris, 1973.

2. *Critique de l'impérialisme: une analyse marxiste non-léniniste de l'impérialisme*, Editions Anthropos, Paris, 1979; *Faut-il refuser le développement?*, Presses Universitaires de France, Paris, 1986.

3. Cornélius Castoriadis, *L'Institution imaginaire de la société*, Seuil, Paris, 1975, especially pp. 214-51.

4. Latouche gives a systematic exposition of his social science perspective and method in a separate book, *Le Procès de la science sociale*, Editions Anthropos, Paris, 1984. There he describes his position as a sort of *realism*, but neither empiricist nor essentialist. On fundamentals of epistemology and ontology, he adopts the view that there is no *discourse of truth*, meaning that reality cannot be exhaustively described (even in principle) by theory. The position is in some ways akin to that espoused by Jean Baudrillard in *Les Stratégies fatales* (Grasset, Paris, 1983; English translation as *Fatal Strategies*, Semiotext(e), Pluto, London, 1990), of the real *(réel)* as the enigmatic limit or boundary condition on theory – never rendered transparent by theory but determining obscurely what does and does not work (and how, or how not) as a theoretical proposition.

5. *Le Procès de la science sociale*, op. cit, p. 198 and passim. Also, although this is not a connection Latouche himself makes, the theme of social reality permanently *inachévée*, torn and fragmented, and traversed by contradictions, resonates with some critical feminist analyses of culture, politics and difference. Cf. Trinh T. Minh-ha, *When the Moon Waxes Red: Representation, Gender and Cultural Politics* (Routledge, New York and London, 1991). It should be emphasised that the primacy Latouche accords to the cultural dimension of analysis, leading on to the view of development and the 'economic logic' as specific artifacts or institutions of Western culture, is the result of a *choice*. This choice involves the adoption of postulates, metaphysical and theoretical, whose validity cannot be demonstrated nor definitively refuted. The primary appeal is to the fecundity of the approach, yet what is judged fecund or desirable depends partly on the value judgements, ethical precepts and notions of knowledge, internal to the position.

6. See especially *Faut-il refuser le développement?*, op. cit. The citations and paraphrases come from chs 1 and 6. Although the book as a whole is not translated, these two chapters are available separately in English translation. The Introduction, published under the title 'Should one say no to development?' is in the English edition of the French-Canadian review *Interculture*, no. 95, pp. 26-35 (Spring/April 1987, Centre Interculturel Monchanin, 4917 St Urbain, Montreal, Quebec). Ch. 6, titled 'Under-development is a form of deculturation', translated by Martin O'Connor and Rosemary Arnoux, is available as *Working Paper in Economics No. 62* (August 1989, Department of Economics, University of Auckland, New Zealand). In both cases, reproduced with permission of the French copyright holders, Presses Universitaires de France.

7. Cited by Latouche in *Faut-il refuser le développement?*, ch. 1, op. cit.

8. This is a theme that Latouche explores in detail in ch. 2 of *Faut-il refuser le développement?*

9. These arguments are most systematically laid out in ch. 6 of *Faut-il refuser le développement?*, op. cit.

10. Resource limits and ecological constraints to 'development' are not extensively discussed by Latouche, nor does he seek to judge their severity as material limits – being aware of scientific uncertainties, demographic imponderables and the importance of culture in determining perceptions of and responses to 'crisis'. He views the ecological problems in general terms as signs of the foundering of the Enlightenment project of 'mastery of nature', and he cites them, along with related issues like health, as contributing causes of the looming 'shipwreck of the grand society'. But there is also the distinct suggestion that, even if coexistence of cultures were *materially* feasible, it is by no means clear that an aggressive West, with its intolerance of difference, could stomach it.

11. In the Introduction to Latouche's *L'Occidentalisation du monde: essai sur la signification, la portée et les limites de l'uniformisation planétaire*, La Découverte, Paris, 1989, pp. 8-9.

12. Ibid., pp. 9-10.

13. See Chapter 5 below. For example: 'if one proclaims that "good development is primarily putting value on what one's forebears did and being rooted in a culture", it amounts to defining a word by its opposite. Development has been and still is primarily an *uprooting*.'

14. *L'Occidentalisation du monde*, op. cit., p. 109.

15. Ibid., p. 83. Chs 3 and 4 of *L'Occidentalisation du monde* are devoted to the themes of 'the West as planetary uprooting', 'deterritorialisation' and the 'demise of the nation-state'.

16. As the historian J.B. Bury wrote in 1932: 'Will not that process of change, for which Progress is the optimistic name, compel "Progress" too to fall from the commanding position in which it is now, with apparent security, enthroned? A day will come, in the revolution of centuries, when a new idea will usurp its place as the directing idea of humanity. Another star, unnoticed now or invisible, will climb up the intellectual heaven, and human emotions will react to its influence, human plans respond to its guidance. It will be the criterion by which Progress and all other ideas will be judged. And it too will have its successor.' In *The Idea of Progress*, Dover edition, New York, 1955, pp. 351-2.

17. From Chapter 2 of this book.

18. From the Introduction to *L'Occidentalisation du monde*, p. 10. The theme is amplified in ch. 5 of the same book, titled 'Au-delà ou ailleurs' (Beyond or elsewhere), ibid., pp. 111-28, which in effect is a preface to Part II of *In the Wake of the Affluent Society*.

19. From Chapter 4 below.

20. The point is, says Latouche (see Chapter 4 below), that the usual economic interpretations *already choose* to privilege certain characteristics, in such a way as to exclude the possibility of reading the evidence another way. To point this out 'certainly does not allow me to assert that my analysis of the informal is the "true" one, but simply that it is a legitimate interpretation, as legitimate as the others, and overall just as plausible in what it suggests'.

21. *L'Occidentalisation du monde*, op. cit., pp. 138-9.

22. From the Conclusion to *Faut-il refuser le développement?*, op. cit., p. 202.

Preface

Rigour, passion and observation

Talleyrand is credited with the immortal words: 'What is excessive is insignificant.' Extravagance does indeed undermine itself. However, 'the intoxication of the thinking process' is not so easily resisted. It is always tempting to adulterate rigorous argument with rhetorical effects, springing from an exalted conviction. At times, efforts at proof may yield entirely to such effects. It is important to draw a distinction between excess flowing from passion, and excess born of theoretical analysis. The conscientious thinker has a duty to pursue to the ends of the earth those ideas he has started – and their consequences – even if they make his head swim. Rigorous thought admits no tactical compromises such as have a place in action.

My earlier book on the Westernisation of the world and the process of uniformisation of societies[1] has been generally well received, but the arguments advanced in it have been considered by some critics to be 'excessive rantings'.[2] It is true that I have not struggled very hard to keep my passion for my own ideas in check. It seems to me, however, that the accusation of excess and rage is slightly misplaced, the disquiet being rather at the truly radical nature of the conclusions being deduced from my stated premises, conclusions that cannot fail to plunge the reader into a kind of dismay. The principal reproaches levelled at me are that I paint the West entirely black, and that I exaggerate the extent to which the world is being Westernised. According to the first criticism, I underestimate the positive roles of democracy, human rights and progress as brought to the world by the West, hence my far too pessimistic vision. As the first part of the present book deals with positive aspects of the West at some length, I shall limit myself at this point to the observation that if at times I play the prophet of doom, it is not to help bring about that doom, but to try to avert it. Burying our heads in the sand doesn't impress me as a strategy for limiting probable catastrophes. It is incumbent on the intellectual to arouse people's awareness of possible dangers, not to lull them into complacency through the media.

The second criticism seizes on my presentation of our planet as subject to a general drive towards uniformity, a move which is radical and irreversible. I go so far as to talk of the West as a steamroller crushing all cultures in its path. Doubt has been expressed as to whether this phenomenon is indeed general, whether it is radical and whether it is irreversible. One critic has remarked:

> A French nurse who has worked for two years in rural Bangladesh, and with whom we raised Serge Latouche's thesis, replied without hesitation that 'talk of a Westernisation of Bangladesh makes no sense at all'.[3]

Admittedly, a great number of differences do survive, and many of them seem in fact to be irreducible; as such they indicate various paths which social evolution might follow. I find no difficulty here. As to the question whether the premises I have adopted are themselves excessive – I do not think so. My analysis of the West as an anonymous and soon-to-be global megamachine churning out homogeneity is no doubt open to debate. Plenty of people will reject it out of hand, but it is not an extremist analysis, and variations on it are quite widespread.

Westernisation of the world: economics, culture and difference

The social and political processes, as well as the economic and technological mechanisms by which we are moving towards uniformity, have been mapped out by commentators for quite some time. In the middle of the nineteenth century, Alexis de Tocqueville argued that the ineluctable march towards equality of conditions also led towards a uniformity that risked being slavish conformity:

> Variety vanishes within humanity. The same modes of action, thought and feeling are to be found in each of the four corners of the world. Peoples come to resemble each other even though they are not specifically copying each other.[4]

In this regard he carried further the prophetic analyses made by Benjamin Constant, who in 1813 had written:

The great word today is uniformity. ... The same code, measures, rules, and if it can be managed gradually, the same tongue: all this is acclaimed as the pinnacle of social organisation. ... It is a shame that one cannot tear down the towns and rebuild them all on the same plan, and level all the mountains so that everywhere there is flat terrain! And I am astounded that no one has yet issued a proclamation that local people everywhere must wear identical costume, so that the eye of the master may be shocked no more by irregular motley designs and outrageous variety.[5]

This satire, directed at the bureaucratic centralisation of the Napoleonic era, holds just as good today when applied to the trends towards worldwide bureaucracy exhibited by transnational corporations, state apparatus and political organisations. The homogenising effects of the world economy do not need further proof; this is recognised as a fact by both supporters and adversaries of capitalism and the marketplace, whether they see it as a matter for joy or grief. In recent years Jacques Ellul has given a searching and pertinent account of the uncontrolled and uncontrollable progress of technology, its spread worldwide and its impact on the destruction of cultures. These three dimensions of uniformisation – the socio-political, economic and technical – can often pull in contradictory directions; the megamachine is not absolutely coherent. But such incoherencies are only secondary, and are not serious impediments to the headlong drive towards the obliteration of difference.

This planet-wide movement towards uniformity in no way excludes some forms of social differentiation. I have, in fact, been at pains to emphasise how attempts to universalise Western styles and standards of living have failed. This assertion lies at the root of the present book too. Social differentiation in the sense of a diversity of consumer preferences, diverse lifestyles, and so on, is of course a feature of the modern world. But I would not say that this motley array of individual consumer fantasies, stimulated by the media and conditioned by rising income, can be a true substitute for cultural diversity – as some of those singing the praises of post-modernity would have us believe. The basic question for me is the following. If, as I argued in the whole second part of my *L'Occidentalisation du monde*, fundamental differences are being maintained and renewed, and if resistance continues to arise and logical bases for differentiation are plainly visible, does this amount to breakdown for the West (which is my argument), or are these phenomena compatible with the generally accepted trend towards uniformity?

The only way to support the latter point of view is to consider economy and culture as two primeval dimensions of human experience, conforming to two antagonistic logics. The first, founded in egoism and individual interest, pushes inexorably towards uniformity. The drive for profit is a mechanism beyond space and time, and the economic dimension operates everywhere through a process of continuous rationalisation. This rationalising force clashes, however, with the cultural dimension of life, which expresses the quest for identity grounded in experience of a collective life and solidarity. This second impulse shows itself in the diversity of forms that spring from the imagination: it is the domain of play, art, beliefs, feelings. A kind of eternal conflict inevitably emerges between these two titans: economy and culture.

This dualism accounts – supposedly – for why, in the heart of homogeneity through economic rationalisation, differences still persist. In contrast to *Dallas*, a caricature of planetary uniformity, we can point to the flourishing production of original programmes by TV Globo in Brazil and Televisa in Mexico. Series produced by these two chains are actually exported to Hispanic speakers in the United States! The astonishing degree to which Japanese culture has been preserved can be given a similar explanation.

This is a seductive thesis indeed: some kind of dialectic between economy and culture would be both source and guarantee of diversity. Many UNESCO analyses are based on this sort of view. Such a dualism underlies all discourse on the *cultural dimension* of development, that is, culture as a factor that must be taken into account and introduced into the strategies and models of development with which experts busy themselves. One can on this basis account for the phenomenon of the spread of non-Western cultural traits in diverse milieux of development and social change: Chinese cuisine, Black music, Hindu wisdom, and so on.

Two weaknesses are evident, however. First, this dualistic perspective does not account for the phenomenon of ethnocide, and secondly it treats the economic as weightless compared to the social. In fact the techno-economic megamachine has made thousands of cultures disappear. The graveyard of assassinated cultures is overflowing. While some cultures have found effective ways to resist extinction, others –

unprotected – are going the same way as extinct and endangered species. The Yanomami people in the heart of the Amazon are right now being exterminated in the course of the complex play of economic and political interests at both local and transnational level. Is this a manifestation of the complementarity of the economic and cultural 'dimensions', or of an outright incompatibility?

Moreover, supposing that culture is an autonomous force separate from the economic dimension of life, the question may be posed, where does the economic dimension originate? From human nature? The economic, this domain or dimension of calculating rationality, is not a natural reality. On the contrary, it is an historical and cultural invention, which in the modern West has been given an unprecedented pre-eminence. If, as anthropologists think, culture is the response of human groups to the problem of existence, then the economic is nothing other than one dimension of *our* culture. Not only is the economic not complementary to culture but, in the West, it is tending to become a substitute for culture, by absorbing all expressions of culture into itself (e.g. as choices of lifestyle, commodity bundle, investment and management of capital, and so on). More and more, utilitarian calculations come to replace play, art, feeling and beliefs by devouring and colonising them. Economic and instrumental reason does not readily tolerate competition.

The character of this book

The predominance of *negative* conclusions in my work tends, no doubt, to reinforce an impression of excess. On the other hand, the excessive use of the phrase 'it's easy to criticise' as a term of abuse, is entirely in line with the operational obsession of the technocratic universe. What we need, one often hears, are concrete approaches and realistic proposals for intervention.

There is, here, an important distinction to be made. It is one thing, and quite legitimate, to attempt to spell out through critical analysis of social and economic evolution, both historical perspectives on that evolution and directions for individual ethics. It is quite another thing to formulate precise plans of action for others. In doing that, one risks betraying one's vocation as an intellectual.[6] The commitment to analysis does not necessarily lead to an output of prescriptions for concrete 'action'. The demand for such 'action' is itself an imperative of the techno-economic system, which simply presupposes that analysis and thought, if they are to be useful, must have an instrumental role in producing actionable recipes.

All leaders have need of counsel, and there are people paid to give it. Ordinary people have a practical need, also, to understand the world in order to achieve some degree of self-determination as free subjects; civil servants, by contrast, merely need a set of instructions in order to carry out their tasks. One of the misfortunes of our times is that we have confused these two roles – those of the free citizen and of the official – to the point that understanding and liberty tend to be reduced to the instrumental level of informed choice.

My book *L'Occidentalisation du monde* clearly falls into the category of work seeking to understand the processes of social change and to explore possibilities for individual ethical life in our world. Perhaps excessively so! The present book, however, sets out to remedy that excess, while still remaining in the same 'genre'. It is not strictly a sequel to the first book. But it is a 'Part Two' in the sense that it proceeds from the same premises, intuitions and conclusions as the first.

My central theme is the possible future of the world *post*-West, the world *after* the Western civilisation has disappeared – *post*-development, in other words. This imagined future is explored via its early real beginnings in the nebula of the 'informal' society. The book examines the problems which the millions of people around the planet who have been shipwrecked by development must resolve if they and their descendants are to survive. It looks at life 'outside' the confines of modernity and the 'formal economy'. Speculations briefly sketched in *L'Occidentalisation du monde* are here pushed much further, to the brink of science fiction. However, the book is not entirely speculative. Much of it is concerned with analysing the causes of the 'shipwreck', that is, of the breakdown or collapse of the West. The first part consists of an exhaustive analysis of the reasons for this collapse; the second part is an interpretation of actual and possible responses of development's castaways in the domain of the informal.

So this is not a wholly new book, rather a second essay on the same vast theme of the Westernisation of the world. The first was concerned mainly with the triumph of the West, but hinted at something beyond this, outside the cultural, political and economic confines of the modern West. This second traverse starts from the contradictions of

the Western myth and explores just what the basis for such a new world
'elsewhere' might be.

Empirical sources and interpretation

It might be taken from all this that the thesis of the 'wreck of the grand
society' – the partial or total collapse of modern affluent and 'liberal'
society as we know it – is an imaginative projection based on theoretical reflection; while conversely the exploration of the 'planet of the
castaways' is a fiction grounded very much in observation of the
terrain. This impression is accurate enough, except that it would be
fraudulent for me to present my revelation of the 'dark continent' of
informal societies as the result of field research carried out personally
in Africa and elsewhere. To avoid such a misunderstanding, let me
assert that this work, despite numerous references to first-hand observations, is first and foremost the fruit of theoretical and critical
reflection.

I lived for two years in the heart of Africa (in Zaire); and I made
forays into neighbouring countries (the Congo, Angola, Rwanda) and
most countries on the western coast (Ivory Coast, Senegal, Gabon,
Nigeria, Liberia, Cameroon, Togo, Benin). I also spent a year in Laos,
with trips into Thailand, Cambodia, India, Nepal, Pakistan and Burma.
However, this experience belongs to a distant past. My preoccupations
were very different then, not to say diametrically opposed to the
concerns I hold now. I was campaigning then for planned development. African and Asian values seemed to me to be obstacles which
needed to be destroyed, despite my curiosity about local customs.

Since then I have had the opportunity to make brief stays in Black
Africa, particularly in Burkina Faso, Benin and Mauritania, in North
Africa and even in Papua New Guinea. These travels have yielded
observations precious to me. All the same, the visits were primarily
devoted to university work (conferences, meetings, teaching) and not
to local research – and anyway they came after my main hypotheses
and interpretations had been formed. At their best, such brief visits
acted as soundings to test out and confirm my intuitions.

These remarks on the primacy of a theoretical dimension in my
work are, obviously, not meant to deprecate the work of researchers
engaged in the collection of detailed concrete observations. Without
such people, in fact, this book would have been impossible. I have not

had much opportunity to gather my own data, and in some ways I would not be very sure how to go about such work. I have come to regret not having spent more time in direct observation. Yet the truth is that I am naturally inclined to armchair reflection. I prefer to apply my critical wisdom to the observations of others rather than to add my own observations to an already ample supply.

This last remark raises an important point. Even in limiting discussion to Black Africa, we have at our disposal an impressive and often unexploited stock of 'raw material' on Third World societies and the informal. Yet it is not as simple as just 'mining' this stock. First of all, in a domain where 'material' is created by the interaction of the observer and the observed, nothing can really replace personal observation. On the other hand, it happens that I have been trained in a particular discipline, economics, which prides itself on the amassing of impersonal (so-called objective) observations. One result is that I am not ideally equipped to undertake personal field analyses. At the same time I must struggle to prevent the domain of personal experience and observation from being invaded and overrun by the cult of the impersonal. The current trend, facilitated by the availability of new technologies for data storage and numerical computation, is to accumulate fabulous supplies of data, without taking the time necessary to make good use of them, let alone to think critically about their interpretation. This opens up the danger of theoretical myopia. A moment's thought reminds us that the social sciences were constructed in the eighteenth and nineteenth centuries on the basis of a very small number of observations. The foundations of the social and economic sciences on which we depend today is essentially a product of a *theoretical* effort dominated by a few influential analysts writing under very particular social conditions. In this respect, our epoch is threatened by the exact inverse of excess: it is threatened by a poverty of interpretation and by the risk of exclusion of the full richness of human experience.

For all these reasons, at the same time as acknowledging my great debt to those who have been my sources of empirical observations, I make a strong claim for the legitimacy of my own procedure of theoretical reflection and interpretation. Fortunately, high-quality observations of Black Africa do exist, along with intelligent and pertinent reporting. There are not very many of these, nor are they exhaustive, but they do exist. In particular there are a dozen or so documents written by Africans or foreigners who know and love this other planet, which can teach us more than the vast data banks where everything is itemised except the precise information which one wants. Without these particular studies and documents, it would have been impossible for me to evoke the planet of the castaways in the way that I do.

Acknowledgements

Most of my sources are identified in the text. However, especially regarding the informal economy, the authors in question are usually discussed in a critical way. So I wish here, at the outset, to acknowledge my debt to the works of pioneers Jacques Charmes, Philippe Hugon, Marc Penouil and their research teams. This book owes a great deal also to the discussions which followed the publication of *L'Occidentalisation du monde*. Indeed it was written almost as a spontaneous response to the comments and criticisms received from many quarters: students at universities in Ouagadougou and Nouakchott, students at Lille-II and the Institut d'Etude du Développement Economique et Social (IEDES) at Paris-I, activists in the Institut d'Etudes Occitanes, numerous non-governmental organisations (NGOs) including Terre des Hommes, Frères des Hommes, Artisans du Monde, environmental activists and others. A special mention must be made of my friends in the South/North Network: Cultures and Development based in Brussels, and in the Mouvement Anti-Utilitariste dans les Sciences Sociales (Movement against Utilitarianism in the Social Sciences, MAUSS). Finally, particular thanks are addressed to Catherine Aubertin, Alain Caillé, Saïd Doumane, François Gèze, Jean-Louis Rapin, François de Ravignan, Robert Schilling and Toon Van de Velde, who were kind enough to read the manuscript and share their judicious comments with me, and to Janine Bourgeois and Sylvie Lamirand who patiently typed it.

Notes

1. Serge Latouche, *L'Occidentalisation du monde*, op. cit.
2. For example Pierre Drouin in *Le Monde*, 24 February 1989, titled his review: 'The "terrifying strength" of the West. The salutary and sometimes excessive ragings of Serge Latouche' ('La "force terrifiante" de l'Occident. Les colères salutaires et parfois excessives de Serge Latouche').
3. Michel Chauvin, 'Déculturalisation et sous-développement', CDTM (Centre du

Documentation Tiers Monde de Paris), no. 3, August 1990, p. 22. See also, by the same author, *Tiers monde: la fin des idées reçues*, Syros, Collection Alternatives, Paris, 1991, p. 105.

4. Alexis de Tocqueville, *De la démocratie en Amérique*, Gallimard, Paris, 1986, p. 266. (English edition: *Democracy in America*, the Henry Reeve text, edited by Phillips Bradley, 2 vols, Vintage Books, New York, 1960.)

5. Benjamin Constant, *De l'esprit de conquête*, Librairie de Medicis, Paris, 1947, pp. 53-4.

6. Cf. the analysis by Julien Benda, *La Trahison des clercs*, Grasset, Paris, 1927.

Part I

The Shipwreck

Even as men wrecked upon a sand
that look to be washed off the next tide.
Shakespeare, *Henry V*, Act IV, scene 1

1

Development's Castaways

Two planets

From one air terminal to another, from one Hilton to another, you may travel the world, east to west, north to south, without ever feeling yourself to be a foreigner, without ever feeling dislocated. Everywhere you'll see the same glass and steel architecture, the same motorways, the same congestion. The same plastic, the same television sets, the same sportsgrounds. And the same Coca-Cola bottles. Right down to the exotic souvenirs produced for the world market in the same factories.[1]

No one would dispute this jaded traveller's comment. Standardisation is sometimes even deliberate. The Novotel chain furnishes its hotel rooms around the globe exactly alike so that its clients suffer no feeling of disorientation!

When you land in the darkest heart of Africa, at Ouagadougou, capital of Burkina Faso, you will find in the official town centre the same glass and steel architecture, the same motorways (although only for a few miles), the same congestion. One has to admit that the climate, local colour, the run-down state of installations, people's strange way of wearing foreign cast-offs, do all create a certain unavoidable sense of dislocation. Yet the centre of the capital, with its infrastructure, machinery, administrative buildings, economic and financial installations, vibrates to the rhythm of the 'transnational technopolis'. This little metropolis of distant Africa is grafted onto the great city-world. The world is a step away from becoming a village.

But once you move beyond the checkpoints marking the town boundaries, you see an *immediate and radical* change. You are truly *on another planet*. The red African soil and its deep spicy odour seize you by the throat. Straight away, you notice the dried mud Mossi huts flanked by their little round storehouses with Chinese-straw-hat roofs looking like little fortified castles, the wandering herds of livestock (zebus and goats), the savanna – in some parts still tree-studded, in others stripped bare by deforestation – giant baobabs and vultures; and finally you come across men, women and children who seem to live outside time, far from the strange speculations of the town. This is not the age-old Africa still to be found among the Lobi, deeper in the country around Gaoua. There, you can still pay for your market purchases in *cauris*.[2] There the three-tiered rituals of initiation – the *joro* – remain a fearsome and feared mode of integration and control in a society which has refused the White way.[3] At the gates of 'Ouaga' rusting car frames and packing cases lie around on the crust of the soil; mopeds pass, carrying huge earthenware jars for *dolo*, the millet beer, raising in the process an acrid red dust that creeps into everything. This strange planet is a planet of people excluded by development – the unwanted and have-nots.

All over the town, development is touted on placards. Development slogans of various sorts flourish along the main streets according to the whims of government operations, international money-lenders or non-governmental organisation (NGO) projects. The dignity of woman is proclaimed, the merits of literacy or vaccinations, faith in progress and in the ideas of the Enlightenment. But this modernity is a downtown spectacle, a ritual display in French (a language understood by a minority only, and read by a mere handful of nationals). It does not go beyond the police posts which separate the town from the rest of the country.

You may see strange sights even in the town itself. Stepping off the two or three main streets which are exactly like any other official main street, you plunge into a world quite different from the 'techno-cosmos'.[4] Vividly illustrated signs point out an amazing variety of little shops and services, ranging from fast-foods (e.g. 'tender young chickens as on TV', spit-roasted behind glass) to African hair-dos, *dolo*-sellers (women who make and sell millet beer), and all kinds of repairs. Innumerable street hawkers behind their tables clutter the footpaths; day and night in the markets, trade of the most unexpected kinds takes place; all sorts of tools are made from recycled scrap iron, shoes from old tyres, marvellous cast bronze statuettes from crank-cases and dynamo wheels salvaged from wrecked cars. Here too is another planet. The division is less marked than between city and country, because this other world exists in the very heart of the city, linked to it by many complex strands. Yet the vitality, the creativity, the dynamism of this *informal* sphere has nothing to do with the farce of modernity, and everything to do with the strange world which surrounds the town. Though by the nature of things development has more relevance for them than for their brothers in the countryside, these people of the urban margins are among those excluded from the 'grand society'.[5]

Poor, without necessarily being in constant misery, these marginalised people of town and field form the vast planet of the castaways of development. My earlier book *L'Occidentalisation du monde* hinted at its probable existence as a 'new world' awaiting discovery and exploration. The informal is, in actuality, a new world in the making. The present book thus pursues, as an intellectual journey, the voyage of hypothesis, exploration and discovery of this world.

The outcasts from the consumer society's banquet

What you see in Burkina Faso is what you see, more or less, throughout the Third World. At Kinshasa, Cotonou and Nouakchott, police or military barriers separate town from country, development from its inverse. Everywhere, modernity is given its ritual downtown parade with all the trappings of transnationality: concrete buildings, steel and glass, asphalt roadways and dense motor traffic, publicity or propaganda on display in the international languages unknown to the illiterate masses, and so on. And everywhere, when you break free of the urban boundaries, you land on another planet. Outside Nouakchott is the desert; its nomad populations are fast disappearing. The mega-machine bureaucratises, then it forces people into settlements. Nomadism and development do not keep good house together. The nation-state cannot escape the logic of modernism and development. A nomad nation-state, whether in Mongolia or the Sahel, does not escape the rule of law. There is a downward slide towards the most radical form of settlement, urbanisation. Elsewhere, settled farmers, finding themselves more and more marginalised, head towards the urban zones. The outcasts of development are to be found throughout the less densely populated country areas, but also in the cities – usually in shantytowns. A 1990 estimate puts the number living in these shantytowns at around three hundred million. The global village is really a huge suburb. Third World towns are growing at an annual rate of 5%. At this rate, the urban population doubles every fifteen years. The murderous giganticism suffered by Mexico City is well known. In Argentina, Uruguay, Chile and Venezuela, 80% of the population lives in urban areas. Already more than 25% of the Congolese live in Brazzaville!

Less and less can we talk about a distinction between the developed and modernised town, and the traditional and neglected countryside. The same distinction applies right in the middle of urbanised areas. The communications revolution may have reduced the planet to a village, thereby turning humanity into one great family, but it is a family full of tensions and contrasting situations.

The outcasts have a thousand faces. You may find them anywhere on the planet, north or south, east or west. There are many processes of marginalisation, resulting in life-patterns which are varied but always dramatic. And the levels of degradation are infinite.

First there are the radically outcast, those whose decline ends in death. Each day, 40,000 children die of poverty. Whichever image one chooses to illustrate this, an Auschwitz every three months or a dead child every two seconds, the thing is itself shameful and monstrous. No place was kept for these children at the great banquet table of the consumer society. No place is kept either for the hundreds of thousands of unfortunates who disappear each year in the innumerable conflicts which ravage the planet, or who lie down in silence, victims of lack of care, weakened by various food deficiencies.

The three or four billion outcasts who more or less survive still get a very unequal share of the crumbs and leftovers from the feast. Internees or refugees, neglected in the countryside or uprooted in the towns, unemployed, without work or protection, this vast company of people live in a sort of enchanted – or disenchanted – limbo, outside the law, concealed within the global village.

Refugees, whether victims of conflicts or of natural cataclysms (these latter often made more severe by human negligence), are a rapidly growing species, with a permanent population of some twenty million. Generation upon generation of refugees are coming into existence. They live out their earthly life crowded in camps in sub-human conditions, victims of situations that the political world-order is powerless to rectify. These are outcasts in more ways than one; no one wants them so everyone tries to pass them on to someone else. They are beggars in spite of themselves, and when they do manage to survive, it is only thanks to meagre world charity and their own resourcefulness in dealing with a concentration camp universe.

There are also outcasts among the outcasts, victims of discrimination among the poor themselves. A recent sociological film, *La Caste criminelle* (The criminal caste), showed the life of millions of Indians penned in camps half a century after independence. These groups were considered dangerous by the British, and they and their descendants are still the objects of a monstrous discrimination.

Then there are the indigenous victims of colonisation by the erstwhile colonised, where the new invasions are harsher and more savage than the old: for example the Dravidian tribes in India, the Papuans of Irian Jaya (the Indonesian-occupied section of New Guinea), through to the Tibetans under China. Around the world there are innumerable peoples struggling for recognition, excluded from political rights, prey to unseen wars, victims of silent genocides: the black animists of southern Sudan, the Karen of Burma. In recent years we have seen intercommunal clashes multiply, based on ethnic or religious divisions: Tamil insurrections in Sri Lanka, Sikh terrorism in the Punjab, recurrent riots in Kashmir and Sind, bloody clashes in Rwanda and Burundi, civil wars in the Eritrean, Tigrayan and Ogaden regions of Ethiopia, struggle among the Sahrouis in Morocco, age-old claims still made by the Kurds in Iraq and surrounding regions.

Only slightly more fortunate are those farmers of the Third World who manage still to cling to some land, but of a kind which no longer nourishes them. They too are outcast. Demographic growth and a globalised economy have destroyed traditional agrarian systems, a situation made worse by aberrant policies of drought and flood management. As a result, rural societies have been plunged into crisis. Even the Lobi of Burkina Faso, shuttered in their tradition, have undergone this trauma. The young men go off to hire themselves out, if they can find work, on the plantations of the Ivory Coast, leaving women, children and elders to keep things more or less running while they are away. The Third World countryside is being left more and more in the hands of old people, women and children, NGOs and their projects for improvements. The men are leaving to try their luck in towns or in other countries.

When they reach town, what are their chances of finding well-paid work under the modern transnational economy? Multinational companies are the acknowledged base of the world economy, and their dynamic was not slowed by the crisis of 1974. They have created around 15 million jobs in the South in the last twenty years. This is hardly a negligible amount. But 500 or 800 million jobs would have been needed to reabsorb the workforce made expendable by the various processes of exclusion. At this rate, it would take six centuries of multinational expansion to find everyone a job. Meanwhile, the numbers continue to grow, and in less than a century the world population may reach 10 billion. Moreover, these jobs are being created while the North is experiencing higher and higher unemployment. Forty million people were counted poor in Western Europe in 1991, 20 to 30 million in the United States. As one homeless person in Casablanca declared:

> This here is a dead space; a space with no substance, no strength, no vitality, no desire, no life. We wrap ourselves in cotton wool; nothing makes sense, nothing is interesting. We don't live, we survive. ... Society is skidding towards unconsciousness, absurdity, rot.[6]

The millions of outcasts crammed into the shantytowns of Bombay, Sao Paulo and Abidjan would most probably agree.

Theology has a word for this state of material and moral abandon, a word which carries a further implication of disgrace or divine curse: *dereliction*. This seems to correspond well to the situation in which these billions of human beings find themselves: at one and the same time invited to the great feast of human brotherhood which the Western dream has conjured up, and then condemned to stay by the door and devour leftovers and crumbs, while rendering polite thanks.

The end of the Third World and the three 'Fourth Worlds'

There is no longer a Third World, now that the newly industrialising countries are joining the developed countries. For these NICs, poverty has virtually ceased to exist. They are about to enter the grand society. Thanks to the trickle-down effect, that is, to the dilution of growth via spin-off benefits from the rich to the poor, everyone experiences the benefits of development. This is the theory in Taiwan, formerly considered an underdeveloped country; likewise in South Korea, Hong Kong and Singapore. That means about 70 million lucky beneficiaries.

But the trickle-down effect operates poorly in Brazil, and not at all in India. There are still billions of people for whom the end of the Third World has spelt nothing but the end of a great hope.

This hope was born in Bandung in 1955,[7] and has been reaffirmed year by year with the rise of the Third World, or at least of its influence within the United Nations. The apotheosis came on 1 May 1974, when the UN unanimously proclaimed the new international economic order. After the political decolonisation of the 1960s, which saw the emergence of acceptance of the *rights of all peoples to self-determination*, it was possible to believe that prosperity for all and the *right to development* were next in line. The oil crisis in 1973-74, with its quadrupling of the price of oil, seemed the first manifestation of a new distribution of the cake.

Today, however, the great hopes placed in development have obviously been dashed. Every day the non-aligned group disintegrates further, and the socialist camp becomes more fragmented and in danger of disappearing altogether: first of all the Sino-Soviet conflict, then Sino-Vietnamese conflict, Cambodian genocide, war in Cambodia and Vietnam; now the crumbling of the Soviet empire, bloody conflicts in former Yugoslavia, etc. In the 1960s the Third World was unified by anti-imperialist ideology. Today that ideology becomes little more than a ritual incantation, as political conflicts and economic antagonism multiply in the South itself. In reality there is no longer a Third World; new groupings are crystallising with the emergence of new interests: the newly industrialising countries, the oil-exporting countries, the so-called semi-developed countries, and so on. Not even the debt crisis has strengthened Third World solidarity or given it a boost. There are great contrasts in situation, and it is not obvious where a common interest lies.

Twenty years ago a somewhat romantic *tiers-mondisme* (Third-Worldism), the ideology of planetary revolution which accorded to underdeveloped countries the messianic role in creation of a just socialist order which the proletariat had failed to fulfil, could capture the imagination. Now it is dead. Interestingly, a large part of Western bad conscience has somehow disappeared along with it. People in the West behave as though the end of a simplistic ideology of worldwide transformation – its credibility destroyed by practical complexity – has wiped the reality of poverty from the face of the earth. The fall of Eastern socialism, and widening belief in the marketplace as the sole creator of prosperity, are all working together to increase people's myopia towards the worsening realities of exclusion.

The down-and-outs, the rejects, never totally eliminated from the rich countries even in most prosperous times, have come to make up a 'Fourth World', a world which has inspired the creation of organisations dedicated to 'the relief of suffering'.

Looking at the rich countries, the plain fact is that economic growth generates maladjusted people. But to the moral suffering created by the stress of daily life in the grand society, is now being added greater and greater material suffering. More and more we encounter the *new poor*. New technologies have created unemployed with no rights, even in middle-management and amongst those traditionally protected through union membership. Above all, as techno-economic competition becomes more and more transnational in character, national solidarity is weakened. We are seeing an unprecedented development in modernised poverty. This in its turn stimulates the phenomena of drugs, crime and insecurity. How many people are we talking about? As we saw, the poor in Western Europe were counted at 40 million in 1991. If we add the 20 or 30 million North Americans living below the poverty line, and the other poor in Eastern Europe, we go well beyond 100 million.

The second group of outcasts are the native minorities throughout the 'developed' world: the Lapps or 'Sami' of the Great European North, the Eskimos or 'Inuit' of Canada, Greenland and Alaska, the Amerindians of North, Central and South America, the Australian aborigines, native Melanesians, and the Tsiganes (gypsies) spread throughout Europe. Here we have a collection of cultures who are very much minorities, often scattered across several nations, immovably set against modernity. There are between 200 million and 350 million human beings among them. These are the last 'Indians' who have refused to be good by refusing to die, and who are making desperate claims for their right to live according to their customs on their ancestral lands. Modernity has touched them all the same. Most of these indigenous people live in jeans and T-shirts, listening to Japanese transistors when they are not waving Kalashnikov rifles in support of their claims like the Mohawks of Quebec. They persist, however, in refusing to be integrally assimilated for as long as society at large refuses to recognise their right *not* to dominate nature and *not* to exploit her 'riches'.

The third group of outcasts, by far the most numerous at present, belong to the 'least advanced countries' (LACs, or equally LDCs, least developed countries). Here rejection is not confined merely to isolated individuals or ethnic groups, but extends to whole nation-states and their populations. Confronted with the dereliction visible in these nations, the international community throws up its hands: what can be done? The debt burden under which these countries are sinking has destroyed the naive illusions of the 1960s. When, in the 1960s and 1970s, the banks agreed to lend, they were convinced that investment, export and repayment were all possible. They believed sincerely in the ideology which said 'everyone can win'. The IMF, in imposing 'structural adjustment' policies based on the restoration of export capacity, still shows its faith in the complementary tenet of the game, that somehow 'all countries in the world can export more than they import' – a fallacy of cumulation and far from obvious! Now, however, we are forced to recognise that these countries can furnish nothing of interest to us. They are good only for placing in receivership or for the wrecker's yard. No one seriously thinks or dares say that they can still join in the 'international leap-frog competition'[8] and catch up with the others. Who would want to bet on Bangladesh, Ethiopia or Burkina Faso? What chance have these countries of entering the technological race, or of putting up their own telecommunications satellites? Or of rebuilding a high-performance industry? In the present context, absolutely none. It wouldn't matter whether they adopted a liberal, socialist or any other conceivable approach.

Populations in the throes of demographic expansion suffer the cruellest blows under modernity. They aspire to join in a feast where they are not wanted. Notwithstanding their misery, they do have enough cash to acquire chemical or bacteriological weapons. They do have sufficient technical and chemical knowledge to cobble together terrifying engines of death. There is already a black market in sophisticated weaponry at ridiculously low prices. It is not beyond the bounds of possibility that these countries might build or obtain nuclear weapons. Manufacturing death and insecurity is becoming much easier than transnational economic success. The idea of a community of nations was always more or less a fiction; now it has broken down completely, and this, along with decay in the social fabric of the rich countries, poses a major threat to the functioning of the whole system.

The techno-economic machine of modernity can move forward only provided that there is a modicum of social order.

However, while these three 'Fourth Worlds' engendered by the productivist machine threaten its continued operation, they also constitute a milieu in which cultural fermentation can take place: they are the laboratories of a possible future.

The planet of the vanquished

In spite of the gulf that separates them, the three 'Fourth Worlds' exhibit a certain number of common traits. They are all victims of progress, all in a situation of internal exile under the sway of planetary modernity. The sub-proletariat of the West, aborigines on reserves, or uprooted rural people in the LDCs, are all different examples of objectively identifiable outcasts from the great banquet of over-consumption, who live out their sentence in their improvised cultures of poverty. Relations with the outside world, with agents of power (police officer, judge, teacher, doctor) and officialdom (technocrats, bureaucrats), are strictly limited. For the rejected groups, this outside world wears a hostile or indifferent aspect. The poor of the West are seen as 'savages'. Services for the relief of suffering have to devise intercultural dialogue. Conversely, it is precisely the indigenous 'savages' of Canada, Australia, the United States and Lappland who are the poor of their own countries. Things are getting to the point now, however, where these neglected masses of the former Third World are forming a new and paradoxical collective identity: a veritable society of marginalised people. They can no longer be considered merely as small isolated groups in the midst of a rich society; they constitute an *other* society.

The state to which the dynamism of modernity has reduced two-thirds of humanity is an outright scandal. Black Africa in particular has been left to rot so flagrantly that French newspapers now have a field day with all the new *coups d'état* and each new famine. Afro-pessimism is definitely in vogue. There is something really indecent about this attitude when it is taken up by those who originally helped to chop up the new states and to put corrupt puppet regimes in place. Foreign banks retire, off-shore investors disappear, 'modern' local enterprises close one after another.

Official Africa has collapsed. Yet should we really mourn the fact?

The obsession with success, modernity's driving force, has no great place in the cultures of poverty. For two or three billion people in Latin America, Africa and Asia, there is no ambition to beat a joint team of Japanese, Europeans and Americans. Very few leaders, even when they are quite Westernised, dare set this forth as a clear objective. 'Africa talks business', said a blurb from Air Cameroon; but slogans like this are intended for Western consumption, not for locals. Monsignor Valaro, the president of Caritas (a Catholic aid organisation), once told a story of market day in Madagascar:

A poor peasant settled himself on the kerb with his five tomatoes, his two fish and his kilo of sweet potatoes. Early in the morning a stranger came by who offered to buy the whole stock at a high price. After thinking for a while in silence, the old peasant replied: 'No, the main reason I come here is to get news of friends and family. If I take your money now, I have no profitable reason to stay in the market the rest of the day with everyone else. Laughing with them helps me forget suffering; you must savour the gift of time, it is a gift of the gods.'

The economist Claude Albagli quotes a similar experience when he arrived in Mali in 1973. There, the canniest seller did agree to get rid of all her stock and to forgo the pleasure of dealing with customers and friends, provided she could get the highest price! In effect, wholesale prices are higher than retail prices. A reasonable attitude, concludes Albagli, even if quite the opposite of what we learn in economics manuals.[9]

The Third World is full of these 'unfortunates'. In Laos they 'listen to the rice grow', in India they chant to Brahma and Vishnu, in Brazil they dance the samba. The development experts and project sponsors, evangelical bearers of the good news, have long cursed these recalcitrant and backward people, seemingly 'allergic' to development.

What should be done with the conquered, the weak, the outcast and the recalcitrant? Puritan or Jansenist theology has a perfect hell planned for them. According to the creed of the Latter Day Saints (the Mormons), 'a lazy or indolent man cannot be Christian and be saved. He is destined to be struck down and cast from the hive.'[10] For a long time the West has rejected the swarming mass of the proletariat in their midst, and has viewed them as a horde of layabouts and alcoholics being punished for their sins and responsible for their own state. Just like the proletariat, the inferior races of the rest of the world should submit to the yoke of the elect, and be kept dutiful and moral – by force if needs be. The Afrikaners of South Africa still hold to this traditional 'Protestant' vision. The 'winners' club thus tends to view the rest of the world as a heterogeneous mass of vanquished peoples, losers, doomed to scorn and misery.

This does not imply that a competitive spirit and concern for excellence are foreign concepts amongst non-Western peoples. On the contrary, in most traditional societies you will find bitter rivalries, ritual struggles and unrelenting competition, supposedly for the acquisition of 'wealth'. It is sufficient to recall René Girard's thesis that mimetic (copycat) rivalry lies at the heart of all human relations.[11] Indeed the forms that the competition takes are innumerable, and it is out of the question to do an inventory of them here. The *potlatch* practised by the Indians of British Columbia, for example, is a spectacular form of competition among chiefs, linked with the acquisition of 'riches'. One ought not to forget that the system of recruitment by competitive process which rules in most administrations and even in most large enterprises, was borrowed from the celestial bureaucracy of Imperial China. The ancient Greeks vied with each other in the Olympic Games just as they did in political life. As Hannah Arendt notes:

> To belong to the few 'equals' (*homoioi*) meant to be permitted to live among one's peers; but the public realm itself, the *polis*, was permeated by a fiercely agonal spirit, where everybody had constantly to distinguish himself from all others, to show through unique deeds or achievements that he was the best of all (*aien aristeuein*). The public realm, in other words, was reserved for individuality; it was the only place where men could show who they really and inexchangeably were.[12]

None the less, this rivalry of the Greeks did not result in social exclusion. It was limited to the political sphere and did not invade the material basis of life, which remained part of the private domain. At bottom, the political game was a sort of sport. Modern society has turned this upside down.

The procedure of competition for entry was borrowed by the West from the Chinese because it satisfies the democratic ideal of equal opportunity within liberal societies which have no mechanism for keeping their institutions running on a purely associative basis. More particularly, competition is the natural form of selection for ability in

a 'free society' dominated by the search for efficiency and performance. Private enterprises, which for a long time recruited management
from family connections and conferred favours on family and clients,
have increasingly had to yield to competitive rule. However, it is quite
evident that the competitive processes in ancient China were not
intended to spread competitiveness everywhere; on the contrary, they
were used as a means to help reproduce an immutable social order by
warding off attempts to build feudal groupings.

As for the *potlatch*, it actually allowed chiefs to turn unbridled
ambition to the accumulation of wealth, as an effective way of neu-
tralising that ambition. Amassing wealth was a matter of 'making a
name for oneself'. Thorstein Veblen, in *The Theory of the Leisure
Class*, described this as a way of publicly ranking people by the
socially sanctioned criterion of 'what they are worth'.[13] Pierre Clastres, in his anthropological studies, shows well how warrior rivalry is
neutralised within societies without a state:

> The chief's prestige is harmless; he has no power. Brave warriors are
> allowed to show off their glory provided that in so doing they get rid of
> themselves by killing each other off.[14]

The 'bigman' of New Guinea must redistribute his wealth and can only
'make a name for himself' by these acts of counter-giving. I myself
witnessed a Melanesian member of the New Britain parliament being
'divested' of his suit by his nude compatriots; as a spectacle this is
incomprehensible to the Westerner, yet it does not lack grandeur.
Someone who has made a name for himself furthermore sees his power
and prestige limited by other 'great men'. Among the Baruya, the great
farmer offsets the great warrior or the great shaman.[15]

Speaking generally, competition, rivalry and the effort to excel
have all been recognised and honoured in most societies not as a
natural mechanism at the heart of society, but as social games and
rituals which exorcise the domineering urges that endanger social
equilibrium. The dimension of 'individualism' and the taste for excess
are put on public display and neutralise themselves.

Many analysts of Third World societies have failed to see this
crucial difference: that in 'traditional' societies, competitive elements
are specifically put to the service of group solidarity. Economists, as
they have uncovered the subtle strategies used by the excluded in the
informal economy of Africa and in other regions of the Third World,

have partly revised their pessimistic assessment of the spirit of enterprise among the indigenous population. A new niche is created by and for the intellectual investigator: the idea of management African-style (or any other exotic style). Wherever rivalry and competition are perceived, there can be found the seeds of entrepreneurial activity, the potential emergence of market society. If the rivalries in play in these informal societies are enmeshed with particular cultural imperatives and solidarities, it is hard to imagine how the qualities of ingenuity, shrewdness and resourcefulness which the castaways manifest in making their derelict lives convivial could be 'channelled' by the World Bank into new development projects. But the West would be rejecting its own tenets if it didn't make the attempt.[16]

Hell and paradise

According to world statistics, the average yearly income per capita in 1988 was $210 in Burkina Faso, compared to $16,080 in France, $19,780 in the United States and $27,260 in Switzerland. This might be taken to mean that Westerners are around a hundred times better off than the Burkinaby. Does this mean that they are a hundred times happier? Evidently not, nor do they eat a hundred times more, or dress a hundred times better.[17] If we propose, in line with some sociologists, that the suicide tally is a good indicator of quality of life, then we arrive at very different conclusions. It is possible to live a relatively happy life in conditions of great frugality and even fierce exclusion. The film on the 'criminal caste', mentioned earlier, showed a moving image of an old couple radiating tranquil happiness under very marginal conditions. Also shown was the revolt of the younger generation: too fierce an exclusion creates unsustainable frustrations, while extreme poverty compromises survival. In Northern Uganda, the British anthropologist Colin Turnbull met a population of itinerant hunters, the Iks, whom forced settlement had transformed into a kind of caricature of their wild state. The struggle for survival in this case has taken the route of cruelty and the loss of all sentiments of sociability.[18]

A great many of the victims of the development process, and of Westernisation more generally, are actively responding to their predicament and seeking to ensure their survival. Only rarely does this defensive reaction take the radical and desperate shape offered to us in the desolate spectacle of the Iks. More often there is a creative technical, economic, social and imaginative response. This may go so far as sketching the contours of an authentically *post-modern* society. Technical and economic dimensions here are totally absorbed into networks of solidarity and reciprocity built out of new myths and visions, cobbled together with more or less grace. Whatever the specifics, we are speaking of the informal.

The informal is an enormous nebula which expresses the seething chaos of human life in all its dimensions, with its horrors and its marvels. Employment within the informal is estimated to furnish between 60% and 80% of urban jobs in most Third World towns. As the informal connects also with the countryside, and as it is not limited to jobs alone, it would not be excessive to imagine that the informal nebula involves billions of human beings and encompasses situations of extreme contrast. Without closing our eyes and painting the entire picture rosy, we may assert that we are witnessing a rebuilding of social bonds sufficient to justify some hope. It is a question of how far to forget that the survival and success of informal activities rest on the young girls who wear themselves out for a *dirham* (a fraction of a dollar) a day in the obscure dressmaking workshops in the medina at Casablanca. It is thanks to them that the fake Lacoste shirts which delight the tourists cost so little. There are also the tens of thousands of children of both sexes sold into quasi-slavery in small Thai businesses, and the hammock-makers of Fortaleza (in north-eastern Brazil) who work interminable hours for poverty wages. It is impossible to draw up a final tally of the blood, sweat and tears which have bought survival for the excluded.

It is less common for things to reach these extremes of savage exploitation in Africa, though numerous testimonies to the contrary can be produced. Against all apparent logic, this strangled and divided Africa is surviving, and in many ways surviving better than Latin America and South East Asia, even though the latter have a much higher GNP (gross national product): $1,000 per head in Thailand, $1,510 in Brazil in 1988. The paradox, though, is only on the surface. Africa, which has suffered less destruction and deculturation, and which is less turned towards the world market, has some trump cards of its own, with which to rebuild a new society and invest creativity and dynamism into its own solutions. The preservation or reconstruction of social solidarity works to ease the shocking effects of having been so determinedly cast out from modernity's party. Popular self-organisation leads to some astonishing successes, and the basis for this merits examination.

The grand society refuted

Just about everywhere in the Third World you may come across wise old sages, like the Amerindian chief quoted at the beginning of this book, convinced that the West is running to its doom and that the people crushed in its path yet have something to say. In Oceania as in Africa, strange prophets may be encountered proclaiming the hour of vengeance or more simply the hour of victory for the outcasts of the grand society. These birds of ill omen often have only a superficial acquaintance with the grand society, and are doubtless ill-informed of its durability – even if they have a good intuitive sense of its power. One may question the profundity of their message and their claim to another mode of understanding.

The normal response to announcements that modernity's grand society is collapsing is a sceptical one. Hopes placed on the performance of the barefoot friars who live on the city margins or in the countryside of another age would seem to be fragile indeed. Even the best successes in the informal sector or the achievements of some bush peasant groups look a little derisory beside the opulence of a jet-age society capable of conquering space and manipulating nature. Only a real optimist could see in these patchings and mendings the annunciation of another society. None the less, the very existence of this 'informal nebula', of this lean-to adjacent to modernity, a patchwork of hangovers from the past and borrowings from modern techniques, materials, myths and ideologies, amounts to a *fundamental challenge* to the exclusive pretensions of the grand society.

The grand society is *exclusive* in the sense that it is based on values that are claimed to be both unique and universal. It alone embodies the destiny of humanity, the pathway of human progress and social evolution. So it becomes inconceivable, once exposed to this true path, not to follow it – unless, of course, one is excluded from it. The grand society is, according to modernity's own mythology, the unique and definitive expression of reason in human affairs. Modernity alone is rational and embodies rationality *par excellence*. Moreover, there could not possibly be two fundamentally different modes of social organisation that are each rational, because reason is singular. So all other forms of sociability prior to modernity must, being irrational, disappear in modernity's path. Other societies are, at best, only *earlier forms* of modernity; they rest on irrational foundations, mystifying superstitions and restrictive traditions. Their only chance is to melt into the grand society through modernising; otherwise they are doomed to disappear, as being too archaic or rigid to recognise their inevitable future.

Considered in these terms, the informal is a serious threat and a paradox for modernity. Understandably enough, its existence was for a long time denied outright by Western analysts – it was trivialised as being the mere vestige of a disappearing past. But finally it has had to be tolerated in the face of evidence that it refuses to go away. It is still, however, considered to be provisional or transitory, never recognised for itself. Why not? The existence (or admission) of even one single contemporary social form fundamentally *different* from the grand society would be like the 'crucial experiment' in science which 'proves' that the rule or hypothesis is not true. A single negative observation, according to the philosopher Karl Popper, is sufficient basis to declare a law false. In this sense acknowledgement of the informal nebula as a distinct and viable social form in and for itself, overturns the exclusive and universalist pretensions of the grand society.

It seems that the grand society, whose own rationality decrees all other societies to be irrational and which acts the self-fulfilling prophet by exterminating them, has ended up by creating and nourishing a new irrational which, refusing to be abolished, must be recognised as incarnating an *other* reason. The proliferation of the informal thus scandalises Western reason. History itself starts to lose sense. If several social forms, even all forms, can coexist, and some of them that we thought were outdated can come back into use, then neither evolution nor progress can be said definitely to exist!

In his book *The Great Transformation*, Karl Polanyi has shown how modern society has blossomed through detaching the economic from the rest of the social dimension. Giving autonomy to 'the economy' by generalising the marketplace allowed the space for rational calculus in the modern sense to develop; and the application of this calculus becomes more and more the norm in every facet of society.[19] This liberation has in turn nourished an uninhibited progress of technology and an endless accumulation of capital and commodities. As part of the same dynamic, though, modern society excludes great masses of people whom it annexes to its purposes along the way. Judged unfit to play a role in the techno-economic machine, these outcasts survive by reactivating solidarity networks and reinventing a lost mode of social interaction. The networks of reciprocity and the logics which permit their persistence and proliferation derive from a *re-embedding* of the economic within the social. This manoeuvre is their ticket out of the impasses of the modern world, the impasses deriving from the dynamic of autonomisation (disembedding) of the commodity realm in the West.

Even if the informal modes of socialising end up being destroyed for one reason or another without leading to the 'alternative' society of castaways, the informal still refutes the universalist claims of modernity. Moreover, it is pretty clear that this refutation entails no triumph by the traditional 'enemies of the open society' (central planning, fascism, etc.), notwithstanding the fact that the outcasts are likely to feel far from friendly towards this society. The liberal and democratic forms of the grand society are threatened by old forms of totalitarianism which are still capable of rising up, for example Nazism or communism. But these forms of totalitarian society are not something radically *other* than modernity; they are only perversions of it. This sort of totalitarianism doesn't destroy the grand society, it takes it over by subverting it from within. Nazism and communism were delinquent forms of the grand society and had Western faces. It is true that the collapse of the grand society may indeed give rise to totalitarian surges anywhere in the world, South or North. However, the features of the castaways' planet that we are about to explore are at the very antipodes of these sinister changelings of the West itself.

Notes

1. Gérard Bonnot, *La Vie c'est autre chose*, Belfond, Paris, 1976, p. 156.

2. Cowries, shells of the porcelain family, *Cypraea moneta* or *Cypraea annulus*, used traditionally as a form of currency and as a symbol of wealth.

3. See Madeleine Pere, *Les Lobi, tradition et changement*, Editions Siloe, Laval, 1988.

4. 'Technocosmos' or 'technical universe' is a term suggested by Pierre Lévy in *La Machine univers*, La Découverte, Paris, 1987, p. 11.

5. As discussed in the Introduction, this concept *(la grande société)* is used to embrace the several facets of idealised modernity, including connotations of Hayek's 'great society' made up of free and freedom-loving individuals; of the 'affluent society'

famously critiqued by Galbraith; of Karl Popper's 'open society' characterised by emancipation through democratic debate and scientific progress; of the community of nations; and more prosaically of the 'world marketplace' which, increasingly, is mistaken as synonymous with the 'global village'. – *Translators' note*.

6. Editorial in the Moroccan review *Lamalif*, quoted by Jean Chesneaux in *Modernité-monde*, La Découverte, Paris, 1989, p. 51.

7. The conference in Bandung, a regional capital on the island of Java, Indonesia, which marked the beginning of the non-aligned movement on the world political stage. – *Translators' note*.

8. In French the expression is *'la partie internationale de saute-mouton'*: the 'international sheep-hurdling festival'; it is a phrase given currency by economist Charles P. Kindleberger.

9. Claude Albagli, *L'Economie des dieux céréaliers*, L'Harmattan, Paris, 1989, p. 161.

10. Max Weber, *The Protestant Ethic and the Spirit of Capitalism*, English translation by Talcott Parsons, Allen & Unwin, London, 1930 (2nd impression 1948), p. 264.

11. René Girard, *Violence and the Sacred*, English translation, Johns Hopkins University Press, Baltimore, 1977. (Original: *La Violence et le sacré*, Grasset, Paris, 1972.)

12. Hannah Arendt, *The Human Condition*, University of Chicago Press, 1958, p. 41. As she notes, already in Homer's time this was the hero's primary concern: 'Aien aristeuein kai hypeirochon emmenai allon' (Always to be the best and to rise above others, *Iliad*, vi, 208); and Homer was the 'educator of Hellas'.

13. Thorstein Veblen, *The Theory of the Leisure Class*, Vanguard Press, New York, 1928; as cited by Paul Dumouchel & Jean-Pierre Dupuy, *L'Enfer des choses*, Seuil, Paris, 1979, p. 40.

14. Jean-Pierre Dupuy, in *L'Enfer des choses*, op. cit., p. 34, referring to Pierre Clastres, *La Société contre l'état*, Minuit, Paris, 1974.

15. See Maurice Godelier, *The Making of Great Men: male domination and power among the New Guinea Baruya*, Cambridge University Press, 1986. (Translation by Rupert Swyer of *La Production des grands hommes*, Fayard, Paris, 1982.) See also Maurice Godelier & Marilyn Strathern (editors), *Big Men and Great Men: personification of power in Melanesia*, Cambridge University Press, 1991.

16. This leads to all sorts of ambiguities in development politics, as discussed in Chapters 4 and 5 below.

17. The fallacies of measures of a 'standard of living' are a central theme of Chapter 6 below.

18. Colin Turnbull, *The Mountain People*, Cape, London, 1973.

19. Karl Polanyi, *The Great Transformation*, Beacon Press paperback, Boston 1957 (original edition 1944).

2

The Myth of a World of Winners

I assert that we live in a marvellous world. We Westerners have the distinguished privilege of living in the best society that history and humanity have ever known. It is the most just, the most egalitarian and most humane society in history.

Karl Popper[1]

The Western dream promises that all humanity shall enter into paradise. The rapid accumulation of wealth by America provided a spectacular beginning to 'this fairytale of modernity'.[2] For all that, the Puritan or Jansenist vision of a world with a small number of elect has not been exorcised from the scene. It is a great and terrible mystery that these two things can coexist: the affirmation that the brotherhood of man exists and is being realised; and the constant preoccupation with the savage struggle to emerge from the lot of the damned and keep one's head above water.

A world of winners

'Europe,' declared Jacques Chirac, 'will be gentle on the strong and hard on the weak.'[3] Salvation is reserved for those who merit it, the strong, those marked with the sign of grace. 'We have four years,' Chirac went on, 'to become strong and that means doing what is necessary to reinforce our national cohesion and our economic and material strength.'[4]

Chirac's message to the French was much the same as what they have heard repeatedly during the 1980s from their President François Mitterrand and socialist prime ministers such as Michel Rocard. The significance of this unison becomes clear when we note that the message is strangely similar to that given by Margaret Thatcher to the English and by Helmut Kohl to the Germans, and that heard by the Italians, the Spanish and the other peoples of the European Community.

Outside the Community, will the world be less competitive and more merciful to the 'weak'? There is good reason to doubt it. Young Japanese children live in a condition one can well compare with the savage exploitation of children in England's nineteenth-century mills. As Michio Morishima has documented, in the contest to get employment within one of the great corporations, 'the children of nearly all social classes are caught up in the ruthless competition of the university entrance exams'. In effect they slave, from kindergarten onwards, for up to thirteen or fourteen hours a day, in order to have a chance in life, and to give best advantage to those businesses to whom they will sell themselves body and soul.[5] The present titleholders, the Americans, are constantly exhorting each other to band together to retain the lead and avoid being overtaken: they are doing their utmost to check their slide down the slippery and irresistible slope of economic decline. Meanwhile, the new industrial countries of South East Asia, named for good reason 'the four little tigers' or 'the four dragons', are imitating the Japanese, sometimes even outdoing their big brother in performance and zeal.

This *drive to win* is not only expressed at the level of the states who take part in the 'international leap-frog competition'. It is also expressed in the most intimate domains of people's private lives. Far from being just a 'rule of the game' in the economic sphere, it is a dictate which extends further and further into the whole of social life. The media exalt it, politicians make slogans of it. Women take it as their inspiration to climb over men to take their rightful place in the sun. Children live it at school and generally adopt the competitive ethos with pride. Formerly confined to the limited sphere of the business world, or in a society formed by Western conquest to whom the self-made man is the rightful hero, the ideology of *mounting a challenge* and of *winning* has little by little invaded the whole social world. Through the effects of advertising, love itself is now ruled by the performance myth. This invasion is all the more striking in France, where Catholic Latin roots have for a long time kept this social Darwinism at bay. Recent presidential and parliamentary election campaigns have been pursued under the banner 'France is winning'. Socialists gaily talk of the win-focused France of 'Tapseg'.[6] There is no real divergence between political parties in this vision – which is, no doubt, the reason for the absence of meaningful political debate.

Does this France which is winning represent all the French people, or just some? Is it a France of some French versus the majority of the others? The France of 'Tapseg' against that of the unemployed? And even if there is an economic solidarity at a national level, and all

French people – or even all Europeans – are included in the fold, what will become of the others still outside? This raises a moral problem which Montesquieu addressed long ago:

> If I knew something which would do good to my country and harm to Europe, or good to Europe and harm to humanity, I would treat it as a crime.

The dilemma of European 'integration' poses a modern-day version of the same problem. As Alain Lipietz puts it:

> The question is not whether the Common Market and the Single Act which carries the economic unification to its full conclusion, are good for France; rather, are they good for Europe? And if they are, are they good for humanity?[7]

The 'Tapseg' discourse of winners is increasingly occupying the political centre stage, displacing an older rhetoric emphasising social and economic solidarity. Bernard Tapie himself is very explicit. On television recently he declared: 'Things are going to change. For once we are going to help winners rather than losers.'[8] Above all this signals a shift in mentality. As Tapie's associate Seguela declared: 'What I am interested in, is not conquering markets, but conquering people's imaginations.'[9] Of course this does not mean an end to business rivalries and corporate takeover struggles; rather it means that the customs of the business world are now spilling over into politics. The winning team, in advertising agency mentality, is the one that wins (success in the presidential election, or in the marketplace); and vice versa. At local level the same sort of argument is heard. For example, in municipal elections during the 1988 campaign in Nice, enormous posters sang an unwearying refrain: 'Nice is winning with Jacques Medecin.' Indeed it was more or less the same rhetoric everywhere, no matter what the party ticket.[10]

This competitive morality has perverted politics and business, and on the rebound has politicised sport and turned it into 'business'. However, as Wladimir Andreff writes:

> If the code 'we must win', including monetary gain, has become a sort of worldwide standard in sport, then by reason of the dysfunctionings I have analysed, 'we won' as a formula starts to lose its meaning and its worth,

becoming less and less able to create common spirit or solidarity (given the methods used to win) outside a fairly narrow nationalism, racism, 'revenge mentality' or parochialism.[11]

The pleasure of the game, calm acceptance of defeat, friendliness with the opponent no matter what the result, all of these things are being trampled under the imperative of victory. The same urgent breath of havoc is communicated to the spectators, whose increasingly savage behaviour puts to shame the warlike customs of so-called primitive tribes. It is hard to escape from this competitive atmosphere. In any martial arts practice hall this 'fever to win' is evident in the stinging assaults and bitter defeats even in the course of friendly training bouts. Equally one has to doubt that the energy spent by individuals in arriving first at the top of a mountain during a summer holiday walk is a simple case of self-mastery and accomplishment for oneself.[12] High performance in the sporting sense becomes corrupted by obsession with 'gain'.

A similar situation holds where our children's schooling is concerned. The timid reforms introduced in France after 1968 with a view to enriching education have not withstood the torrential return of frenzied competition. Some convincing studies showing that excessive individual rivalry and systematic streaming have a pernicious influence on the development of balanced groups, have had negligible impact under the pressure of *cold hard facts*. There's no value, people say, in talking about disastrous psychological consequences; this is not much use when the task in hand is to ensure success.[13]

Is this the result of the progress of which we are so proud – to have reduced all the richness of life to the most radical imperative of survival, even while the people we consider far behind us can still afford the luxury of living?

We're all winners

Since the Second World War, in industrialised countries, it has become clear that continuous growth will eventually benefit even the workers. Thus the belief that we can all win together has become a dogma. Hell will disappear as it ceases to have any significance. The Church has likewise had its day. Development for all becomes, henceforth, the modern scientific rendering of the objective which Bentham, English philosopher and founder of utilitarianism, attributed to social action on his radical platform: 'The greatest happiness for the greatest number.'

Jacques Chirac, in the same speech of January 1989 cited above, alluded to the Declaration of Human Rights and expressed the wish that 'rich countries would take sharper notice of the worsening situations unfolding in developing countries'. He then went on:

> How can the French, the Europeans and the other industrialised countries call themselves holders of a certain philosophy regarding these human rights, which we trumpet and pat ourselves on the back for, if we make no concrete response to the tragedy of the worsening misery of the Earth's poorest?[14]

What is the issue here? Is it a matter of giving alms? Of charity? Having conquered and ruined others, it seems that we now are called upon to try to prevent them from dying. The inconsistencies are plain. Are we supposed to believe that not even the poorest countries, such as the Burkinaby, are 'losers' in the great combat of world economic affairs? If so, how can Europe be hard on its own weaker members, while still holding out a rescuing hand to the weak of the rest of the world, so they can grow strong in turn and win as well?

It would be unjust to accuse the former Prime Minister of France of bad faith and hypocrisy. In any case, his speech is astonishingly similar to speeches made by all the Western heads of state. The rhetoric has hardly changed since President Truman gave his 'Address on the state of the Union' on 20 January 1949, with its famous Point 4:

> We must embark on a bold new program for making the benefit of our scientific advances and industrial progress available for the improvement and growth of underdeveloped areas.[15]

Since that day, belief in the precept 'good deeds equal good business' has become one of the cornerstones of Western discourse. Upheld by heads of state, the same discourse is maintained – with varying degrees of sincerity – by political opposition leaders, the Christian Churches, and a wide range of non-governmental organisations.

While not entirely supplanting the earlier elitist belief in a select few, this generalised will-to-conquer opens up the possibility of everyone emerging victorious from the fray. None the less there is still an obsessive and anxious search for signs of divine election. Within each trading bloc, nation, or commercial enterprise, people are urgently counselled to join forces in order to make sure they win. At the same time we tell ourselves over and over again that this game of the grand society will end in victory for all. How is this seeming paradox possible?

The answers are simple. First and foremost because, supposedly, it is not a zero-sum game. Secondly because, on certain assumptions, competitive cooperation can be worthwhile for everyone. And finally because, at a certain level, the interests of the competitors are in harmony.

However, these propositions hold only under *certain very restrictive conditions*. Closer scrutiny shows that it is impossible to turn this exceptional case into the general rule.

Together we'll win: the proposition that the game is not zero-sum

The argument implicit in Western ideology is as follows. No matter how relentless the competition between people, it is not solely a matter of one side attempting to seize the booty that the other is fiercely defending. Contrary to simplistic visions of class struggle, bosses thrive not by impoverishing their workers but by making them comfortable; great chiefs of enterprise achieve opulence not by ruining their competitors but by fruitful rivalry with them. States themselves prosper more by trade and cooperation than by pillage. Since the eighteenth century the West has celebrated the idea of a 'healthy commerce' which enriches all nations while at the same time refining local manners and customs. It is not a matter of having to share out a fixed amount of treasure. For centuries, even millennia, the essential 'wealth' of the world was made up of a quasi-finite stock of gold and precious stones, objects of finery and display. In such circumstances hard work alone could lead only to small gains of surplus wealth. So theft, pillage, extortion, rape and plunder, piracy in brutal or institutionalised forms, were understandable as ways of turning the wheel of fortune, enriching some to the detriment of others. The game was zero-sum or involved only a very slight net gain.

But then, it seems, progress in science and technology, directed towards industry, changed all that. It is now possible to extract prodigious quantities of *wealth* from nature, and this opens up the prospect of giving everyone what they need – and more – without depriving anybody. Now bosses and workers, businesses in competition, even rival nations, all have a common interest in cooperating in the fight against humanity's primary foe: nature. This old crone must be forced to yield her secrets, her mysteries must be revealed, her formulae appropriated.[16]

It follows that scientific and technical cooperation is imperative if humanity is to triumph. Under the aegis of the United Nations – via its specialised agencies such as UNESCO, WHO, ILO, UNCTAD, FAO, and so on – and also through direct commercial relations, bilateral cooperation and the establishment of communal laboratories, sovereign states carry out trade in knowledge, sharing the results of their discoveries. Indeed, the international scientific community constitutes, through its networks of conferences, journals and other publications, a real force of cooperation whose exchanges often escape state control. Industrial conglomerates themselves, whatever their rivalries, often finance common research institutes, cooperate in setting up experimental plants and testing new techniques, and acknowledge the reciprocal benefits of opening their factories to visits by their competitors. Transcending the innumerable conflicts which divide them is their common interest in furthering the conquest of nature (and thus the triumph of humanity).

The fight against Aids is a classic illustration of this mentality. Notwithstanding the violent polemic which set French and American teams against each other in the race to discover the formula for the retrovirus, cooperation in the actual research prevailed. The rationale for this was self-evident, given what was at stake for humanity – more obvious, anyway, than when a business launches a new perfumed washing powder, or when a state research institution discovers a new toxic gas.[17]

Solidarity among workers and management is just as fundamental. Taylor strongly affirmed this, at a time when the intensity of the class struggle disguised the fact that production is necessarily the result of a common endeavour by bosses and workers. Taylor's message was that scientifically organised work allows increased productivity, through rationalising time and motion and standardising production. Bosses and workers can be winners *together*, as long as both parties are willing to give up trying to exploit each other to the greatest extent possible. It is true that workers are not in control of how they work. But in return for agreeing to be cogs in the machine, they will come to share in a certain opulence. In making *their* business a winner, in accordance with Taylor's precepts, they will share in its enrichment. And in making business as a whole a winner, as with Ford, the workers as a whole come to share in the general prosperity.

The idea is to expend all your energy productively, for the benefit of the team as a whole, just as if you were engaged in a sporting activity. In his analysis of the non-Taylorised factory, Taylor made the explicit comparison:

> When an American worker plays baseball, undoubtedly he gives his all to help his team to victory. Yet when the same worker comes back to work the next day, instead of exerting himself to produce the maximum, in the majority of cases, this man exerts himself to do as little as possible without risking the sack.[18]

Much earlier, Adam Smith had hinted at the gains in productivity that could be expected from the rational organisation of work, with his example of pin manufacture. However, he denounced the negative effects of this forced cooperation in terms that Marx himself would not have disowned:

> In the progress of the division of labour, the employment of the far greater part of those who live by labour, that is, of the great body of the people, comes to be confined to a few very simple operations, frequently to one or two. But the understandings of the greater part of men are necessarily formed by their ordinary employments. The man whose whole life is spent in performing a few simple operations, of which the effects too are, perhaps, always the same, or very nearly the same, has no occasion to exercise his understanding, or to exercise his invention in finding expedients for removing difficulties which never occur. He naturally loses, therefore, the habit of such exertion, and generally becomes as stupid and ignorant as it is possible for a human creature to become. The torpor of his mind renders him, not only incapable of relishing or bearing a part in any rational conversation, but of conceiving any generous, noble, or tender sentiment, and consequently of forming any just judgement concerning many even of the ordinary duties of private life.[19]

The present crisis of Taylorism and Fordism is, indeed, encouraging a greater emphasis on active cooperation between workers across all levels of a business enterprise. The introduction of new technologies, in particular the effective operation of flexible workshops, depends on better teamwork to eliminate defective items and avoid machine breakdowns. The ultimate aim in the new management style is the 'six zeros business': defects zero, breakdowns zero, stockpiles zero, delays zero, bumph zero, morale crisis zero.[20] The setting up of *quality circles* is the symbol of this new spirit. The workers accept that they must adapt still further to the machines and they must renounce biological rhythms for shift work; they sell their 'loyalty' to the business and make themselves attentive at every moment to the activity of sophisticated machines. In this way the workers collectively make *their* business win; and so, cumulatively, business *as a whole* is the winner, all of which brings benefits back to the workers themselves.

This view is not entirely without basis. But the supposed harmony of interests – all winners together – is simply taken for granted at the outset. This optimistic postulate is what allows industrial society to be seen as a marvellous engine in the service of everyone – rather than, as I propose, an infernal machine.

A 'human machine'

The most marvellous invention of the human mind, without which science and technology could not have progressed nearly as far as they have, nor seen anything like their full practical application, is the 'social machine'. Modernity's project of constructing a society on the base of utilitarian reason alone has given birth to the most prodigious mechanical edifice ever conceived. Modern political, economic and military organisation breaks with tradition in every way. Action does not follow routine, but is driven by the *search for efficiency*. In this context efficiency is just another word for *rationality*. The central precept is twofold: economise on *means* in realising any given objective; at the same time, mobilise *all available means* so as to obtain the best overall result.

The self-interested individual is not a 'natural' entity, but emerges out of the shattering of mutually supportive communities into a multitude of separate members. Once constituted, however, this social atom becomes the building-block of the liberal society. In his search for maximum happiness, he will expend all the energy available to him.[21] He might be a good soldier, a good citizen, a good producer;

the same principle applies in each case. Competition between groups and nations then carries the same logic up to a higher level. However, if the basic purpose of this competitive struggle between people, groups and nations is to be achieved – namely the greatest possible domination of nature – some sort of social organisation is needed to ensure solidarity between the individual agents. The basis for this solidarity is a *contract* ensuring a common interest in this goal. The social contract on which the nation-state is founded is a voluntary association of individuals which ensures maximum rights (peace, security, civil rights) to the parties involved while minimising their obligations (fiscal, juridical). A similar logic is in evidence with the division of labour in the workplace: the work contract on which business is founded aims likewise to maximise production and revenue while minimising costs (effort, investment, raw materials).

The division of labour, it has been said since Adam Smith, is the organisation of people for production in such a way as to allow maximum productivity in a given state of knowledge and techniques. However, this organisation is continually transformed by the forces within society and within the workplace itself: competition between agents, the ways workers interact and communicate, the interface between people and machinery, the invention of new techniques and new instruments requiring new ways of organising workers, new adaptations by individuals to the world of production and consumption – and also interdependently in the social and political spheres. But behind all these changes is an unchanging imperative; what I will refer to as the double law of the *maximine*:[22] maximum results and enjoyment, minimum costs and effort in attaining them. This law is none other than the law of progress: the *perfecting* of all nature, in all its domains, is continuous and cumulative, the march is 'infinite' and 'indefinite'.[23]

This principle of *maximine* is, in essence, utilitarian in the Benthamite sense. It is not by chance that we owe to Bentham himself the introduction of the verbs maximise and minimise. Utilitarianism aspires to perpetual and universal optimisation.[24] Competition reveals successes and punishes the mistakes of individuals, enterprises, groups, nations. This empirical testing-out by the marketplace is the supreme arbiter, ensuring that rationality and efficiency prevail. The social machine as a whole thus realises, in a supposedly admirable way, a synthesis between struggle on all levels and cooperation on all levels, equally to the benefit of humanity, the great winner of the primordial and cosmic confrontation with nature. In this hallowed image of the mechanics of progress, all reference to the possible limits and dysfunctioning of the machine is erased.

The three circles of paradise, or the renewal of old moons

In reality, the social machine is far from perfect. Even in its own terms, this rationality gives rise to innumerable mishaps and wastages. There is no 'natural' solution to the problem of how to organise the components of the machine, and inevitably the human cogs get organised according to technocratic and bureaucratic logics. In most organisations, Parkinson's Law holds total sway, hierarchic structures bend inevitably to the Peter Principle.[25] Incompetence and corruption are widespread. Catastrophes occur on a daily basis, ranging from the personally inconvenient to planning bungles and 'industrial accidents' that threaten entire cities or regions. The obsession with performance does not translate into the capacity to find an infallible means of achieving it. A wholly operationalised society truly obedient to the performance principle is an unrealisable fantasy.

Rigidities and failures allow the proponents of improved performance to denounce the dysfunctionings of existing forms of organisation. Managers and theorists thus find themselves oscillating around rigid prescriptions and the need for flexibility.[26] The same dialectic unfolds at the level of political and economic regimes. Unfortunately there is no stable point of compromise between authority and spontaneity, cooperation and unbridled individualism. This explains the constant reorganising of the machine.

The law is immutable, but prophets change. Today, the exegesis of the performance law exemplified in Jacques Chirac's speech is to be found everywhere. The media spread it all round the planet; heads of business and of state set about giving practical effect to it in the economic and political spheres. Scholars, and most particularly economists, are its guardians – not inventors of the law as such, but certainly the gatekeepers of its successive canonical formulations.[27]

The law of the *maximine* – of rationality/efficiency and progress – has, in effect, seen three major formulations. Each phase is characterised by a distinctive formulation of the rivalry/solidarity synthesis constituting what might be called a *virtuous circle* or a *circle of paradise*. These virtuous circles have given successive blueprints for achieving modernity's unchanged utilitarian project: the greatest happiness for the greatest number. The idea of 'quality circles' is only the latest in the line, the third heaven as it were.

1. The first circle of paradise: industrialisation. The first virtuous circle in historical terms is that of emerging industrialisation. This entailed the movement from the first gropings of capitalism in the putting-out system (outwork), to the factories of the 'first industrial revolution' (steam engine, spinning mill, iron and coal) of the nineteenth century. Its primary theoreticians were the economists of the late eighteenth century (the Physiocrats and Adam Smith) and of the early nineteenth century (David Ricardo and Jean-Baptiste Say).

In this formulation, the division of labour exalted by Adam Smith becomes hitched to the *laissez-faire* credo already proclaimed by the Physiocrats, and announced as the way to ensure the *wealth of nations*. By the grace of this 'invisible hand' the well-being of the casual labourer already surpassed, it was argued, the luxury in which former aristocrats lived. The *harmony of interests* of all members of society is proclaimed via the law of Jean-Baptiste Say, reinforced by Ricardo's law of comparative advantages. The underlying propositions are as follows. The new social organisation, supported by machines, allows unprecedented productive efficiency. This augmented production will not be monopolised by one group to the detriment of another, nor by some nations to the detriment of others. Rather, as expressed by the Physiocrat Mercier de la Rivière, the happiness of one group can increase only through the intermediary of the happiness of others. People will get rich together rather than at each other's expense.[28]

In fact this common interest is never quite demonstrated. According to Say, in the 'law' that bears his name, increased production is sure of finding increased outlets because 'products are traded against products'. Every supply creates, immediately and *ipso facto*, its equivalent demand. Revenue from production is strictly equal to the value of this production. Thus it follows, for example, that if workers' incomes remain fairly low, then it must be that the products of the factories in which they work are luxury products provided for the upper classes. It is tempting (though not strictly valid) further to propose that, similarly, if workers expelled from the factories by the introduction of machines do not manage to get work in the factories which produce these machines, they will still be able to find work as servants. This concept of circular movement of income underpins the view that continual growth of wealth is possible and that it cannot fail to benefit everyone.[29]

The same argument is applied at the international level. Even nations which refuse to introduce the new social organisation for themselves still profit in some ways, while missing out on other benefits. They profit from the cheapness of manufactured products and the resultant increase in the mass of 'wealth' at their disposal. However, their absurd refusal to enter fully into the game of modernity will lead them to *regress* relative to the others; they will fall farther and farther behind.

2. The second circle of paradise: consumerism. The second virtuous circle corresponds in general terms to what is known as the 'second industrial revolution', associated with the general spread of electrical power, the development of the combustion engine (and of petroleum) and thus of the engineering and automobile industries. It was inaugurated with Taylorism, and reached its zenith through Keynesian consumerism *(le keyneso-fordisme)*.[30]

The scientific organisation of work touted by Taylor and Ford amounts simply to the systematic application of Adam Smith's principles of self-interest and 'division of labour'. The breaking down of tasks, the timing of each component movement, the rearrangement of tasks and the setting of norms to eliminate dead time, combined with standardisation of products and components and in due course complemented by the introduction of the assembly line, allows the mass production of goods previously reserved for the elite – cars, electrical household appliances, and so on. Individuals are stimulated by bonuses to work harder, while the climate of competition is sharpened through the spectacular drop in costs and the frequent appearance of new products.

The great crisis of 1929 showed that, notwithstanding Say's Law, the spiral of increasing prosperity shared by all was by no means automatic. Production gains were not matched by comparable rises in income for wage-earners, who were the only potential buyers of this new mass production. Competition within the framework of nineteenth-century industrialisation no longer engendered a harmonisation of interests, so a new dose of solidarity was needed. The answer was soon forthcoming: *all* businesses must follow the Fordist logic and practise a policy of high salaries. The law of performance/prosperity thus takes on the form of the 'Keynesian-Fordist compromise' – the second virtuous circle of growth. Production grows (*en masse*) thanks to gains in work productivity (through scientific organisation) and in capital (through technical progress); there is a sharing of the gains between wage-earners and businesses; and consumption grows (*en masse*) thanks to high salaries and complementary redistribution of income (particularly through welfare state policies). The implicit political contract and workplace contract upon which the social machine is founded are renewed and revitalised in a new social contract drawn up through 'tripartite negotiations' around the green baize table between workers' unions, employers' representatives and the state.

The state is here called upon to depart from the role of 'night watchman' which traditional liberals wished to assign to it. Henceforth it 'regulates' the machine to ensure its smooth running. It arbitrates and enforces the rules of the game, while itself playing a substantive role through redistribution policies, maintaining a high level of economic activity through public spending (the Keynesian policy portfolio, including public works and social welfare spending) – and the wheels of progress are greased by a moderate inflation rate, what Keynes called 'a gentle rise of price level'.

No radically new principle is discovered in this second circle. Mass production and mass consumption already existed; they go hand in hand with the industrial manufacturing system. All that has happened is that the the progression of the system itself has brought about the conditions for its extension and restructuring. The balance between rivalry and solidarity, momentarily ruptured by Taylorism and the second industrial revolution, was re-established through the rise of mass consumerism.

The 'invisible' hand, which was never enough on its own to ensure the harmonisation of interests within society, is now made a little more conspicuous. However, it is still Say's Law – with the help of Keynesian pump-priming – which guarantees the existence of this harmonious organisation of agents' plans. For thirty consecutive years, the thirty glorious years from the end of the Second World War till 1970, more and more cars and refrigerators find more and more buyers. Bentham and the consumer society are triumphant.

At the international level a complementary story is told. Theoreticians demonstrate through their models that not only do previously non-integrated or 'backward' countries come, via international trade, to obtain cheaper and more abundant goods, but further that by this trade they benefit from a more efficient allocation of factors of production. This will tend, on the assumption of equal productivity in all countries, to bring about a standardisation of workers' income levels on a world scale. Moreover, the harmony of interests is reinforced by the politics of international cooperation advocated by Truman and the UN, summed up by the slogan 'good deeds equal good business': enriching poor neighbours is a way of creating future clients. The richer my clients become, the better for my business. Generosity and egoism walk hand-in-hand. I understand perfectly well that in working for others I am working for my own interests.

3. The third circle of paradise: enterprise society. With the 1974 oil crisis marking the end of the 'thirty glorious years', new solutions for the solidarity-prosperity thesis had to be found. Some well-meaning analysts advocated aid to the Third World as a way of re-igniting the world economy. Willy Brandt and others spoke in this way of 'Keynesianism on a world scale'. But according to liberal logic this perfectly understandable generosity is not necessary. Rather, they say, we can all get to the third heaven through entering the third virtuous circle, that of 'quality circles'.

The crisis of the Keyneso-Fordist system of regulation has been analysed any number of times, and the main arguments require only brief recapitulation. One theme is that the saturation of the consumption side of the equation has bogged the system down and brought about a lowering of productivity. The cycle then becomes vicious. Job layoffs lessen demand, and so on.

What is the solution? New technologies are available, but their introduction presupposes further reorganisation of the workplace. Robotics and information technology, for example, allow small-scale production lines so that products can be personalised and better adapted to clients' wishes. The workforce has to be adapted to new requirements. Thus we enter into the era of *quality*. We consume not more but better. We produce not more but better. We work not more but better. The thousands of workers 'liberated' by machines will have to change their role; henceforth they must participate in this quality civilisation by producing services, through the marketplace, to businesses and to individuals.

The basic law of the machine has not changed: we are still looking for the *maximine*. But the new modes of organisation around the quality theme require a new resolution of the rivalry/cooperation dialectic. The assembly lines of the Taylorist and Fordist factories are dying. Business no longer merely needs a blindly functional labour power; now it needs 'loyalty'. Costly and delicate new instruments demand absolute devotion and active intelligence. This is the price of performance. The objective becomes 'total quality at the first attempt' – exemplified in the 'six zeros' mentioned above. If this is achieved, then businesses will develop new market niches, obtain market share, ensure full employment and furnish high salaries. This is the recipe for success. As Alain Lipietz writes:

> We are by now familiar with the recipes of the nations and regions who are 'winning'– Japan, Western Germany, Sweden, Northern Italy, Massachusetts, Michigan. Producers mobilising their know-how, unions and managements resolving their disputes through negotiated compromises, a research partnership between the state and the private sector, and so on.[31]

The recipe for this new way of accommodating the law of *maximine* has been, as we know, fine-tuned in Japan. Morishima characterises it as follows:

> The employees of those companies which constitute the 'national team' of Japanese industry compete with their foreign rivals as a single, united body, and competition among large enterprises to become a member of this national team and be in receipt of various favours from the government is equally fierce. ... In this sense Japanese society is a fiercely competitive society, but it does not produce competition between individuals; the individual has to work at the risk of his life on the battlefield of group competition.[32]

This ethos is clearly expressed in the operations of the new *flexible workshops*, in which the logic of versatile specialisation relies on teamwork as much as on individual initiative. Corporate solidarity is the order of the day. The harmony of interests is, all the same, still guaranteed by Say's Law. As Antoine Riboud, Jacques Chirac's guru and French BSN foodstuffs magnate, puts it: 'The productivity of new techniques lowers the relative prices of goods and thereby frees up more spending power which in turn creates new jobs.'[33]

It is thus that the economic war will be won. It will be won for everyone. Of course, the law will not operate without some snags, since organisations (whether businesses, government administrations or unions) inevitably lack the versatility necessary to adapt themselves perfectly to progress. But victory for all is not in doubt, even if during the battles some are overtaken by others.

The myth of the harmony of interests

When Adam Smith wrote that the butcher, the baker and the brewer owed to their own sense of self-love rather than to benevolence towards others, the ability to supply each other and us with meat, bread and beer in the best conditions, as though an invisible hand had harmonised individual plans to bring about the common good, he was far from sure of how his formula would be received.[34] There were three good reasons for his doubts. First, what he argued was not really new; secondly, it wasn't really very radical at the time; and thirdly, it was circumscribed in application to a very narrow domain.

From the time of the medieval scholastics, it had been fashionable to ask whether a world dominated by sin after the fall of Adam must be condemned to chaos, or whether worldly matters conformed to some sort of *natural order*. The Fathers of the Church had already, for several centuries, interested themselves in the question of compatibility between the common good and individual pursuit of secular ends.

According to St Augustine, there existed a kind of 'balance of passions' (antecedents for which can be found in Plato) between the three great sins – the lusting after flesh, money and power – which correspond to the fundamental desires of man. For example, love of glory serves to limit covetousness of the flesh and greed for money. This idea of a general order emerging out of personal disorders is a theme that runs right through classical and medieval thought. Thus, according to Pascal, collective concupiscence,

> by playing simultaneously on the desires for worldly goods and on the fear of punishment, makes of the weaknesses of its members an admirably secure foundation for the strength of the state; it uses even our madness to

moderate our madness, it creates an order and makes it emerge out of what is the seed of all disorder.[35]

For Montesquieu, a little later on, human passions, though not yet reduced to the single passion for money, are already called interests. But there is still a comparable formula: 'Each individual moves towards the common good, believing he works towards his own particular interests.'[36]

The same examples made famous by Adam Smith, of the brewer and the baker or similar trades, were used over and over again to show that the pursuit by everyone of their own interests can give rise to a certain order. What Smith succeeded in doing was to liberate the economic domain from the clutches of the larger moral realm, through the demonstration that the common good is realised *in this sphere of material interests* when individuals pursue profane and *amoral* ends and are motivated by the sentiment of self-love.

This sentiment is not incompatible with the sympathy for others so much emphasised by Smith in his *Theory of Moral Sentiments*. Smith's argument, however, was that while this sympathy was essential for the maintenance of civil society, it is not essential for realising the common good within the economic sphere *per se*.

Bentham then went much beyond this, arguing that sympathy derives from self-interest; this permitted him to make the step from personal to general interest. Love of self serves as a basis for universal benevolence; and this is what proves that an internal union exists between the interest of the individual and that of the human race.[37]

It is a charming irony that Smith's vision, which found its origins in the meditations of the Fathers of the Church, has in this way been turned to the service of the most profane conception of the world – the utilitarian vision which claims to explain the natural order and the basis for achieving the greatest good for the greatest number without any reference to God or any help from religion, solely by the calculation of utility.

In fact Smith's own formulation was far from radical. It did not go nearly as far as the provocative slogans of, for example, Bernard de Mandeville's *Fable of the Bees*, nor did it have the abstract generality of the utilitarian analyses that followed – not to mention the modern disciples of the latter, the 'libertarians' or 'anarcho-capitalists' who want self-interest to rule everywhere.

For Mandeville, as is well known, 'private vices make public virtues'. For him, the wealth of nations is brought about through the pursuit of immoral ends, whereas good sentiments can actually undermine prosperity. Asceticism, frugality, modesty and the practice of traditional virtues, all no doubt highly commendable, do nothing to foster production and commerce. It is the search for personal pleasure and the creation of 'artificial needs' that are most conducive to general well-being. The traditional liberal creed, as recounted by Jacqueline Hecht, testifies to this same modern economic optimism:

> Each man working for himself works, in seeking his personal interests, for the benefit of those like him, and the interest of one is the interest of all. Even private vices lead to public good and, in this idyllic vision of things, there is no place for desperate competition, nor for vicious struggle between individuals and classes. Rather, trade represents the solidarity which binds mankind, and the harmony of interests is preserved by the invisible hand – or the unseen hand of Providence which wants only good for its creatures.[38]

The utilitarians go a step beyond Mandeville, and make a fundamental change to the moral discourse. Bentham was quite explicit on this point, arguing:

> When Mandeville advanced his theory that 'private vices are public virtues', he did not see that the erroneous application of the terms of vice and virtue was the source of the confusion of ideas which enabled him to plead an apparently contradictory proposition; for if what we call virtue produces a diminution of happiness, and if vice, which is the opposite of virtue, has a contrary effect, it is clear that the virtue is an evil and the vice is a good.[39]

In other words, the individual's search for his or her maximum utility will *in itself* be the good – noting that it can be useful to be generous and disinterested, and that it is in one's own interest to encourage goodwill in others in case one needs to call upon it. The pursuit of individual self-interest generates the common good, that is the greatest good for the greatest number.

Hegel attacked this mode of reasoning mercilessly. 'Utility as the essence of existent things,' he wrote, 'signifies that they are determined as not being in themselves, but for another: this is a necessary [dimension of things], but not the only one.'[40] In disgust at this confusion of ends and means, he was led to reject totally the utilitarianism of the Enlightenment, which he considered to be the height of platitude.[41]

As G.E. Lessing asked nineteenth-century utilitarians, 'And what is the use of use?'[42] The philosophical founders of utilitarianism were aware of this problem. To the objection 'Useful to whom or for what?', they replied: useful to society, to humanity. The foundation of the utilitarian morality is, or would have to be, a utility which is collective, communal, social, universal. But this can lead to a paradox of circular definition. Once it is supposed that society is founded on the utility of its members bound together in the social contract, any distinct moral dimension tends to disappear in the circularity of the logic: the social utility which guides the individual is founded in the last resort on personal utility. Individual interests, as Bentham puts it, are the only real interests.[43] It is hard to avoid falling into hedonism: the view of society built on the cumulation of individual pleasure-seeking.

Hegel, indeed, emphasised in his critique that the world seems to offer itself freely for man's enjoyment: 'Everything is for his pleasure and his delectation, so that when he leaves the hand of God, he walks in the world as though in a garden planted for him.'[44] Taken on its own this may seem to allow that individual utilities may cumulate in the *common good*. So for example, when Adam Smith shows that *in the sphere of commodity production and exchange (the economic sphere)*, the pursuit of personal utility generates society-wide well-being, the coincidence of individual with collective utility is clear. Following this line of reasoning, there is nothing to stop economic logic from invading the *entirety* of society. Any distinctive moral dimension fades away along with the specific content of utility.

Formulated thus, the theory of the harmony of interests is a metaphysical dogma. One might, with just as much (or as little) pertinence, adhere to the contrary thesis, that of the radical incompatibility of individual interests. This was the nub of Hegel's critique. What from one point of view was *served by* the world and by others, was in another respect inevitably *in the service of* the world and other interests:

Just as everything is useful to man, so man is useful too, and his vocation is to make himself a member of the group, of use for the common good and serviceable to all. The extent to which he looks after his own interests must also be matched by the extent to which he serves others, and so far as he serves others, so far is he taking care of himself: one hand washes the other. But wherever he finds himself, there he is in his right place; he makes use of others and is himself made use of.[45]

In fact, neither Adam Smith nor the early utilitarian philosophers upheld the thesis of a harmony of interests in its absolute generality. Conversely, none of the political adversaries of the liberals – such as Proudhon in his *Désharmonies économiques*, Otto Effertz in his *Système des antagonismes économiques*, or Marx with his analysis of class struggle – upheld the opposite thesis of incompatibility of interests in a rigid way. In practice the nuances, restrictions and limitations placed on the thesis of harmony of interests, however strongly enunciated, have tended to be fuzzy additions that do not threaten the basic edifice. (Even with Marx, the announcement of an irreducible class antagonism is the preface to the vision of a classless society where interests are harmonised.) The result is that the utility-harmony principle can and does undergo a quasi-limitless extension. This principle is thus the foundation for nineteenth-century liberalism and for all modern varieties of neo-liberalism up to Reagan and Thatcher. Once the basic principle is asserted, conflicts of interests – whenever they arise – are adjudged more apparent than real, only superficial and transitory; they spring more from bad policies than from the nature of things. The belief in a harmonious and progressive 'natural' order of things becomes an irrefutable dogma which justifies a bland optimism about the workings of self-interest in all domains.

All the same, a collectivity which genuinely rejected tradition as its mode of regulation and denied any transcendent elements, in favour of constructing a social system on the basis of utilitarian reason alone, proceeding from the calculations of individual subjects, would doubtless be doomed to *disorder*. The Marquis de Sade in fact demonstrated this antithesis of utilitarian reason with quasi-mathematical rigour throughout his work. His rejection of the postulate of a natural order and adoption of the counter-thesis of a natural disorder, amount to a far more radical critical perspective than those furnished by Proudhon, Effertz or Marx. First of all, in this unbridled utilitarianism, individual happiness, pleasure and utility are not reduced *a priori* to a supply of bread, meat, beer or gadgets. The crucial question is the compatibility or not of individuals' passions, given that each person is the sole judge of his or her feelings. At the very time when Bentham was elaborating his 'arithmetic of pleasures', de Sade was constructing a true *anti-*

economics with his 'game' of unleashing unbridled passions. His standpoint was that, because of the difference between individuals' experiences (the thesis of radical subjectivity, sometimes called the *no-bridge* problem in the theory of communication), there exists no natural harmony. There is no invisible hand. By contrast with the situation where money units prevail (incomes, prices), there is no *common measure* between the pleasure of one and that of another. Inasmuch as human passions are not all reduced down to a single passion for monetary gain, the pleasure of the butcher need not in any way coincide with that of the baker. On the contrary, one has to suppose that, in striving to reach the highest possible level of satisfaction, each individual will set out to utilise the other in whatever way suits, as an object for the exercise of power, an instrument or an object in the pursuit of pleasure, and so on. In de Sade's own writing, this thesis of self-gratification is expressed in its most 'natural' form: sensuality. And then beyond that, the offences of rape and crime, with all the fine gradations of sadism as described in *The 120 Days of Sodom*, are the substance of the 'indifference curves' designating the preferences of the 'consumers'.

Obviously the voice of de Sade could not be allowed to be heard; his discordant naturalism, his anarchic hedonism and his subversive individualism were too much of a contradiction of the link between order and nature that the Enlightenment had borrowed from the earlier Newtonian mechanistic model. As Alexandre Koyré has written:

> To define 'man' proved to be a much more difficult task than to define 'matter', and human nature continued to be determined in a great number of different, and even conflicting, ways. Yet so strong was the belief in 'nature', so overwhelming the prestige of the Newtonian (or pseudo-Newtonian) pattern of order arising automatically from interaction of isolated and self-contained atoms, that nobody dared to doubt that order and harmony would in some way be produced by human atoms acting according to their nature, whatever this might be – instinct for play and pleasure (Diderot), or pursuit of selfish gain (A. Smith). This return to nature could mean free passion as well as free competition. Needless to say, it was the last interpretation that prevailed.[46]

The triumph of the vision of harmony through competition was, however, neither as self-evident nor as simple as Koyré would have us believe. In fact, the social project (in all its political, ethical and economic dimensions) of Jeremy Bentham, John Stuart Mill and the English school of political radicalism – the utilitarian project which is the kernel of modernity and to whose essential features we still adhere – got off the ground only by virtue of a decisive initial choice. This preliminary step was the suppression of the passions achieved through the Puritan revolution: the reduction of multi-faceted life down to the single dimension of economic interests expressed in the marketplace. This straitjacketing is an indispensable requirement – both in theory and in practice – for constructing the 'competitive' machine. This *business morality* had first to be inscribed in the flesh and impulses of people, as the basis for the emergence of a model of social order – a simulacrum which has absolutely nothing 'natural' about it at all!

The ways in which this moral reformation took place varied from one European society to another. In eighteenth-century France, following the social crisis or disintegration of the social fabric that marked the collapse of the *Ancien Régime*, it was necessary to impose the terrorism of moral virtue in order to contain the excesses of hedonism. According to Jacqueline Hecht, with the Revolution,

> everyone could see for themselves that a spontaneous harmony of interests did not exist, and that the 'natural' (pre-existing) order certainly did not ensure the greatest good for the greatest number, and that the uncontrolled play of natural forces could only harm those individuals and classes least favoured or least protected.[47]

Certainly this general mistrust turned out to be only provisional. But it was necessary to wait a little while – in France for Guizot,[48] in England for Bentham and Mill – for the exclusive triumph of material interests to be seen and the basis for the emergence of economic and political liberalism to be clearly mapped out.

Jean-Baptiste Say summed up this utilitarian reduction of the passions to material interests alone in a neat syllogism:

> The happiness of an individual is proportional to the quantity of needs that he can satisfy, and the quantity of needs that an individual can satisfy is itself proportional to the quantity of products that he can make use of; consequently, the happiness of an individual is proportional to the quantity of products which he can make use of.[49]

Thus, in the progression from Helvetius to Jean-Baptiste Say, we see the constitution of *ordinal utilitarianism* – 'more is better' – which is the leitmotif of modern societies. This utilitarian morality rests on a whole series of reductions which have become accepted as so many unquestionable propositions. Happiness for everyone is the foundation of justice, and collective utility is the measure of happiness; collective utility in turn is the sum of individual pleasures; utility corresponds to anything that brings money (that you can sell) and to anything that can be acquired with money (that you can buy). As every person's interests are measurable in the same way (that is, money value of goods and services), the growth of material product measures the progression of happiness in society.

Karl Marx, in a page full of lucidity and humour, laid out admirably this interdependence of individualism, utilitarianism and the supposed harmony of interests in the modern economy and society dominated by the commodity form:

> The sphere of circulation or commodity exchange, within whose boundaries the sale and purchase of labour power goes on, is in fact a very Eden of the innate rights of man. It is the exclusive realm of Freedom, Equality, Property, and Bentham. Freedom, because both buyer and seller of a commodity, let us say of labour-power, are determined only by their own free will. They contract as free persons, who are equal before the law. Their contract is the final result in which their joint will finds a common legal expression. Equality, because each enters into relation with the other, as with a simple owner of commodities, and they exchange equivalent for equivalent. Property, because each disposes only of what is his own. And Bentham, because each looks only to his own advantage. The only force bringing them together, and putting them into relation with each other, is the selfishness, the gain and the private interest of each. Each pays heed to himself only, and no one worries about the others. And precisely for that reason, either in accordance with the pre-established harmony of things, or under the auspices of an omniscient providence, they all work together to their mutual advantage, for the common weal, and in the common interest.[50]

Belief in the harmony of interests, like the belief in progress with which it is intimately linked, is the key dimension of our collective mythology. Its foundation remains, all the same, both fragile and arguable. It is clearly true that, in certain circumstances, the interests of certain subjects (individuals, groups, states) can be compatible, within defined limits. Thus it is undeniable that, as Halévy remarks acidly, it is 'of interest to the wolf that the sheep be fat and numerous'.[51] In most cases though, there is every chance that interests will clash. What works to sustain the myth of a harmony of *human* interests is the designation of a common enemy, nature, which must be vanquished in the collective interest. Yet this belief that nature is the number one enemy of humanity is also open to question, and is an unverifiable metaphysical dogma. Certainly it seems clear that, far from being definitively vanquished, nature may respond in a hostile way and exact vengeance for the maltreatment inflicted on her. The environmental crisis shows in a dramatic way that there is no natural harmony between the interests of humanity and those of nature. Yet one cannot deduce from this that there *is* a natural harmony to be found within humanity, nor that this harmony (if it exists) can be realised through the domination of nature.

The fact remains that, whether well founded or not, faith in the invisible hand has a very substantial practical effect on our value system. Modernity's ethic decrees as morally sound – because contributing to the general good – all activity validated by the market. This value system thus accords *activity* (by which is meant production and consumption activity) a positive value in itself, and this strongly reinforces the taste for action – new goods, new experiences, conquest of new frontiers – which is at the heart of modernity. The fact of being active, of stirring oneself to get money, is necessarily a good. Ways of being at odds with this activity – such as rest, meditation, slow movement, wisdom, enjoyment of life – are given lower value or condemned outright. Any doubt about the morality of activity-in-the-marketplace becomes almost out of the question. The fact that all this agitation in order to make money might be importunate or might disturb others is not taken into consideration. Yet the mere event of being solicited as a potential buyer/seller can be disagreeable. When it plays on emotions and passions, it can become frankly obnoxious. Everyone has had experience of this, but this evidence is ruled out of court by the crushing affirmation that, by going after my money or in seeking to sell me something, the importunate salesman is contributing to my well-being despite myself – because he or she involves me in trade to our mutual satisfaction (or, if nothing else, informs me of opportunities for trade). There is no longer any respect for decent reserve. We are imprisoned in the implacable logic of utilitarianism.

It becomes a moral duty to drive small entrepreneurs to bankruptcy, even if this serves no survival need, simply because humanity gains the benefits of the competitive effort. In the societies most marked by these beliefs, children are incited from a very young age to enter the search for the common good by engaging in their own transactions. Obtaining money from other people is proof of a precocious social utility. Such beliefs are what make up the moral science of modernity.

Say's Law: good deeds and good business

We have seen the interdependence between the dogma of the harmony of interests and the law of Jean-Baptiste Say. The latter is presented as, at one and the same time, an empirical fact (supply creates demand, products are traded against products), and a rigorous logical deduction – almost a tautology, that revenue generated by production is equal to the value of this production, that the revenue spent on the production is the measure of value of the production. All the same, the 'law' is not demonstrable except through an act of faith in the autonomy of the economy and in its autodynamism.[52] At the root of the entire conceptual edifice, notwithstanding its appearance of being an objective and observable reality, is a metaphysical dogma, that of the harmony of interests.

This dogma is what props up the optimism felt generally throughout the West, and the optimism about the West – that is, about the future of the world under Western leadership. It is what makes 'self-evident' the claims about the benefits of good business practice, those of the marketeers like Antoine Riboud as well as those of generous spirits such as Willy Brandt. For Adam Smith and the liberals, in doing good business you perform good deeds, since you contribute to realising the common good. The reciprocal is true too: in performing good deeds, you will do good business: this is the Keynesian and Fordist variation on the liberal logic. This slightly heterodox vision still shares in the underlying dogma.

President Truman's 'Address on Point 4' clearly enunciated the doctrine back in 1949. In helping the Third World, we help ourselves: 'To increase the output and the national income of the less developed regions is to increase our own economic stability.'[53] Alongside the obvious moral justification, aid thus finds its political and economic justification (which ultimately makes the moral justification redundant). Truman's argument was that to maintain world leadership, we must help the losers. Thus we shall all win, but those performing best will win more than the others (though not at their expense).

Thirty years later Willy Brandt suggested that, in order to extricate the industrial economies from a crisis which should never have arisen – and thus can only be (as we have seen) a momentary crisis of adjustment, and, whatever the cause, will in due course sort itself out – we should reinforce the effect of good business by good deeds towards the Third World. In winning more, we will be helping the most handicapped and the most retarded not to lose.

This logic of self-interested benevolence is verified, in a grotesque fashion, on the sporting plane. Twenty-four African countries and four Latin-American countries had decided not to participate in the 1990 'World Games', because of the direct and indirect costs and because they had no chance of winning anything due to their lack of means (prohibitive prices of players, trainers, equipment, etc.). The rich countries responded with a proposal for financial support for participation, to be financed by the receipts of the event – along similar lines to what already happens at the Olympic Games.[54] The World Bank has likewise made this solidarity formula its credo. As it declared in its third Annual Report of 1947-48:

> The more advanced countries, too, have a vital interest in promoting the development of the underdeveloped areas, for the more effective utilisation of the vast resources of those areas will result directly in an increase in trade between them and the more developed countries, to the substantial benefit of both.[55]

The scandal of the losers

Thus the message of the grand society is access to abundance for all – or at least, for the most impoverished, to some degree of prosperity. The prospect is inevitably enticing. Traditional societies were frugal for everyone, or for the great majority; they were sometimes materially poor, with occasions of insecurity and precarious survival (being vulnerable to famine, war, natural catastrophes, and so on).

Adam Smith, in announcing the new age, asserted the benefits of the unparalleled development of productive forces in a capitalist system. He took the precaution, however, of underlining the numerous dangers of this mode of operation for a human society. By contrast with the ultra-liberals who have since reclaimed him as their fountainhead, he was far from seeing everywhere an invisible hand dispensing the greatest good for the greatest number. For him, decent society is not simply the spontaneous result of individual competition and the pursuit of maximum self-interest. Rather it rests on sympathy. Moreover, political power is needed to correct the dysfunctions and dangers that the free play of interests in competition produces in the economic field. The dangerous effects of the marketplace range from the degeneration of the labouring classes to the extermination of foreign peoples. 'For the American Indians', notes one of Smith's commentators, 'there was no "invisible hand" leading their nations to the summits of wealth.'[56] So Adam Smith himself was far from believing that what is good for capitalists is good for the rest of society.[57] His view was, indeed, that free competition and economic liberalism could mitigate some of the negative effects of capitalist activity and generate a certain common good within a limited domain. Only the ultra-liberals like Gustave de Molinari or the American libertarians have subsequently pushed to the extreme the belief in a spontaneous natural order emerging from the free play of individual interests.

The liberal tradition in the broader sense has always recognised the legitimacy of the political order. Its Leviathan is variously envisaged as an enlightened despot, a night-watchman state, or a providential welfare state; and in practice, the liberal state may even degenerate into a totalitarian perversion. This shows that there is a certain haziness as to the exact principles and practice of political organisation in the grand society, the exact basis for its social functioning and its internal coherence. Certainly, notwithstanding all such differences and variations, modern Western societies do all participate in the grand society, and are founded on the belief of the greatest good for the greatest number, the belief in a game where all are winners. If, however, one adopts a more agnostic position and places a question mark over the corollary beliefs in a natural harmony of interests and in an autodynamism of the economic system, one is led to look more closely at this conviction that all can win, and to see the paradoxes it involves.

If we were to suppose that happiness, the stake in the game, is measured by material well-being, this in turn being measured by production in the sense of economists and national accountants, then we have to admit the indisputable growth in the supply of human riches since the industrial era. Undoubtedly everyone *can* win something in terms of absolute magnitudes. So it is indeed possible that the well-being of the poor, including the poor of the Third World, does now (if we may paraphrase the classical economists) embrace objects which constituted luxury for the affluent classes of former days or were even unknown to them. In some ways this is clearly true. Take a walk in the shantytowns and note the television antennae, count the wrecks of cars or listen to the transistors. From this point of view, the old Marxist thesis of absolute pauperisation induced by capitalism is difficult to sustain.

However, there are other features of modernity also to be considered. In this game, some can lose everything. There are no guarantees against radical exclusion. In the Fourth World, these total losers are rather numerous. In the winning countries, on the other hand, nearly everyone wins to some degree; this fact illustrates perfectly the success of Fordism as we have analysed it. In the variety of intermediate situations, some win a great deal and a great many win very little. Thus it has been said of Brazil that it brings Sweden and Indonesia together in one country, a very rich country with a growth dynamic and 15 million inhabitants, and a miserable country with 80 million outcasts.[58] It is possible to theorise this situation in terms of 'exclusive' development. The rich parts can generate their own dynamic of capital accumulation, with a strong interior market for the opulent sector. So one can get a situation where, as the Brazilian president Emilio Medici is said to have remarked: 'The economy is going very well, the people not.'

Now, in a game, what counts in the end is not the final result in absolute numerical terms so much as the placing. One has to say, therefore, that in the development game in the grand society, the greatest number do *lose relatively*. Even hard-headed statisticians admit that the poverty line rises with GNP; and many sociologists suggest that the subjective feeling of decline and exclusion rises even faster. The result is widespread impoverishment even when average income increases. All of this is completely consistent with the margi-nalist economists' abstract reasoning about the diminishing marginal utility of money. As Alfredo De Romana notes:

> The marginal utility of income (its usual value, or the well-being gener-ated by the goods it buys) differs greatly according to the level of income of each: 500 dollars makes an interesting difference to my budget, but it

represents only crumbs to the Rockefellers, while for a family dying of hunger, it is the difference between death and luxury.[59]

The situation of those outcasts blessed with a rising per capita income is still degraded in comparison with the winners that they are unlikely ever to join. With their jeans and transistors, one cannot even assert in most cases that they are better nourished, better clothed, better cared for, than they were before modernity. In agreeing to play the game, one accepts the stakes and the rules. The stakes in this game – money wealth – is equally the criterion for evaluating what is gain or loss, what defines happiness. As we shall see (in Chapter 6 below), application of the economic criteria of well-being actually works to destroy the riches of the non-Western peoples. The societies of the Third World are, in this respect, definitive losers in this game: what they esteem is denied, devalued; and what they previously scorned becomes over-valued. Most candidates for modernity are condemned to be shipwrecked from the moment they set foot on the gangplank of the grand society. So it is in all their interests, if they can, to invent other games and to 'remake' themselves to become *nouveaux riches* in other ways.

Taking these features into account, once we break out of the straitjacket of economic reasoning and evaluation, the Marxist thesis of absolute pauperisation can be seen to contain a true intuition: the grand society is simultaneously a society of workers and a society of wreckers. It feeds its indubitable social dynamism on the destruction and negation of those different from itself. While operating to enrich them, it works simultaneously to impoverish them.

Marx thought he could formalise this intuition using the classical labour theory of value. If the value created by society is equal to the quantity of work expended to generate that production, then we are dealing with a fairly constant magnitude, not very sensitive to technological changes. In these terms, the 'game' of class struggle is indeed a zero-sum game: what one group gains in surplus value the other group loses in wage income. The aggrandisement of wealth smacks of robbing Peter to pay Paul. However, the thesis of absolute pauperisation, if understood in this material sense, clashes with the commonsense impression that there is a bigger total product to be carved up. Not only does the Marxian exploitation argument rely on a 'metaphysical' conception of value which economics has managed to dispense with, it also fails to identify the central mechanisms bringing about the dereliction of the greatest number. In terms of quantity of goods, the economic game is not zero-sum. However, while only relative when considered strictly in economic terms, pauperisation on a world scale becomes absolute when one reasons in terms of the *social status* of those who 'lose'.

Notes

1. 'Conversation on economics', *Revue française d'economie*, no. 2, Autumn 1986, Fayard, Paris, p. 63.

2. The phrase is taken from Bertrand de Jouvenel, *Arcadie: essai sur le mieux-vivre, Futuribles*, Sedeis, Paris, 1968, p. 132.

3. Jacques Chirac, the Mayor of Paris and prominent figure of the French Centre-Right (and for a brief time Prime Minister in the mid-1980s), quoted in *Le Monde*, 6 January 1989.

4. Ibid.

5. Michio Morishima, *Why has Japan 'Succeeded'? Western technology and the Japanese ethos*, Cambridge University Press, 1982, pp. 174-93.

6. Bernard Tapie and Jacques Seguela are successful French businessmen who are prominent in political debate. Seguela is an advertising executive; Tapie is a corporate raider turned politician who is also prominent in sports management and sponsorship – voicing clearly that sport and business are facets of the same competitive 'game'. – *Translators' note.*

7. Alain Lipietz, *Choisir l'audace: une alternative pour le XXIe siècle*, La Découverte, Paris, 1989, p. 136. We return shortly to resolution of this question, in discussion of the pretended moral foundations of business practice.

8. Quoted by Michèle Manceaux in *Le Fils de mon fils*, Plon, Paris, 1989, p. 118. She adds: 'He is rapt in his formula and in himself. He repeats the word "terrific" over and over again. He is terrific, we are terrific. Worse than in America.'

9. Quoted by François Brune, in *Le Bonheur conforme*, Gallimard, Paris, 1985, p. 203.

10. Confronted with this imperative of 'winning', it is not at all surprising that the old-style Communist Party, which denounces 'winners' as corrupt under any circumstances, has no viable alternative to offer. On this point, see the tract by Francette Lazard, director of the Institut de Recherches Marxistes: *'Les "gagneurs" en crise?'*, October 1988. While clearly Stalin, Khrushchev and Gorbachev all promulgated ideologies of 'winners', these were images of collective winners which played on notions of common purpose rather than individual glory.

11. Wladimir Andreff, *La Diversité des pratiques sportives et la 'marchandisation' du sport*, photocopied document, UNESCO, 1988, p. 38.

12. The other side of the coin is that each year in the European mountains, many dozens of people die through stupid accidents, ill-preparedness and misfortunes while trying to 'prove themselves'.

13. I often remember how shocked my wife and I were some years ago, when a Canadian friend proudly showed us the *educational games* she had placed in her

newborn baby's crib. 'Tomorrow's world will be hard,' she said. 'We have to equip our children from the very start of life.' Who knows if, tomorrow, my own daughter will be able to avoid hanging such monstrous prosthetics in the cradles of our own grandchildren?

14. Op. cit., *Le Monde*, 6 January 1989.

15. Harry S. Truman, 'Inaugural Address on the state of the Union', on 20 January 1949, in *Harry S. Truman: documents*, Government Printing Office, Washington DC, 1961, p. 103.

16. This imagery of subjugation was particularly vivid in the writings of Francis Bacon (1561-1626), one of the founding fathers of modern scientific tradition and its accompanying vision of technology. See Carolyn Merchant, *The Death of Nature: women, ecology and the scientific revolution*, Harper & Row, San Francisco, 1980.

17. Subsequent events in the Aids drama show the ambiguity of the 'everyone wins' formula. Once the virus was identified, the major French and American players (the Institut Pasteur in Paris and the National Institute of Health in the US) have been engaged in a multi-million dollar squabble over their respective share of the royalties, reflecting their relative roles in the discovery; see *Le Monde*, 18 September 1992. This is analogous to a fight over trade-marks, patent rights and market share. Undoubtedly the lawyers 'win' along the way. – *Translators' note.*

18. Quoted by François Stankiewicz in *Les Stratégies d'entreprises face aux ressources humaines*, Economica, Paris, 1988, p. 10.

19. Adam Smith, *An Inquiry into the Nature and Causes of the Wealth of Nations* (the Glasgow Edition, edited by R.H. Campbell, A.S. Skinner & W.B. Todd), Clarendon Press, Oxford, 1976, bk. V, article II: 'Of the expense of the institutions for the education of youth', pp. 781-2.

20. As described by Jean Chesneaux, *Modernité-monde*, op. cit., p. 11.

21. What follows is a condensed recapitulation of a variant of the methodological individualism that underpins most 'liberal' political economy and political philosophy. In French, *cet atome social* has a masculine gender. It seems appropriate to render it in the masculine in translation – he, his, him – if only because the individualism here being analysed is very male-oriented and phallocentric in its character. – *Translators' note.*

22. In arriving at this choice of a neologism to designate explicitly the *twofold* obsession with optimisation inherent in economic rationality, I have tried to find a term distinct from several similar expressions already in use. For example, the term 'minimax' would be inadequate because it does not indicate the primacy of maximisation over minimisation that I want to convey; and it is, in any case, used in a precise technical sense in operational calculus. The principle of the 'maximin' is used in a precise sense in the mathematical theory of decisions in an uncertain universe, and also is taken up by Rawls in his theory of justice. However, these concurrent expressions evidently share with my principle of the *maximine* – the idea of a *maximum minimorum* – the evocation of a double optimising obsession.

23. Progress is, in effect, the cumulative effect through time of the efficiency imperative. In the *maximine* there is on the one hand the efficiency drive, to *economise on means* in realising any given objective; and on the other hand the quest for more, to mobilise *all available means* so as to obtain the most possible. This double imperative can be given a precise formulation within the confines of (static) neo-classical equilibrium theory, where resource endowments, technologies and agents' preferences are taken as 'given'. The view of 'economic progress' over time arises on the assumption that each step in accumulation builds upon what has been previously achieved. However, as will be seen, the application of the twin imperatives – the most, and at least cost – becomes inherently fuzzy and ambiguous when the parameters of history are opened out, for example with questions of population growth, equity and an indefinite time horizon. – *Translators' note.*

24. This is admirably demonstrated by Jacques-Alain Miller in 'Le despotisme de l'utile: la machine panoptique de Jeremy Bentham', *Ornicar*, no. 3, May 1975.

25. Parkinson's Law holds that in administrative structures work expands to fill the time available. The Peter Principle affirms in its turn that in a hierarchy, each person tends to rise to their level of incompetence, where they stagnate and multiply their mistakes.

26. The comprehensive blueprinting of production has always seemed, in the eyes of social engineers, the most rational way of organising the social machine. But the human being becomes merely a mindless cog. This is the case with Taylorist organisation of the workplace, which reduced the worker to a mere executant of the rational plan inscribed in the assembly line. However, experience has shown that a result of this abstract rationality is the destruction of individual energy and initiative – leading to a much reduced real efficiency. Social cybernetics now teaches us that the efficient working of the whole depends on supple articulation of the parts. Taylorism is condemned as inferior to new types of organisation which call upon personal initiative and commitment rather than the abdication of worker intelligence. Discipline is replaced by self-discipline.

27. The main difference between the slogans of gifted practitioners like Antoine Riboud and those of economists is that the former are interested primarily in their own affairs, so they say crudely and simply what the latter group disguise in useless and pretentious garb to try to make out that everyone has a common interest in playing the game.

28. Cited by Jacqueline Hecht, 'De la Révolution scientifique à la Révolution culturelle: l'enseignement de l'économie politique', in Michel Servet (editor), *Idées économiques sous la Révolution 1789-1794*, Presses Universitaires de Lyon, Lyon, 1989, p. 42.

29. One fallacy is evident. The unemployed workers may *not* be reabsorbed into the circular flow; this is one of the problems with Say's Law that Keynes was later to address, and that is clearly a real issue for many Third World populations. – *Translators' note.*

30. The French term '*keyneso-fordisme*' signals the bastard provenance of this formulation: on the one hand the Keynesian public policy programme of high investment to sustain economic activity (and, particularly, employment) levels; and on the other hand the famous Henry Ford policy of paying workers high wages so they could afford to buy his standard-model cars. – *Translators' note.*

31. Alain Lipietz, *Choisir l'audace*, op. cit., p. 77.

32. Michio Morishima, *Why has Japan 'Succeeded'?*, op. cit., p. 193.

33. Antoine Riboud, *Modernisation, mode d'emploi: rapport au Premier ministre*, Editions 10/18, 1987, p. 31.

34. One can recall Adam Smith's famous line from bk. I, ch. ii of *The Wealth of Nations* (Glasgow edition, op. cit., pp. 26-7): 'It is not from the benevolence of the butcher, the brewer, or the baker, that we expect our dinner, but from their regard to their own self-interest. We address ourselves, not to their humanity, but to their self-love, and never talk to them of our own necessities but of their advantages.' In the received wisdom, this idea is then juxtaposed with the statement Smith makes in bk.

IV, ch. ii (ibid., p. 456), in the context of import controls: 'He generally, indeed, neither intends to promote the public interest, nor knows how much he is promoting it. [... He] intends only his own security; and by directing [his] industry in such a manner as its produce may be of the greatest value, he intends only his own gain, and he is in this, as in many other cases, led by an invisible hand to promote an end which was no part of his intention.'

35. Pascal, quoted by Simone Meyssonnier in *La Balance et l'horloge: la genèse de la pensée libérale en France au 18ème siècle*, Editions de la Passion, Montreuil, 1989, p. 78.

36. Charles de Montesquieu, *De l'esprit des lois*, bk. III, ch. vii; originally published in Paris, 1748; new edition Belles Lettres, Paris, 1950. (English edition: *The Spirit of the Laws*, translated and edited by Anne Cohler, B.C. Miller & H.S. Stone, Cambridge University Press, 1989.)

37. The passage comes from a French translation of passages of John Bowring's rendering of Bentham's *Deontology*: 'Déontologie', in *Revue du MAUSS*, no. 5, 1989, p. 93. Bentham's essays on his utilitarian deontology were never completed, and exist only as a collection of manuscripts. However, compare the following passage taken from original manuscripts: 'And thus it is that out of the self-regarding affection rose by degrees the sympathetic affection; out of that, the power of the popular or moral affection – and both of them, in their main tendency, operating in conjunction to the increase of the aggregate of happiness.' In *The Collected Works of Jeremy Bentham: Deontology*, edited by Amnon Goldworth, Clarendon Press, Oxford, 1983, p. 204.

38. Jacqueline Hecht, in *Idées économiques sous la Révolution*, op. cit., p. 43.

39. Translated from 'Déontologie', op. cit., p. 88. Compare the following from Bentham in *Collected Works: Deontology*, op. cit., p. 160: 'Thus if the effect of virtue were to prevent more pleasure in any shape than it produced and at the same time to promote more pain than it prevented, the practice would, according to the persons affected by it, be either wickedness or folly...' – and *vice versa* for vice.

40. G.W.F. Hegel, *Lectures on the History of Philosophy*, Part 3, Section II (ii, D), 'The German illumination', translated by E.S. Haldane & F.H. Simson, Kegan Paul, London, 1896, vol. 3, p. 403.

41. G.W.F. Hegel, *Phenomenology of Spirit* (original edition 1807); English translation by A.V. Miller, Clarendon Press, Oxford, 1977, Part C (BB: Spirit), B/II 'The Enlightenment', pp. 328-55.

42. Cited by Hannah Arendt, in *The Human Condition*, op. cit., p. 154.

43. Bentham, *Théorie des peines et des récompenses*, French version published in Appendix to Elie Halévy, *La Formulation du radicalisme philosophique*, Alcan, Paris, 1901, vol. 2, p. 230. Republished in *Revue du MAUSS*, no. 5, 1989, pp. 70-6, Paris. Cf. also Bentham's *Deontology*, op. cit.

44. Hegel, *Phenomenology of Spirit*, op. cit, p. 342. See also Jean-Louis Bouche, 'De l'utilité dans la pensée économique pendant la Révolution française', *Revue du MAUSS*, no. 8, 1990, pp. 142-62.

45. G.W.F. Hegel, *Phenomenology of Spirit*, op. cit., pp. 342-3. This 'vocation' is not a matter of voluntaristic choice, it is the simple and ineluctable correlate of coexistence in the world. This Hegelian view of the dialectic of user-and-used undermines the proposition of an additive character of individual utilities. There is, certainly, a 'harmonisation' of activity in the sense entailed by the simple coexistence of things and activities; but this encompasses death, antagonism and violence in all their forms, and is far removed from the 'harmony of interests' of the idealised liberal society. The postulate of the 'radical incompatibility of interests' is just the converse side of the Hegelian dialectical coin. – *Translators' note*.

46. Alexandre Koyré, *Newtonian Studies*, Chapman & Hall, London, 1965, p. 22.

47. *Idées économiques sous la Révolution*, op. cit, p. 75.

48. Guizot was a prominent conservative politician in the 1848 administration of Louis Philippe, the period of triumph in France of the new bourgeoisie.

49. Jean-Baptiste Say, cited by Jean-Philippe Platteau, in *Les Economistes classiques et le sous-développement*, Presses Universitaires de France, Paris, 1978, vol. I, p. 180.

50. Karl Marx, *Capital*, bk. I, pt. 2, ch. 6, 'The sale and purchase of labour power', Penguin/New Left Review, paperback edition, 1976, p. 280.

51. Elie Halévy, cited by Philippe Mongin, 'Le libéralisme, l'utilitarisme et l'économie politique classique dans l'interprétation d'Elie Halévy', *Revue du MAUSS*, no. 10, 1990, p. 163.

52. 'Autodynamism' is the view that economic growth and accumulation are in some way 'natural' or 'spontaneous' tendencies (at least after a certain take-off threshold is attained). But Latouche rejects the idea that there is anything automatic about the development process. In his earlier book, *Faut-il refuser le développement?*, op. cit., he argues, retaking a celebrated line from Marx, that economic development is '*not* the law and the prophets', *not* the *telos* that fulfils and transcends all pre-existent cultural and historical specificity. He postulates, instead of the autodynamism of capital accumulation, a dialectically inverse characterisation: the *entropy of capital*. That is, denuded of the impetus of particular cultural imperatives, there is no unequivocal tendency towards accumulation, rather a tendency for dissipation. The well-documented 'obstacles' to the modernisation process in many Third World societies may be seen as *prima facie* evidence against the spontaneity of take-off and growth. It may also be noted that the pertinence of Say's Law (irrespective of its validity) further depends on the assumption that all relevant objects of produced and reproduced wealth and sources of utility are integrated in this 'circuit', or alternatively that those not integrated are not adversely affected by the operations of the market circuit. This point is developed in the section that follows on 'The scandal of the losers' and at length in Chapter 6 on the vicissitudes of the 'standard of living' concept. – *Translators' note*.

53. Harry Truman, 'Address on Point 4', 24 June 1949, in *Harry S. Truman: Documents*, op. cit., p. 106.

54. Wladimir Andreff, *La Diversité des pratiques sportives et la 'marchandisation' du sport*, op. cit., p. 52.

55. World Bank (International Bank for Reconstruction and Development), *Third Annual Report 1947-1948*, p. 15.

56. Spencer J. Pack, *Capitalism as a Moral System: Adam Smith's critique of the free market economy*, Edward Elgar, Aldershot, 1991, ch. VIII.

57. Ibid.

58. Peter Berger, *Les Mystificateurs du progrès: du Brézil à la Chine*, Presses Universitaires de France, Paris, 1978, p. 176. Numerous other imaginative expressions have been launched in the same vein, such as 'Belgindia' (Belgium plus India) for Brazil, 'Norwegypta' (Norway plus Egypt) for Argentina, and the slightly shocking formula for the region of Sao Paulo: 'A Switzerland surrounded by 20 Biafras.'

59. Alfredo L. De Romana, 'L'économie autonome, une alternative en gestion à la société industrielle', *Interculture*, no. 4, 1989, Centre Monchanin, Montreal, p. 110.

3

The Shipwreck of the Grand Society

Anyone who pretends that the earth and sky will founder doesn't know what they are talking about. And anyone who says that they will not founder is equally in error. Whether or not the world will end, is something we know nothing about.

Lie-Tsu[1]

In defending the 'open society' based on the market economy against its enemies, liberal ideologues have not only sought to show the superiority of Western countries over those of the socialist bloc, they have also magnified the 'great society' as being the best ever produced in history.[2] Western society is *great*, according to them, not only because it is tending to a planetary scope with its vocation of embracing the whole of humanity, but also because it permits the greatest possible realisation of each person's potential. In short, this society alone will bring the greatest happiness for the greatest number. René Girard, hardly the most obvious partisan of the market economy, persuades himself that 'no other society has permitted so many people to escape from conditions that I would continue to define as "subhuman" '.[3] But this optimism is based on a limited vision. The 'foundering' of the grand society, whose first moments we are perhaps seeing, does not result from the loss of confidence of 'free men' in their city, a phenomenon much feared by liberal authors, but rather from the contradictions that this marvellous utopia itself produces. While the grand society has allowed a great number of people to escape from conditions that seem subhuman to us, it also condemns a greater number of people to a radically inhuman condition than any other society found in history. According to the World Bank itself, a billion human beings live *below* the poverty line.

The ambivalence of modernity

It has become commonplace to evoke the two-sided character of modernity. Most often, the attempt is made to dissociate the two faces of this new Janus,[4] so as to preserve the 'good' side and jettison or forget the other. The 'good' aspect of the West is emancipation, usually expressed in terms of human rights. The bad side is imperialism, both economic and political. If one proposes that, with decolonisation, political imperialism is dead, and that economic imperialism (at least in its Leninist and *tiers-mondiste* sense) is inconsistent and contradictory, there remains for the West just the elegant face of liberty and democracy. A lot of people see it as the propagator of a 'liberty without frontiers'.[5] Many intellectuals in the Third World let themselves be seduced by this beguiling image, and come to see the West as the instigator of liberty in the South.[6] Thus: liberty, democracy – and prosperity?

Clearly, prosperity is also one of the many faces of the West. But here things become less clear-cut. At the heart of the West's dynamism is the drive for technological progress and the systematic war against the stinginess of nature. Yet this war against misery and against the servitude that misery entails does not necessarily proceed via liberty and democracy – despite what some people try to have us believe. Modernisation, in the sense of the enterprise of economic rationalisation, is a veritable rape of tradition and of ancestral values; it has rarely been a purely spontaneous process, more often the doing of an 'enlightened despot' and sometimes of a despot with very little enlightenment (Stalin, Pinochet, Ceausescu, and so on). It is a matter, in practice, of *changing people's outlooks* and of mobilising all available potentialities. Those leading the modernisation always fear that the individual energies suddenly liberated in a traditional society will not be deployed in the *right* direction. Peter the Great, Kemal Atatürk and Meiji himself, all the great 'modernisers', set about their task with cudgel firmly in hand.

Convinced libertarians will, of course, point out that brutal and authoritarian modernisation does not bring about prosperity. They will add that economic liberalism conforming to the emancipatory face of modernity is the true vector of economic development. There are all sorts of reasons for not believing them on this last point. It should first be noted that economic liberalism is not necessarily accompanied by democracy and civil liberties. (The example of South Korea is always available to remind us of this.) Furthermore, this economic liberty is widely suspected – and not without foundation – to leave the weak defenceless and at the mercy of the goodwill of the strong. The critiques of the early socialists have lost nothing of their pertinence on this point. According to Lacordaire: 'Between the strong and the weak, it is liberty that oppresses and constraint that protects and frees.' Or as August Bebel puts it: 'Economic liberalism is the free fox in the free chickencoop.' And François Brune observes: 'Those in a situation of dominance always confound freedom with the right of steel and guns against wood and stone.'[7] Already in the eighteenth century Jacques Necker, refuting Turgot's liberalism with the lucid cynicism of an enlightened conservatism, spoke of an 'obscure and terrible combat, where one loses count of the number of unfortunates, and where the strong oppress the weak with the protection of the law'.[8]

Conversely, of course, any form of regulation or protection may result in 'perverse effects'. The libertarians and other ultra-liberals use this as an argument for condemning any form of constraint. Yet they do not demonstrate that these perverse effects are inevitable in every circumstance, nor that they are necessarily worse than the perverse effects of absolute individual liberty. Only an unshakeable faith in the harmony of interests and a narrowly utilitarian and pessimistic vision of human nature justify their rosy image of the market society – an image which, in fact, no society has yet really tried to implement, notwithstanding its supposed conformity to 'natural law'.

The democratic ideal, which is perhaps the most noble product of the Western imagination, in practice has been implemented hand in hand with the destruction of cultures through the rise of technology and the market. We can see the seeds of the irresistible march towards equality of conditions in Europe, so well analysed by de Tocqueville, in the medieval movement for emancipation of the towns (freeing them from the feudal yoke of royal and baronial control).[9] But can we plausibly claim to discover, behind the real and imaginary dynamic of Western democracy, the seeds and values of an authentically universal democracy? Or should we, as Louis Dumont argues, denounce *Homo aequalis* in favour of *Homo hierarchicus*, and expose the fallacies of democratic aspiration in an effort towards more *communitarian* (or holistic) conceptions of social organisation that emphasise the benefits of a well-tempered hierarchy? The question is not easy to answer, but it is useful at least to explore it.

The two faces of modernity are much more difficult to separate than might initially appear. We do not really know of any 'rational' economic system apart from capitalism, and in spite of all its reforms and reinterpretations capitalism remains tainted by the accusation of *exploitation*. For the worker anyway, it is the incarnation neither of economic democracy nor of emancipation. This ambivalence is, in fact, inscribed right into the foundations of the project of modernity. It derives from the *antinomies of reason* and from the impossibility of dissociating means and ends given that the two are comprised of the same thing: utility.

The construction of the rational society involves a double movement which engenders a contradiction. This relates closely to the imperative we have designated the 'principle of the *maximine*'. This principle demands, on the one hand, using the least effort to accomplish a given objective, in other words the economy of means. Following this line of thinking, one can propose that modern society, being in theory more disinclined to effort than primitive communities, sets out to free the individual more and more from servile tasks, to reduce the hours of work and transport times, and to simplify the burden of housework. It holds out the promise of a leisure civilisation. Socially and politically, it reduces constraints and limits obligations. Security and civil peace are, ideally, achieved with ever-decreasing resources committed to policing, and with fewer and fewer restrictions of any nature on the activities of individuals.

But this liberation, this freeing of the individual, is equivocal because it offers leisure time only while abolishing the free enjoyment of it. Time is economised because it has value; and this means precisely that at all costs it must not be lost or wasted. It can be economised (saved) only in order that it be better invested (used productively).

The other aspect of the *maximine* principle meanwhile demands that, *at the same time* as one 'saves' time and effort, there should be a mobilisation of *all* available energy to produce the maximum 'utility'. The economised means (time, resources, energy, labour) liberate modern man only in order better to subordinate him. How can effort be reduced? Through the maximal mobilisation of all resources; through the competition of individuals and groups; through the invention of new machines, both technical and social, with ever-increasing production and ever more intensive utilisation in both production and consumption. The overall objective of the greatest happiness for the greatest number has no precise quantitative meaning. In practice it translates into the imperative of more and faster: the production of ever-greater masses of commodities, through the endless creation of new needs yet to be satisfied, through the accumulation without limit of capital, through the growth of collective power over nature and over people themselves, and perhaps even through the production of the greatest number of human beings.

Because of this indeterminacy about the distinction of means from ends, the growth in consumption is accomplished only in the growth in production, and *vice versa*. The growth in power subordinates citizens supposedly in order better to liberate them; but it liberates only in order better to make them subservient. The fantastic growth of productive forces which, we are told, puts at the disposal of each member of the rich societies the mechanical equivalent of 35 slaves, fails to make life as 'easy' as the possession of one single slave made it for the beneficiary in the societies of antiquity.[10] The gain of time from rapid-transport systems serves only to encourage the further extension of communications systems and the lengthening of distances between home and work. The West is precisely the man spoken of by the Taoist sage Chuang-Tzu, who runs faster and faster in a vain attempt to get away from his own shadow.

The minimal social cohesion needed for individuals to deploy their energies in an effective manner ends up taking a perverse form under the effects of this liberated energy, becoming the implacable constraint of a social regimentation which transforms agents and users into cogs of the machine. The nostalgia of modern humanity for authentically universal values derives much of its force from the fact that modernity has produced little more than a *phantom* of democracy and of freedom.

The myth of the grand society

Going beyond the ambivalence of modernity, what underpins the myth of the grand society is the elevation of life as supreme value. Through all its vicissitudes and despite its rough edges, the West has managed to make life – in the sense of biological survival – into a universal value. The first, the most indisputable of human rights, is life: life pure and simple. And in this respect, the progress achieved is indisputable, objective, verifiable. The programme of putting death to death – the eradication of death – has had some clear success on the three fronts of miserable death, violent death and natural death. One might quibble about the degree of success on the first two counts, but not on the third:

the victory over natural death is striking. The number of people on the planet has grown dramatically by virtue of modern medicine and hygiene. This demographic growth must be good, we are told, because it is the outcome of a good thing, namely the reduction of mortality.[11] Life expectancy even in the most poverty-stricken countries is now much higher than it was around the beginning of the twentieth century, having gone up on average from 46 years in 1960 to 62 years in 1987. Success in the eradication of epidemics has been striking too. Remaining targets such as cancer are only a matter of time. The Cancer Research Association has set itself the objective of eliminating this menace between now and the year 2000, and of obtaining a recovery in at least 75% of cases. The television advertisement for this Association in France shows Professor Jacques Crozemarie pronouncing emphatically the slogan 'Choose life!' Who would choose death, after all?

So the utilitarian programme has succeeded remarkably well in its second goal: it has produced the greatest number. If life is the greatest of goods, utilitarianism has fully succeeded – but in a sense closer to that of Malthus (who was also a convinced utilitarian) than of Ricardo, who located happiness in abundance.

The fetishisation of health care demonstrates well this obsession with hunting down death everywhere and at any price. The Aids virus, for example, is an ultimate test. If the West is not capable of mastering the virus, this will put in danger its whole pretension to incarnate the value of life. Marc Augé puts it very nicely:

> We have shown up to now a sort of vanity from the fact that we have mastered (or pretend to have mastered) all of the epidemic or endemic diseases. It is indeed on the basis of this capability that the West has brought its civilising message to the peoples it colonised. Consequently, the inability to master a sudden assault by death would have a very great significance for Western civilisation, since if we were no longer capable of stopping death, the very kernel of our power would be placed in doubt, and our whole secure universe (shored up by vaccinations, the prolongation of lifespan, etc.) would be at risk of collapse.[12]

This valuing of life by the West is purely *quantitative*. It refers to life in its biological sense, survival, with various prostheses at whatever price. If, however, human life is cultural before being biological, its price cannot be measured in these terms. The quality and intensity of life, as defined according to an infinite diversity of systems of meaning in traditional cultures, are what constitute life's value. However short it may appear in the eyes of a stranger, a life has always been well filled if it has accomplished the objectives asked of it. The salvaging of human lives at all costs amounts, by contrast, to a monstrous indifference to all that constitutes the *humanness* of a life.

This discounting of the humanness of the individual, and the privileging by contrast of the biological mechanism, is evidenced in the monstrous marketing of the body and in the repugnant trafficking in organs that is taking place under our eyes on a planetary scale. Far from abuses flying in the face of medical humanism, these phenomena are the inevitable consequences of the medicalisation of the human being. The newspaper *Le Monde* reported on 23 March 1989, that Turkish peasants were offered 21,700 French francs (about US $4,000) for giving up a kidney which would subsequently be grafted onto a patient in Great Britain. The article went on to say that the organiser of the traffic confirmed all the facts, and claims to have acted out of humanitarian concern rather than for profit. And why not believe him? In any event, according to the British Department of Health, trade in kidneys for transplantation, if not encouraged, is not illegal.[13]

Profit is not necessarily at the centre of such commerce, just as it was not when, last century, a traffic in corpses for use in scientific analyses was organised on a grand scale. On the other hand, the new bodysnatchers are engaged in a transnational financial speculation, organised in part to dodge national regulations.[14] So, for example, there is an impressive flux of flesh and blood flowing out of Latin America to save North American lives. One can debit one's body piece by piece and sell each morsel individually on the retail market. After all, what basis could there possibly be for respect for the physical integrity of the sacrosanct individual in the generalised market society of which the anarcho-capitalists dream?

In sum, the quantity of life produced by the grand society conforms to the law of the *maximine:* the maximum of life for the least cost, the distribution being made according to the highest bid. Given the fantastic expense of the sophisticated medical equipment now employed (scanners and so on), health policies increasingly push individuals into taking responsibility for their own health, in the sense of managing their life-budget: insurances, cost-benefit trade-offs, and so on. The market in bodies and lives further extends to children, and indeed to religious vocations! The trade in child prostitution is well known. Equally, the search for children from the South for adoption in the North sometimes goes as far as outright kidnapping. In Italy a veritable trafficking in young Indian women in response to the deficit of religious vocations in the North was recently unmasked. The cult of life for life's sake thus ends up by inducing the greatest disdain for human life.

The economic war and the reality of competition

The true face of the humanistic West, supposedly peace-loving and respectful of life, is made clear in the picture of economic life furnished by economists, managers and the related specialist media. This *game*, from which everyone should emerge a winner, is in reality a veritable war. A bellicose and aggressive vocabulary dominates in the language of both the captains of industry and the young wolves aspiring to the top. Industrialists love to adopt the language of sport. The chief executive of one company engaged in equipment manufacture thus declared: 'In this industry, international competition is a Formula One contest.'[15] One knows what to think henceforth about sportsmanlike behaviour: every trick can be used.

As François Brune has analysed, the discourse of advertising agencies amounts to a 'perpetual military metaphor':[16]

> They speak of 'niches', define 'targets' (preferably 'sharply outlined'), establish 'strategies' and launch 'campaigns'. There is even 'combat marketing'. For example a seminar theme might be: 'How to illustrate marketing operations through playing a *war game* with a military campaign map showing consumer preferences.'

Who, asks François Brune, will be the victim of this assault? As guests on the French literature and commentary television programme *Apostrophes*, on 14 December 1979, a group of advertising agents glorified their daily combat: 'It is like being a boxer, being hit all over the place throughout the day.' The interviewer asked: 'So you are the Goldorak of advertising?' 'Yes,' came the reply, 'in the sense of a man who never stops winning.'[17]

Advertisers are, of course, not alone on the battlefield; indeed their war is just the preliminary skirmish. French industrialist Antoine Riboud makes clear the pervasiveness of the military mentality:

> It is obvious that the economic battle is rough and unequal. It will be won only by those who are strong, courageous, tenacious, imaginative, and also capable of communicating, listening, and understanding. ... It is clear that in order to do battle and win, business must have freedom.[18]

With regard to new technologies, he goes on:

> It is exactly in this domain that the world economic war is taking place. And it begins with the battle for social efficiency, a battle which France could well lose.[19]

The *game* between nations, linked intimately to the game between transnational corporations, is a pitiless fight. The existence of a minimum of common interest in the common fight against nature is what permits maintenance of a minimum degree of cooperation; but for all that it is clear that it is not a matter of all winning together but of conquest. This is made plain by Riboud with reference to new technologies. These are, he says, too costly and too complex to be profitable without expansion and differentiation of markets. All firms in the industry thus have an interest in expansion of the markets. But, at the end of the day, a carve-up must take place:

> It is with market shares and nothing else that wealth and jobs are created. If this pursuit of increased market shares is not continued, then impoverishment of the nation and social conflicts will be the paradoxical consequences of technological progress.[20]

This is all very well, but where are these market shares to be found? Within France? That is difficult, because the market is already saturated and introduction of new technologies has already resulted in many redundancies. Will new market shares be found in Germany, or Japan? Perhaps, in certain niches, but don't the Germans and the Japanese, who themselves continue to introduce new technologies, also have need of market shares? Riboud points plainly to the contest:

> We are in the process of catching up as fast as Fiat to the productivity level of our most efficient competitors, the Japanese. We were 50% less efficient

three years ago. This catch-up is significant but still insufficient, however, because if we were to visit a Japanese automobile factory now, we would observe programmes of training, skill-development and management that will allow a further gain of 100% in work productivity within three years.[21]

Bravo! A round of applause, please! And will the Burkina Faso nation be able to follow suit, also introducing new technologies, increasing its market share in France (or elsewhere)? No one tells us so. In order to avoid 'the impoverishment of the nation and the social conflicts that would be the paradoxical consequences of technological progress', the Japanese must also increase their market share. Here in France? In Burkina Faso?

In theory, one might conceive that the Japanese market could enlarge in France, while the French market share could enlarge in Japan. Since it is not a zero-sum game, each player gets richer and the market gets bigger. One would arrive, thus, at an equilibrium à la Jean-Baptiste Say, but at a higher level of economic activity after the elimination of the weak, mediocre and inept. The French Cabinet minister Claude Cheysson seems to see it this way:

I had thought, believed, and declared for a long time that the markets of these countries (Burkina and others) that we would need, were not going to be there for us. But this was to neglect the new needs of our consumption society, along such lines as progress in electronics, computer and information technologies, the expansion of services. The experiment has now been made: a market that is smaller in terms of the number of consumers but is more dynamic and demanding more frequent renewal, assures for the most advanced – whose advance never stops increasing – a growth that our financiers and economists consider to be unequalled and that they laud on every possible occasion.[22]

Antoine Riboud is not a theoretician like Jean-Bapiste Say. He knows how things work in practice, and puts it very well: it is necessary to enlarge market share *first*, and enrichment comes after that. Unfortunately, what can be said of successful entrepreneurial behaviour at the micro-economic level is not *universalisable* to all those in the game. Not only must there be losers in order that the market shares of others can grow, but the whole process can go backwards if there is not a gentle push from somewhere to place the market as a whole on a growth trajectory. One might one more time call upon the generosity of the brave Burkinaby people. Even though they are very poor, by tightening their belts a little bit more, they can still buy a few French and Japanese cars for their elites. This gives rise to a feeling of optimism about sales potentials in the South, which encourages the French and Japanese to continue their investments so that they end up buying each other's new models. By virtue of repeating endlessly that the potential for development in the South is immense, that the prospective markets are enormous, one can end up believing it and acting accordingly. Thus there will be no losers, other than the French and Japanese competitors who were incapable of staying on the racetrack and who, by producing at too high a cost, were damaging to the well-being of humanity (including the Burkinaby).

Of course, the prospects for the Burkinaby of building a car industry that is competitive with the French and Japanese sectors recede a bit further. That aside, have things changed in any fundamental way from the time of Cecil Rhodes, a practical man and a humanist like Antoine Riboud, who declared that imperialism was the only solution to relieve the misery of the English working classes? As Rhodes' friend Stanley argued to the Manchester Chamber of Commerce in 1877, if the English managed to convince all those negroes who are going around naked to cover themselves (even if only on Sundays!), what a fantastic market opening that would be for the cloth industry! They knew already: 'It is with market shares and nothing else that wealth and jobs are created.' François Partant writes:

> Whatever the liberal economist might think, we are not involved in a cycle race. If we have to compare the capitalist world to something, it should rather be to an undisciplined dinner by cannibals, where the strong eat the weak. But the individual fattens more than in proportion to what he swallows, and this is the source of growth.[23]

As for competition between individuals, this is a very particular sport. Economics has focused only on the individualist aspect of modernity, and has completely misunderstood the dimension of solidarity-cooperation. Or rather, it proposes that this solidarity-cooperation can be made to emerge from individualism through a contractual agreement of equals. Cooperation founded exclusively on the individual interests of the parties to the game presupposes, however, a confidence that cannot be justified on the basis of interest alone, notwithstanding all the fancy acrobatics of the 'prisoner's

dilemma'.[24] Moreover, everyone plainly knows that a business enterprise is not an association of equals and that competition between
members within the organisation (between top executives, within
middle management, between groups of salaried employees down to
the lowest paid wage workers) is not the same as that taking place
between companies. A competent and reliable labourer will usually
be a loser in relation to even the most mediocre manager. As François
Partant writes:

> The unfortunate thing is that individual success (for the capitalist) limits
> singularly the realisation of potential for others – for the rank and file
> workers, for less successful competitors. ... Yet the capitalist who has
> succeeded will always assert that competition is a 'healthy rivalry' and
> the source of all progress.[25]

One of the often ill-recognised features of modernity is that each
individual does have some chance, if circumstances are very favourable, to win in one domain or another (sport, media, film, business,
politics, art, etc.). In industrial societies today we have the situation
described by Andy Warhol in which 'each person has, or will have,
been famous for at least ten minutes'.[26] With news and current events
programmes on the one hand, and TV games on the other, who will
not sooner or later end up on the small screen? But even so, could
anyone be made to believe that everyone has the same chance of
becoming the boss of a transnational firm or a world-renowned artist?

The division of labour and its systematic control constitute, without
doubt, a rational mode of organisation from the standpoint of the
maximine. But it is impossible to derive these features from application of individualist precepts. Certainly workers can, formally
speaking, optimise their situation within a universe not of their choosing. But the universe of modern business cannot emerge simply from
the interactions of *Homo oeconomicus*. Entrepreneurs in the modern
universe necessarily do not follow the same logic as their 'rational'
employees. What interests them must be something other than the
limited pleasures obtainable through material commodities, which
most often they already have. They are motivated necessarily by a will
to power, not by a desire for pleasure. They are interested in the power
that the dynamic of profit can permit them to acquire. They do not
seek to minimise their efforts and pain in pursuit of bourgeois com-
forts; rather they mobilise all their resources (that is, money, the pains

of others, and their own time and energy) to maximise their position of power.

The specificity of the entrepreneurial activity, and even more so of executive power, reflects the fact that *'the satisfaction afforded by power is not something one can share out'*.[27] Only a small number can succeed in this pitiless fight for a place at the top. It is not live and let live. As in any war, the law is that of *vae victis*, too bad for the losers.

Fortunately for the great mass of those who are vanquished without combat, who do not aspire to the top, they are utilisable as front-line troops in the army of the conquerors. But the combats themselves give rise to even greater masses of *outcasts* who are the *absolutely vanquished*. In effect there are several distinct 'markets', partitioned off and hierarchised: that of the kings of the castle who do battle for power in high finance and major industry; that of middle-managements concerned with their paypackets; down to the rivalries among the low-paid workers. All these groups are entered in the economic game, even if the bulk of them are coming last. But there are others as well, who are left out of the game entirely.

The price of opulence

The material wealth that modernity promises has among its costs the abdication of citizenry at the Centre and the loss of independence on the Periphery. Getting abundance at lowest cost presumes not only that maximum energy be deployed, but also that this deployment be in forms over which the individual has no say. Even on the political level, the objective of maximum power at the price of minimum relinquishment of rights implies an abandonment of the substance of citizenry. In the factory, the office, the market and daily life, the productive agent, the passive consumer, the manipulated voter, the user of public services, the citizen, becomes simply a *cog* somewhere in the vast techno-bureaucratic machinery. We touch here on one of the great contradictions of the project of modernity: the free society of free citizens is a form denuded of the very essence of its content. The attractive project of democracy is emptied of all substance. Where is liberty on the production line? Where is democracy when the citizen, at the end of a day of hassles, comes home only to find innumerable problems (children's homework, taxes to pay, social security forms to fill out, and so on)? He is lucky if, somewhere between dessert and the washing up, he feels up to watching on television the president he has elected (or for whom he has not voted; what difference does it make?), inaugurate a nuclear power station on which his views have never been sought. And even if his views had been sought?

It is well known that modern production in its mechanistic and centralised form (whether capitalist or socialist) implies a *submission* both formal and real of the worker. Taylor went further than this when he reputedly retorted to a worker: 'No one asks you to think; there are people paid to do that.' Because of this separation of the tasks of conception from those of execution, the affluence promised by Fordism/Taylorism comes on the premise of reduction of the worker-citizen to the status of blind servant of the machine. And, comments Alain Lipietz, 'with the loss of mastery over the productive processes, the working class loses all ambition for self-management. It gets in exchange the welfare state and consumer society.'[28] François Partant writes in the same vein: 'The nineteenth-century industrial worker lost the right to choose what he should do and how to do it; and then with Taylorism he lost as well the right to know what he is doing.'[29]

Of course it will be said that this negative state of affairs has been left behind, and that technological progress now permits the restoration of active participation within productive enterprise. Thus Antoine Riboud, for example, insists on the participation of *all* workers in the firms using the new technologies. Information, he says, 'relates to the very fundamental theme of democracy in the workplace, and to the right of workers to obtain as much information within their workplace as they receive as citizens within the nation'.[30]

This is a derisive irony. Do they really receive much information as citizens? Is it necessary to confuse information in the sense of a limited but sound knowledge needed to make a decision, with the media avalanche of messages whose very quantity (whatever might be its inherent value) leads to the *disinformation* not only of citizens but very often of the decision-makers as well? As nicely put by Jean-Pierre Garnier: 'the modern communication technologies turn out to be, for the majority of people, techniques of excommunication more than anything else.'[31]

The new technologies do demand, in fact, an active involvement on the part of the workers, a purposeful and if possible intelligent attentiveness. Yet in the flexible workshop the digitally controlled machine means that workers can no longer come and go as they please; the machine decides. 'The worker becomes his own taskmaster directing his self-exploitation, self-managing his exploitation.'[32] Is this new manner of working really more democratic or liberating? Doesn't it, on the contrary, indicate a further stage of alienation? The two are not necessarily mutually exclusive, in the sense that, at the price of a severe mutilation through renunciation of a part of his private life and person (which we know to be pushed very far in Japan), the new-style worker can obtain the reward of feeling recognised as a member of the collective enterprise. This is not nothing. But what scope remains for him (or her) to exercise, and take pleasure in, his roles as a free citizen in the civil world? We know equally that, in Japan, democracy is a pure fiction. The clan-rivalry between political factions and between industrial conglomerates concerns individual citizens only in terms of the end-results imposed on them. In the contemporary world the workers, if they have indeed adopted the enterprise's stance, demand from the political world only that they each be left to work in peace to facilitate the operation of the machine.

And in the office, which increasingly is the norm as work milieu, what democracy is there, what freedom? The workers are totally integrated into a huge and anonymous techno-bureaucratic machine. Self-management is just the final word for obtaining as much of their effort as possible; the enlightened design of working conditions has this in view.

For the societies *lagging behind* in the modernisation process, those of the Third World, the route to opulence is through absolute submission to the therapies of the experts. The first act necessary for take-off is acknowledgement of the diagnosis made by foreign experts. The societies outside modernity must begin by becoming aware of their misery. Then a long treatment commences. The renunciation of bad habits, of customary practices and ways of thinking is a necessary stage; after that comes adoption of a development model. Whether this model be liberal or socialist, it must be imposed in authoritarian fashion. To the processes of constraint and submission characterisic of the modern business and industrial state, is here added the forced imposition of outside values. All of this in the name of liberty and democracy! Modernity unveils here its true face. The 'natural' order reveals all its artifices. And when opulence does not arrive, it is always easy to pretend that this failure has nothing to with the non-universality of modernity, but is due to the momentary incapacity of the societies in question to modernise themselves.

The affluent society consists, for the people of the rich countries, of a rather illusory reality; and for the people of the poor countries, of a very real illusion. For both, it amounts to a veritable enchantment from which it is almost impossible to escape.

Business ethics and economic *raison d'Etat*

It would be a mistake to suggest that ethical considerations do not figure in the grand society's discourse and the project of modernity. The common good, collective well-being, improvement of the condition of humanity, are the expressly stated objectives of the project. Certainly it is not demanded of individuals that they take care of others. The modern morality knows nothing about personal sacrifice, renunciation, privation, altruism. Nor has it retained the 'private vice' of Bernard de Mandeville, having rather domesticated it and transformed it into good. The objective of the common good being defined as some degree of material abundance, all that is required is a concern for oneself and a vague sympathy for one's neighbour. The basis of respect for others, and hence of moral conduct, is the contract. In contracting with another, I consider him or her as a free subject and I respect his or her liberty. All justice, wrote the liberal economist Courcelle-Seneuil a century ago, 'consists in the according of wills, and should be sought after nowhere else'.[33]

Now it is true that by adding – as do the interventionists preoccupied with the condition of disadvantaged social groups – the proviso that one should not confuse business conduct and matters of charity, the door is opened to another moral criterion. But if business conduct itself conforms to justice, what place is left for charitable conduct – other than signifying a human foible which, while certainly excusable, is hardly to be advocated? In fact this respect for the freedom of others, independent of the concrete situation, becomes for the ultra-liberals and libertarians an absolute rule. Inside a contract, anything goes (the individual subject is free to take drugs, free to sell himself or herself in small pieces, and so on); it is only outside a contract that it becomes a case of theft or evil.

The desire to prevail over others, while respecting them, is thus presented as a morally sound attitude. The morality of this utilitarian ethic has its basis in the presumed universalism of modernity's project. When each individual fights to win, not everyone wins; yet society wins because because the greatest happiness for the greatest number is generated. Moreover, because the greatest happiness for the greatest number is generated, is is possible that no individual absolutely loses, because there is a bigger pie to be shared around. This is the *ethics of business:* fight while respecting others, respect others in a world of constant warring.[34] More and more this is becoming a public morality, imposing itself across the whole of social life. Antoine Riboud, for example, takes it for granted: 'It is necessary to respect an ethic and the duties it imposes, in order to benefit from mankind's resources which are unlimited if he feels so motivated.'[35]

In fact there is a common interest in having a definite restraint over individual 'instincts' such as the desire for power in the exploitation of others; otherwise the very existence of a social order would be undermined. In market societies there is a real risk that the fight to win will override the respect for others, meaning that the minimal ethic of calculation of interests by free individuals is always in danger of being trampled upon. Fraud and deceit by the strong is a fact of life in Western societies. This deceit is manifest in the non-respect of basic principles when elementary rights of the person are refused to others, to refugees, to immigrants, etc., in the name of self-interested preservation of what one has acquired. It is expressed as a private economic *raison d'Etat* in industrial espionage. This takes place even with major sporting events. At the time of the 1983 America's Cup yachting contest, the Canadian team sent a frogman to try to photograph underwater the keel of the boat *Australia II*, which indeed was wrapped in canvas and under constant guard. A double violation: of proper business ethics and of sporting ethics.[36]

The same duplicity is manifest in still more flagrant fashion in the non-respect of contracts with the weak. The various treaties that the Whites entered into with the Indians and other indigenous peoples were systematically violated. The work contracts of the nineteenth century in Europe were subjected to all sorts of abuses (misrepresentations of hours worked, unjustified deductions). The regularity of wage labour, a requirement for the smooth working of large-scale industry, has been obtained only by virtue of all sorts of coercive measures (laws, union action, strikes), going quite outside the freedom of contracts. The nineteenth-century worker, calculating freely his pleasures and pains, typically chose to work 'part-time'.[37] The across-the-board mobilisation that the enticement of new needs is supposed to have induced 'naturally' has been achieved through constraint.

This omnipresence of coercion, duplicity and deceit does not menace the existence or the importance of an ethics of business. But it does limit what convincingly can be claimed for it. Despite all their efforts, the new sophists have not been able to make their morality emerge from the prisoner's dilemma. *Deceit always pays.* Machiavelli knew this. It pays, but equally it makes impossible an individualist society founded uniquely on personal interest. Jean Baechler, who has tried to construct a political theory on an individualistic axiomatic basis, acknowledges this. Respect for engagements one has entered into is, he concludes, an indispensable virtue which does not result from self-interested calculation.[38]

Radical individualism implies that the incommunicability of subjective worlds (the 'no-bridge' problem) is insurmountable. From this point of view, the Marquis de Sade is the only authentic utilitarian: he made deceit and manipulation into an entire mode of conduct. Each individual can and should take advantage of the opportunities that his or her situation offers, deceive others when convenient (while avoiding getting caught out), indulge in hypocrisy and encourage the virtue and generosity of the weak in order that they may be more easily duped. These are the logical consequences of 'liberal' tenets pushed to the extreme. Of course, such a world with neither faith nor law is an *anti-society*, and any social cohesion is impossible: it is not even a society of thieves. The Iks described so vividly by Colin Turnbull come fairly close to this non-society, with the sole qualification that they renounce extreme violence.[39]

In order for the passion for business to have triumphed over all others and to inhibit their unbridled effects, it has been necessary for the worship of the golden calf to come to prevail exclusively, bringing with it a certain moral code. On the American greenback is inscribed quite specifically: 'In God We Trust.' The most utilitarian of societies, the United States of America is not mistaken in believing it necessary to invoke religion to guarantee the law of the dollar. In the business world, the 'misleading' statement (if not outright lie) is so widespread a practice that it is no longer considered to involve disrespect for rules of proper conduct. With regard to economic policy and affairs of state, it is always a case of a 'diplomatic lie'. Advertising permits in a similar way the most preposterous assertions. When it is asserted that a particular brand of mineral water allows you to 'digest even bricks', or that with certain disposable nappies 'even wet they stay dry', there is no question of trying to mislead the consumer! False invoices and tax declarations are a national pastime. In public offers on the Stock Exchange, the most shameless lie with hand on heart is a precondition of success and in no way discredits the perpetrator. It is clear that, in the economic war, deceit costs nothing and can bring big rewards; it is a weapon that even the most honest businessman could not imagine doing without.[40]

A human being cannot live in society without some sort of ethics; and ethics cannot be reduced to a set of imposed rules. In particular, in a liberal society where the state is supposed to minimise its directive role, the necessary ethical norms have to be internalised by the citizens. Since there is a fair risk that citizens individually may not be much inclined to respect these norms, public opinion plays an important role in imposing this respect. In the Anglo-Saxon countries of Protestant tradition, public opinion plays this role with great force, particularly given the fact that social morality has already been pretty much reduced to this minimal ethic. The whole of life tends to conform to business logic: buying and selling, trades, contracts between individuals; and so the ethic of business becomes that for life. At the same time, the lack at the personal level of a strongly felt ethic is compensated for by the attention accorded to the theme of ethics in public opinion and in the media.

In Catholic countries, although the end result is the same, the flavour of the process can be slightly different. There is more readiness to pose questions about the relationship between 'necessary economic efficiency' and the 'requirements of faith'; so the problem of ethics in management is one of 'succeeding while maintaining integrity'.[41] By contrast with traditional Christian moral theorists, who sought to define the proper place of the economic on the basis of an *other* morality, it is here a matter of finding the place for an ethic starting from economic logic. For example:

Placing themselves resolutely at the heart of the triumphant liberal system, the authors of the manual *Ethics of the System and Management* explain how to make honesty a genuine tool of management and how to promote an ethical component within firms on a par with communication services and quality control.

As Machiavelli would have said, what counts is not to be moral, but to give the impression of it. Equally, Werner Sombart writes: 'It suffices, in the interest of business, *to be considered* as possessing the bourgeois virtues, not necessarily to have them in fact.'[42] According to a survey done in 1987 in the United States, 63% of American managers think that ethics contributes to the success of business. So, as Didier Pourquery concludes, investment in a clear conscience is a useful form of marketing. We are still very much within the schema of 'good deed, good business'.

All the same, in utilitarian logic there is no discernible difference between 'being moral' and 'giving the impression of being so'. This is the origin of the great hypocrisy that reigns in countries where morality is grounded in utilitarianism backed by public opinion.[43] In real terms, as has been seen, the obsession with winning leaves little place for concern with respect for the other. Winning means *winning at any price*. How can a barrier be imposed against exploitation of the other, when nature has already been sacrificed? The domination of nature, the founding principle of modernity, in fact implies having no respect for the other living species, nor taking any account of ecological balances, nor concern with cosmic order. How, given that, can one be expected to respect other humans, not to be tempted to 'naturalise' them and treat them merely as a means to an end? Slavery and apartheid reveal clearly the way things can go. Is wage labour compatible with an authentic respect for others?

The business ethic restricts the respect for others to the respect for private property; and even this is not rigorously applied, with a retreat to the more limited domain of civil law. Mere respect for the laws, even if the laws have their inspiration in *ethics*, does not and cannot amount to an ethic. Any sort of transgression becomes possible, merely if no law is enforced against it. So conformism tends to take the place of a rule of good conduct, and success to establish its own legitimacy.

Business ideology is, indeed, really a type of social Darwinism, justified by the supposedly higher interest of business. This amounts to a kind of *raison d'Etat* operating in the economic domain. Whenever the higher interest of business demands, any other moral consideration should be put aside. This higher interest of business is, evidently, very vague and arbitrary. It can be linked to state policy: for example when the fight against unemployment is made a priority, eyes will be closed not only to questions of personal ethics but even to the non-application of existing laws (e.g. concerning social security and welfare entitlements, employment conditions, environmental damage, safety). In the competition with neighbouring countries, almost any tactic is allowed in the name of realism.

If orders are not forthcoming without under-the-table payments and bribes, then such payments are part of the game. If the balance of payments demands export of armaments, then let us export armaments. In competition between firms, the same thing goes. The survival or profitability of the enterprise is the ultimate justification. If respect for business ethics is compatible with profit, or even permits one to make greater profits, then go for ethics. If respect for ethics compromises the survival of the enterprise, then to hell with ethics! Business creates jobs, creates affluence, contributes to the greatest good for the greatest number. How could we not want the means, if we desire the outcome?

This overriding *raison d'Etat* is always premised on collective utility. The *general interest* (or equally, public interest, national interest, interests of humanity) is 'the first principle and the unique principle of all the actions of kings and leaders'.[44] When this general interest takes on an economic form, quite naturally the *raison d'Etat* becomes economic in character. So the state enters into collusion with business firms, as in the industrial-military complexes. The projects of the industrial giants are imposed on and against everyone. What is good for General Motors is good for the United States; what is good for Electricité de France is good for France; what is good for IBM is good for humanity.

In the developing countries, economic *raison d'Etat* allows every sort of crime to be justified in the name of devlopment. A Brazilian politician recently declared: 'It is now *our turn* to pollute.' The Amazonian forest is casually massacred, with the remaining Indians at the forefront. Peter Berger spells out this implacable logic as follows:

> Event X has given rise to terrible suffering for a great number of those who have had to live through it. But at the end of the day, it amounts to a good rather than an evil, because it has led to event Y.[45]

Event Y is, of course, the development eternally awaited; and X may be the assassination of a culture, the rape of populations, and so forth.

The sacrosanct principle of economic *raison d'Etat* can be summed up in the adage: you can't make an omelette without breaking eggs. The only thing is, although the eggs get smashed, one never sees the promised omelette.

Moreover, this morality is extremely elastic. Up to what threshold can one throw toxic wastes into the environment without showing a lack of respect for others? Will employment of women during the night continue to be proscribed (which, in law, is still the case in France) out of respect for the human person, while it is accepted for men when the machinery demands it? How many decibels are tolerable for workers without failing to respect their persons, knowing that techno-logical progress without such nuisance is a great deal more costly? Take the example of a totally automated milk and cheese factory that I happened to visit in the Auvergne. The performance of the techno-logy is truly impressive. Five hundred thousand litres of milk can be transformed each day into soft paste, with an extremely small work-force. Everything is clean and sterile. Two or three technicians in a soundproofed room control the whole of the process and its workers, including those who empty and rinse the vats and prepare the cheeses. However, the dozen or so women and men who carry out the comple-mentary tasks of equipment maintenance, supply and surveillance up close are engaged in feverish activity in an infernal din. The contrast is total between technological prowess and disdain for the human being. If even a tiny fraction of the energy, ingenuity and capital consecrated to the functional perfection of the system had been de-voted to ensuring for the minions of the machines a pleasanter way of working, the lives of these latter would have been substantially im-proved. The absolute indifference to this *minor* problem is striking. Progress is technical progress, not that of the working conditions of the machine's auxiliaries.

Respect for the human person is assured, the businessman will respond, when each partner contracts freely. We know where this leads in terms of the freedom of the unemployed and of those in poverty. Even if freedom of contract has its merits, it has its limits too. No existing or conceivable morality is content with the 'free contract' between the drug-trafficker and the addict. The Mafia also operates with free contracts. The supposed autonomy of persons upon which individualistic society reposes is both a fiction and a norm. The real inequality of people's situations empties this autonomy of much of its content on the economic plane, and the 'social construction' of indi-

vidual subjects (leading to such and such capabilities, wants, preferences, etc. being taken as 'givens' by the economist) is a delicate
process which rarely leads to wholly satisfactory results at a psychological level. The conscious, mature, healthy adult, who is
well-balanced and capable of looking after himself without being
excessively dependent on others and doesn't feel the compulsive need
to control others, is a rare species, even in the most 'advanced'
countries. The free citizen is indeed more a utopian ideal than a reality.

The modern ethic proposes nothing that would permit a movement
towards this ideal. The inversion of ethical grounds which takes place
in modernity poorly disguises the way in which the ethical is reduced
to the role of alibi. During the many centuries before the Enlightenment in the Christian West, the question was posed as to how to ensure
a morally acceptable character of economic life. Utilitarianism turns
this upside down: henceforth it is economic principles that penetrate
into the ethical domain. The question becomes: What morality compatible with economic imperatives can still be preserved? The only
solution amounts to proclaiming that the economic law of free contract
is morally sound from the outset, by virtue of its universality (or, at
least, its universalisability). But since, in practice, this universality is
far from evident, there is every cause to suspect that the business ethic
is only a fig-leaf to mask the nudity of a shameless cynicism. Economic reason and *raison d'Etat* go hand in hand in this Machiavellian
farce. Didier Pourquery, already cited above, observes justly:

> The 'moral majority' discourse of the Reagan Administration, which has
> much to do with the latter's successes, seems in flagrant conflict with the
> discourse of the media-glorified heroes of the corporate takeover years:
> these *raiders* with all the Borgia ambience engendered by their vocabulary
> of financial shark, black knight, poisoned pill, liquidation and 'rationali-
> sation' of firms.[46]

Yet the real Machiavellis are not these Borgia golden boys with their
excesses, but rather the directors of transnational industry, good
fathers, good husbands, living a strict life (or giving the impression of
it), who through the enigma of their cold calculations strangle entire
peoples and mutilate their subordinates, all the while 'sponsoring'
charitable organisations and non-governmental organisations.

The business ethic is insufficient to assure the respect of persons within a social body, and it cannot in any case derive from the logic of business alone; somewhere there is a need for 'virtue'.

Public demoralisation

The spectacle of the modern world and the opportunistic behaviour evident in business, politics and public life generally, have widespread demoralising effects on individuals. The most gross utilitarianism is used to justify individual behaviour: 'The seeking of mere individual pleasure leads to its pursuit through aggression and violence. At the limit, every pleasure being allowable, every violence to get it is also permissible.'[47] Material interest in the form of advancing one's career, in particular, serves as an alibi for the most detestable excesses. Citizens who are otherwise 'honest and decent', who have succeeded in controlling their passions and emotions, will impose the worst inconveniences on their friends and close companions without a scruple and without remorse. 'It was in my interests, I couldn't do otherwise' will be the excuse.[48] To pursue one's interests becomes the *categorical imperative* of modern times.

Yet social life rests, none the less, still very much on the love of couples, the attachment of spouses to each other, tenderness towards children, and relations of friendship and camaraderie, and correspondingly on jealousy, envy, antipathy and hate. These human relations cannot be reduced to a calculus of interests. Such ties, essential to the social fabric, imply an ethical dimension whether implicit or explicit. Friendship, it is said, creates rights and duties. These relationships are maintained and lived through exchanges and freely consented obligations. They conform to an ethic which is not that of business, and therefore value conflicts are inevitable. If my employer offers me a promotion through eliminating a work comrade, should I follow my career interest or the duties of friendship? If I can succeed in some deal I'm involved in through sacrificing the woman I love, how will love weigh up compared with money? Should even the renunciation of hate for a matter of pecuniary interest be considered as a virtue? Respect for laws does not give a solution to these intimate conflicts. Conformity only glosses over the problem; it provides a solution only for the morally lazy. The tyranny of public opinion in business societies tends effectively to impose this solution: surveys of public opinion are used to provide the answer to all problems not solved by business morality. Since economic utilitarianism is widely dominant, one can bet that the surveys will tend to result in a crushing of other ethical principles. In a utilitarian society, comments A.W. Gouldner, 'traditional values become transformed into superficial ornaments: graciousness, courage, courtesy, loyalty, love, generosity, gratitude'.[49]

The cynicism of the dominant utilitarian individualism has its home territory in the business domain. But it is remarkable how far business life extends its empire to the whole of life. Without this spillover, there would be nothing to stop the overflowing of passions into the street. What we come to see, though, is that love and friendship, and their opposites, are relegated to the hidden realm of private life – and, perhaps, tend even to atrophy. The utilitarian foundation of modern societies in this way becomes a self-fulfilling prophecy.

This 'positive ethic' of the winners finds an aspect of its positivity by reference to social Darwinism, one of the founding myths of modernity. The transposition to social life of Darwin's theories of natural selection keeps not much more than the idea of the fight for survival and competition between species. There is a tendency to forget the necessary complementarities of species and the generalised interdependency of nature – aspects already much downplayed in . Darwin's own theories, as in all allied Western thought. The neo-liberal ideologues see in the natural selection mechanism an historical dynamic of trial and error which ensures the triumph of the best-performing institutions. The minimum of social organisation on the basis of which calculating individuals can compete most fruitfully, is supposedly engendered through self-interested competition under forms that have already survived the test of past competition.

The war of all against all brings about the common good, at the same time as being the law of nature. The selection of the fittest which this conflict ensures can even be presented rather cynically as a version of the common good. The Christian version of 'everyone winning' (all souls can be saved) is replaced by 'the best will win' with the unstated sub-text 'and down with the rest'. Social competition is a 'natural' mechanism for selection of elites. At the international level it has produced superior and inferior peoples. The latter are condemned to be dominated or to disappear. In 1849 the US President Andrew Jackson, having gone against a Supreme Court judgement in permitting the State of Georgia to deport the Cherokee Indians so as to seize their tribal territories, declared:

> We should not lament the fact that a race of Indians has returned to the dust, because it is necessary, for the full advance of civilisation, that nations disappear and die, and that each generation is succeeded by another and cedes to it.[50]

Here, with perfect cynicism, the brute fact of dispossession was presented as moral norm. Today, in leaving the Yanomamis Indians in Brazil to be massacred and poisoned by *garimpeiros* (goldhunters) and other traffickers, in contempt of solemn undertakings, Brazil's President Sarney followed the same line, with lack of will perhaps substituting for cynicism. It becomes even more odious when the Brazilian government, through one of its influential ministers, declares explicitly that the Indian culture is mediocre and not worthy of respect. In front of the external affairs commission of parliament, General Gonclaves calmly observed that an economy like Brazil's cannot afford to let itself be guided by romantic impulses.[51]

This ideology of a sort of inevitable demise completes the demoralisation of civil society. The adulation and respect accorded to the winners adds moral lassitude to absence of scruples. Max Weber perceived it well when he said:

> Unconsciously, we side with those who are on the way up, because they are stronger or will become so. The simple fact of having won is taken, thus, as demonstrating that these forces are an 'economically superior' form of humanity; and only too easily do historians bend to the idea that, in the struggle, the triumph of the 'developed' parties is automatic, and that defeat in the fight for existence is a symptom of 'backwardness'.[52]

The fascination of victory induces the support of the masses. As Hannah Arendt has commented, this effect 'may not be moral, but it's very strong'. Fascism, Stalinism and Nazism have all, in their time, been nourished by these ways of thinking.

A minimum amount of reflection shows that this 'morality of the strong' does not hold up. Nature is quite indifferent to what we call strong or weak, inferior or superior. These categories reflect human judgements, human points of view. Social life cannot be reduced to a 'natural' process; it is impossible to have a society without some sets of values that owe nothing to nature or that enter somehow into contradiction with the supposed processes of 'natural selection'. On the other hand, the selection process can operate conversely to what the ideology proposes. Nature can, in effect, favour the 'weak' or the 'backward' or even the 'flawed', who come eventually to survive and flourish at the expense of the elite whose very 'superiority' may have contributed to their downfall. In modern market society, all sorts of incoherencies can be pointed out. The competitive process in fact excludes cultivated workers, works against healthy consumers, and tends to result in miserable and even 'degenerate' masses. Max Weber condemned in these terms the elimination of the free Germans of the East to the profit of 'inferior Polish elements'. Neo-fascist ideologues, who generally like the social Darwinist theory, happily contradict its tenets in their objections to the invasion of immigrants and the rise of inferior peoples. This naturalist bulwark of the business ethic functions only as a sidelight which can be used as convenient to justify the occasional elimination of any moral consideration.

The truth about development assistance: aid that kills

The devil of philanthropy pretends that those who steal by the bushel can reimburse by the thimbleful the poor people that they have pillaged, and that through this they will gain a great reputation of virtue and have no further need for self-improvement.[53]

One part of the myth of the grand society is to extend a helping hand to the handicapped, so as to help them not just to survive but to enter into the club of the strong. The only definitively vanquished party is nature; all humans can win. The form that this brotherly assistance takes is aid. This rather fuzzy category of 'aid' includes gifts of materials, technical or humanitarian assistance, financing of development projects, loans with concessionary terms. This aid comes from independent states, from the international community, from private charitable organisations and various other sources. One thing is sure: in general the aid is not a bad thing for the donor. This is not to say that they are sordidly self-interested, but the ambiguities are clear. Non-governmental organisations put to work funds that, very often, are obtained through the generosity of citizens (not necessarily themselves rich) of the rich countries. Aid in this way redeems the uneasy conscience of the affluent countries at the same time as emanating from a real wish for solidarity and a feeling of fraternity. The NGOs must first of all ensure their own survival and payment of their staff; their *modus operandi* after that can vary a lot, but most often there are genuine good intentions. Aid from states and from the international community may also be provided with sincere intent. Yet political and economic calculations are clearly present, especially in the case of state-given aid, and the weight of bureaucratic apparatus of the multilateral aid agencies tends to have a sterilising effect.

Aid ends up itself becoming a veritable 'business'.[54] The aim is to exploit the 'aid market' through effective use of the resource potential of the rich countries. New NGOs with a high media profile take over the market to the detriment of the older charitable organisations. The ability to 'sell the argument' counts for more than capability to 'deliver the goods'. In some extreme cases, the budget for public relations and internal operations eats up the better part of the funds gathered by the NGO. Business firms further 'sponsor' aid organisations, which is good advertising for them. In France, the wine distributor Nicholas founded a campaign on the slogan 'Drink wine and they'll have water'. The Gibbs company proposed 'Choose our toothpaste and we will help UNICEF'. By eating Kellogg's Cornflakes, you help finance Médecins sans Frontières. And all, clearly, in the logic of good deed/good business.

It should be made clear that if the results of this aid are, at best, *globally* insignificant and at worst very negative, this is not for want of good intentions. The belief that it is possible to help others without real cost to oneself is extremely widespread. Very few aid agents could be accused of cynicism. One can be astonished at the capacity for blindness of these agents who otherwise live their lives in accordance with economic reason, but this is how things are.

Is it necessary to argue the case that aid fails to achieve what is sought? Others have done this, and perfectly well.[55] It does not seem required at this point. Yet whatever the amplitude and seriousness of the arguments about the ineffectiveness or noxious effects of aid, it is impossible to demonstrate that aid is necessarily bad, or even improper. Making full allowance for all the differences in perception about life and death between cultures, the facts remain that the vision of a famine is intolerable *for us*, and that it is quite valid for us to give a bit of what we have left over to those who do not have enough.

Moreover, if we look closely, we could almost certainly find some small-scale projects supported by NGOs which have 'succeeded', meaning that they have improved the well-being of local populations in the long term. It is more difficult, on the other hand, to find a country which has, as a whole, *genuinely* profited from aid, notwithstanding the great number of countries that have received massive aid. In 1988 the organisation Secours Catholique celebrated its hundred-thousandth small-scale project. This is but one of about 550 development NGOs in France, and of about 2,542 inventoried in the OECD in 1990. Small projects are therefore counted in the millions. Despite all this, the least developed countries remain the least developed countries, Burkina Faso is still Burkina Faso, and the province of Yatenga remains a zone of abandonment.

The fact of this repeated failure around the globe, as with non-development more generally, does not stop the myth from operating. The occasional cases of success must be admitted, and one can always find circumstantial explanations for the failures: corruption of the intermediaries, bad choice of projects, incompetence of the agencies, unconducive environment, inappropriate attitudes of the local people, and so on. All the same, the overall ineffectiveness of aid can be seen as a necessary consequence of modernity's dynamic of exclusion. To aid Burkina Faso in a genuine way would mean helping the country to become a winner, giving it the means to fight us on our own grounds – not giving alms that simply prolong the agony into which the Centre's very success has plunged it. Even if that assistance were sincerely wanted, it is unclear whether we could provide it. How could France, for example, which is always lagging behind Germany and threatened by ferocious world competition, set out effectively to solve others' problems when it has not resolved its own?

In fact, aid is possible because it is relatively inoffensive and can even contribute to solving the Centre's own problems – and this is above all true *because* the aid does not have the envisaged effect for the recipient. Taking the case of Switzerland, an official government report estimated that 95% of the amount dedicated to international aid either remained in Switzerland or returned there.[56] Of course, the same is not necessarily true for aid from NGOs. But the important fact remains that, when it is effective, aid is furnished within the interstices of economic rationality. When, as occasionally happens, the product of aid emerges onto the national or international economic stage, the harsh winds of competition usually destroy it. Local initiatives, whether wholly autonomous or supported by micro-level aid, may also encounter hostility from the state. This is not surprising, as the administrative apparatus and governments of the Third World countries are largely dependent on the existing world order, and they cannot afford to go systematically against the interests of the dominant powers in the use of aid on which their survival depends.

The most effective aid that public-spirited groups and organisations in the North can give to the poor in the South is undoubtedly to combat the 'infernal machine' and to impede some of its mechanisms, at the same time mobilising public opinion concerning the machine's 'misdeeds' through counter-information campaigns. Attempting to 'rehabilitate' development's castaways amounts to impeding them in their efforts to find their feet in the islands of the informal and organise themselves. An honest person cannot, at this point, avoid admitting the ambiguity of any course of action.

The mechanics of exclusion

Modernity's techno-economic machine functions to exclude, not only because it is based on generalised competition, but above all because the game cannot be extended to all comers. It has been shown at some length that the economic and social competitiveness that stimulates individual and collective energies in the world system is a veritable war. As with any war, it has its victors and its vanquished. By contrast with a game or sport, the defeated parties do not have any rights: neither consideration nor respect need be shown. They are at the mercy of the victor and can only hope for pity.

In practice, the human solidarity that one might have hoped would encourage a generous attitude on the part of the winners is doubly limited. First, the fight to the death tends to induce a devaluation of others to the point of their *dehumanisation*. For the Nazis, as is well-known, the inferior races were merely fleas to be crushed. The Reverend Malthus was not a great deal more generous about those 'not invited to nature's banquet'. Secondly, the cult of life in its biological dimension (survival needs, etc.) restricts the generosity of the well-meaning to basic support. This falls far short of the truly sportsmanlike gesture of 'shaking hands' and assisting the loser to prepare for the next contest. Quite on the contrary, the losers are not given the chance to get their revenge in the next round or game, rather they are definitively *excluded*.

The dominant mode of thought which exalts this unchecked competitiveness pretends none the less that *everyone can win*. If the 'game' is not zero-sum, then in theory the losers could still be winners. In the war of humanity against nature, the booty is ever-increasing. Nature is the sole party definitively beaten; all the human participants can come out with a profit. It is a bit like a global-scale party game, with the prizes coming out of the treasure-chest dug up from nature with the aid of technology. There is nothing to prevent even the 'losers' coming away with a little prize, thus being better off than at the outset.

The high priests of the established order are unceasing in their efforts to *prove* precisely this win-win nature of the game to us, through objective statistics. The poorest countries in Africa have more miles of road, more railways, more ports, and more factories of all sorts than before colónisation. The life expectancy of the populations has gone up, and the numbers prove that in spite of everything, production *too* has increased. The number of schools, hospitals, literate people, etc., has grown enormously.

All that is hard to deny.[57] But beyond that? Are those the real stakes of world competition? It is only modern society that has propagated the belief that *true wealth* is a stock of objects and kilometres of roads. Most of the hundreds of thousands of cultures in human history have not been greatly interested in the creation of new objects and new needs. The remaining survivors of non-Western cultures continue to show a grand indifference to most of our gadgets and an even greater allergy to the logic of their production. They are interested only when they find they can bypass them and give them a role in their own strategies within a quite different social game. In the cultural scheme of things, the quantity of objects does not *ipso facto* have any significance. Goods are not the Good. However:

> A new order is now in place. Of its nature, it marginalises the weak, the handicapped, and the defenceless. Amongst the excluded are a growing number of countries of the Third World, as well as a Fourth World in rapid expansion in our own societies.

This lucid observation comes not from a critic of the *status quo* but from the already-cited former socialist French Minister of External

Relations, Claude Cheysson.[58] (One might ask in what respect is this order new?) He then concludes:

> It will naturally be like this, as long as the sole criterion of progress is growth, and as long as our society's value system is focused only on wealth and material prosperity.

Clearly, the little qualification, 'as long as', allows all sorts of optimistic escape-routes, in particular the delusion that a bit of redistribution will solve all the problems without there being any questioning of the basic rules of the game.

The shipwreck of the grand society is due to the very success of the techno-economic machine in engendering outcasts. Modernity entrammels the whole of humanity within its process of planetary uniformisation. The uprooting touches each and every individual, and the imposition of the West's 'cultural model' of desires and needs has reached everybody. But after having invited everyone, willing or unwilling, to participate in the Olympic Games of social life, the machine abandons the losers to their fate. The three 'Fourth Worlds' – this international community of paupers, refugees, misbegottens, billions of malnourished, badly housed, in short all these cast-offs of development and modernity – are witnesses to the sinking of the grand society.

Notes

1. Cited in *Philosophes taoïstes*, Gallimard, Bibliothèque de la Pléiade, Paris, 1980, p. 379.

2. See in particular Karl Popper, *The Open Society and its Enemies*, 2 vols, Routledge & Kegan Paul, London, 1945; and Friedrich A. Hayek, *Law, Legislation and Liberty*, 3 vols, Routledge & Kegan Paul, London, 1973-79.

3. René Girard, in his 'Postface' to *L'Enfer des choses* by Paul Dumouchel & Jean-Pierre Dupuy, op. cit., p. 265.

4. Janus was the ancient Roman god with two faces, looking both ahead and behind at the same time.

5. Liberté sans Frontières is the name of a foundation linked to the France-based organisation Médecins sans Frontières (roughly translatable as Doctors International, a network concerned with the provision of health services and medical care in the Third World) which has made a speciality of this cultural niche through its colloquia and publications.

6. This idea is encapsulated in the title of a typical work of this genre, by Mahmoud

Hussein, *Le Versant sud de la liberté* (The South slope of liberty), La Découverte, Paris, 1989.

7. All citations from François Brune, *Le Bonheur conforme*, op. cit., p. 233.

8. Jacques Necker, *Sur la législation et le commerce des graines*, in *Oeuvres complètes*, vol. 1, p. 79. New impression in series 'Scientia Antiqua' by K. Schill, 1971.

9. See in particular his two great works: Alexis de Tocqueville, *Democracy in America*, op. cit.; and *The Old Regime and the Revolution*, Doubleday, New York, 1955.

10. The figures are roughly for the 1980s. Hannah Arendt writes, in *The Human Condition*, op. cit., p. 171: 'A hundred household appliances and a half a dozen robots in the cellar will never replace the services of a good housekeeper.' Then, paraphrasing Aristotle, she adds: 'because slaves are not tools to make, to produce, but to live, life consuming their service unceasingly.'

11. Jean-Claude Chesnais, *La Revanche du tiers monde*, Laffont, Paris, 1987.

12. Marc Augé, interview in *Le Monde* on Tuesday 20 December 1988, entitled 'La société, le sida et le diable' (Society, Aids and the devil).

13. Showing a commendable reflex based on non-utilitarian value principles, and under the pressure of public opinion, the Council of the British medical profession condemned those responsible for this odious trade, at the same time pointing out that in Japan, moneylenders sometimes obtain reimbursement from bad debtors in the form of a kidney. (Reported in *Le Monde*, 6 April 1990.)

14. It was reported in *Le Monde* on 15-16 October 1989 that a Dutch organ-trafficker had provided a kidney for transplant at a price of 240,000 francs (about US $40,000), which provoked something of a scandal in France.

15. Cited by Antoine Riboud, op. cit., p. 148.

16. François Brune, *Le Bonheur conforme*, op. cit., p. 18.

17. Ibid., p. 12. Goldorak was a TV warrior-fantasy figure in vogue at the time, with plastic replicas sold for kids, a cross between a Japanese martial arts champion and a futuristic sci-fi character. François Brune adds: 'In focusing this way on the heroism of their trade, our horsemen conveniently neglect to speak of their very real victims.'

18. Antoine Riboud, op. cit., pp. 15-16.

19. Ibid., p. 35.

20. Ibid., p. 39.

21. Ibid., p. 25.

22. Claude Cheysson, in a brochure from *Le Monde Diplomatique* titled 'La paix des grands, l'espoir des pauvres', published by *Le Monde*, 24 February 1989. Cheysson, of a socialist persuasion, initially saw the problem of inadequate markets as an impetus to an international redistribution of wealth, and thus from a *tiers-mondiste* point of view not a negative thing. But now it seems that, if the affluent countries can solve amongst themselves the problem of creating markets, the fate of the LDCs becomes irrelevant to them.

23. François Partant, *Que la crise s'aggrave*, Solin, Paris, 1978, p. 104.

24. This is a favourite situation considered by liberal theorists of social choice. Two prisoners, in separate cells, can save their heads if they support each other, but each separately has an interest in denouncing the other. The argument is that experience will teach them to see the value of cooperation (if they live to learn by experience). Let us hope so!

25. François Partant, *Que la crise s'aggrave*, op. cit., p. 64.

26. Cited by Jean Baudrillard in *America*, Grasset, Paris, 1986, p. 116.

27. Jacques Austruy has analysed this well in *Le Prince et le patron*, Cujas, Paris, 1972, p. 71.

28. Alain Lipietz, *Choisir l'audace*, op. cit., p. 77.

29. François Partant, *Que la crise s'aggrave*, op. cit., p. 40.

30. Antoine Riboud, op. cit., p. 122.

31. Jean-Pierre Garnier, *Le Capitalisme high tec*, Spartacus, Paris, 1988, p. 36.

32. Michel Perraudeau cited by Michel Kamps, *Ouvriers et robots*, Spartacus, Paris, 1983, p. 36.

33. Courcelle-Seneuil, *Journal des économistes*, February 1889. Cited by André Vianes, 'La pensée du 19ème siècle face au premier centenaire', in Servet (editor), *Idées économiques sous la Révolution*, op. cit., p. 439.

34. Clearly this does not imply that everyone will get an absolutely (even if not relatively) bigger share of the pie; so there is a hole in the logic of the argument. Usually it is presumed to be filled by the (rather specious) assertion that since private property and person are respected in market activity, no one is actually dispossessed of something they previously owned. It is true that, commencing in a state of absolute destitution, it is difficult to end up with less. But does market society really guarantee to each individual the 'minimum' that they need for health and comfort of person? The hole in the logic remains; the 'losers' are respected while being weeded out in the process of natural selection. This is a sort of doubletalk closely allied to the deceit referred to in the paragraphs that follow. – *Translators' note*.

35. Op. cit., p. 16.

36. As reported by Wladmir Andreff, *La Diversité des pratiques sportives et la 'marchandisation' du sport*, op. cit., p. 13. Similar, and indeed even more extreme, episodes have marked subsequent America's Cup campaigns, where the financial stakes run into hundreds of millions of dollars.

37. One has the well-known example of the 'sublime Parisian' of the nineteenth century – the elegant bum who worked the minimum needed to keep body and soul together, and enjoyed a 'life of leisure' in the city.

38. Jean Baechler, *Démocraties*, Calmann-Lévy, Paris, 1985.

39. Colin Turnbull, *The Mountain People*, op. cit.

40. See Didier Pourquery, 'Le mensonge, une arme économique', *Le Monde*, 12-13 November 1989.

41. See for example the article in *Le Monde* on 21 April 1989 reporting on a symposium on business activity and ethics, 'Les profits de l'éthique'.

42. Werner Sombart, *Le Bourgeois*, Seuil, Paris, 1928; citation to 1966 impression, Petite Bibliothèque Payot, p. 122. In particular, under this heading of 'bourgeois virtue', Sombart places commercial loyalty and private honesty.

43. The tendency towards hypocrisy is aggravated by the fact that 'public opinion' seems unfortunately not to be held in high esteem by businessmen: a survey published by the *New York Times* on 29 April 1986 revealed that 53% of Americans thought that the business world was basically dishonest.

44. Lionel Rothkrug, 'La réforme laïque: les précurseurs de l'utilitarisme', *Revue du MAUSS*, no. 5, 1989, p. 123.

45. Peter Berger, *Les Mystificateurs du progrès*, op. cit., p. 167.

46. In *Le Monde*, 21 April 1989.

47. Paul-Henry Chombart de Lauwe, *La Culture et le pouvoir*, Stock, Paris, 1975. Cited by François Brune, op. cit., p. 83.

48. See Alain Caillé, *Critique de la raison utilitaire*, La Découverte, Paris, 1989.

49. Alvin W. Gouldner, 'La classe moyenne et l'esprit utilitaire', *Revue du MAUSS*, no. 5, 1989, p. 30. (French translation of ch. 6 of *The Coming Crisis of Western Sociology*, Heinemann, London, 1971.)

50. Cited by Michael Jackson, in 'Un nouvel agenda pour les promoteurs des droits humains: les droits collectifs des nations autochtones', *Interculture*, no. 103, Montreal, Spring 1989, p. 32.

51. Reported in the *New Zealand Herald*, Auckland, New Zealand, 22 April 1989.

52. Max Weber, from 'Leçon de Fribourg', *Revue du MAUSS*, no. 3, p. 52.

53. Leon Tolstoi, in 'L'enfer reconstruit', in *Inédits*, Bonard, Paris, 1925, p. 293.

54. See Bernard Kouchner, *Charité business*, Le Pré-au-Clerc, Paris, 1986.

55. For example Brigitte Erler, in *L'Aide qui tue*, Editions d'En-Bas, Lausanne, 1987. The author concludes (ibid., p. 91): 'All my experiences show that development aid is in total contradiction with the noble moral goal that it is supposed to serve, namely fighting against hunger and misery, and contributing to the independence of the developing countries. The community of interests that supposedly exists between the people of the developing countries and ourselves is only a chimera.'

56. Reported by Gilbert Rist, at the colloquium *South-North Network, Cultures et Développement*, 22-25 November 1989. Rist adds: 'If one adds in the activities of the World Bank, the rate of return is about 200%. Who would still speak of "aid" or "gift"?'

57. The book *La Revanche du tiers monde* by J.-C. Chesnais, op. cit., relies on arguments of this sort.

58. Claude Cheysson, 'La paix des grands, l'espoir des pauvres', op. cit.

Part II

The Island Refuge

The 'new barbarians' will shake the very foundations of the empire with a creativity which is the evidence of a new society in the making. They are the new historical subjects, now emerging side by side with those who, in the bowels of the existing society, mobilise and struggle for a different social order.[1]

The foundering of the grand society is an anguishing spectacle not just for its members, but also for those excluded from it. Developed and underdeveloped, elites and marginals, we are all in the same boat. The Westernisation of the world is a *fait accompli*, whatever might be the limits to the process. Given that, to a greater or lesser degree, we are all Westernised, the bankruptcy of the West touches us all. Even if Westernisation is a synonym for dereliction for the planet's growing masses, its definitive collapse could have still more disastrous consequences for them. Whether in the form of a nuclear apocalypse, ecological catastrophe, or gradual decomposition of the world economic and political system, the crisis of the West could well signify, for development's castaways, a dead-end pure and simple. The problem of the technological and financial dependency of the Third World is something open to argument, and is perhaps surmountable. But the dependency for food supplies, especially in the case of urban populations, has reached such a point that any breakdown of trade relations would have immediate disastrous effects.

In my preceding book, *L'Occidentalisation du monde*, I sketched a less catastrophic possible way out. Development's outcasts, here and now, are not all sinking in an ocean of despair. As Jean-Jacques Gouget writes, 'in the Fourth World perhaps resides a vision of the world which can be humanity's saving grace as an alternative to productivism. The culture of poverty is certainly a lot richer than the cultural void of consumer society.'[2] This assessment was made with regard to the poor of the West itself, but it is even more well-founded for the other 'Fourth Worlds'.

Those who no longer have any chance, at least for the meantime, of getting back on board the grand society and attaining affluence, find themselves setting up camp – more or less comfortably – either on the coasts where they have been abandoned, or on islands to which they have managed to swim. This archipelago of the informal where the castaways have made their camps can be considered as a possible prefiguring of an *other* society. Such a suggestion will undoubtedly excite a sceptical response from some and lead to all sorts of questions. Can one really found such hopes on the informal, made up of a bit of anything and everything? Isn't it so much interdependent with the formal economy that the disappearance of the latter would bring about disappearance of the informal along with it? And even if the informal ended up giving rise to something discernible, wouldn't this new form still be a 'development'? How might this society of the castaways fulfil the hopes placed in it; and in any case what will it look like? How might it resolve the contradictions stemming from its double inheritance of the West and of a lost identity?

These are my questions too. The purpose of my analysis of the foundering of the grand society is precisely to furnish plausible responses to these questions, at this crossroads between rigorous reflection and science fiction.

Notes

1. Leonardo Boff, 'Eo povo que se organiza para a libertação,' *Jornal do Brazil*, 3 May 1981, p. 6. (Translated from the Portuguese through the French.)

2. Jean-Jacques Gouguet, *Du quatrième ordre au quart monde, les plus pauvres dans la démocratie, hier, aujourd'hui et demain*, presented at the colloquium of the Mouvement ATD Quart Monde, Caen, October 1989, p. 3.

4

The Archipelago of the Informal

We are the architects of our own houses,
The doctors of our sick people,
Our children's teachers,
Our own building site engineers.

Popular chorus from the Peruvian barriadas

In presenting the *informal,* in *L'Occidentalisation du monde,* as the embryo of a new society – or rather as something that could give birth to this new society – I insisted on the need to understand properly the meaning of the *formal* if we are truly to grasp the significance of the informal.[1] One must be on guard against the *economist's* bias, and not interpret the informal in *economic* terms alone. For the informal is above all a form of social life, an authentic culture of poverty. The basis for the very existence of the informal, and for its viability, is its reinsertion of the economic within the larger social texture of life, to the point that sometimes the economic is completely absorbed within this texture. We will have to return time and time again in different ways to this point, for one can overcome some forms of prejudice only by repeated insistence. It is hard to wipe out habits of thought grounded in several centuries of involution of economics.

People tend to object that the informal is a bastard category, obtained by lumping together New-Age craftspeople making things out of second-hand materials, along with drug traffickers, ordinary small-scale business enterprises which elude the taxman and the statisticians, and shady civil servants. The mere fact of being distinguished from the formal economy, as a matter of definition, is not enough to turn it into a unified whole. The International Labour Office (ILO) defines the informal sector as 'made up of the sum of all unregistered activities as well as registered activities having similar characteristics in the corresponding economic sectors' (degree of organisation, scale of operations, technological level). This is a compromise between economic and statistical criteria, adopted mainly for purposes of data collection.[2] However, the informal is not really a *sector.* It is often present at the very heart of the formal economy and functions in close interaction with it. The classic example is the civil servant who benefits from the 'corruption' inherent in his position (bribes, misappropriation of goods, etc.), while also engaging in bits of other work on the side. This is not necessarily reprehensible in itself. Businesses, employers, consumers and citizens have one foot in the formal, the other in the informal. The symbiosis is total and constant. It would, moreover, be unfair to reduce the informal to a form of parasitism on the formal sector; the opposite is just as true: the formal economy often has need of the informal, for obtaining raw materials, as distribution and sales outlets, and for maintaining the tissue of relations with wider civil society and public bodies. Even in the most developed countries, there exists a shadow economy, exemplified most clearly by domestic work, which operates and evolves parallel and complementary to the official economy.[3]

Finally, it might be objected that this informal activity has always existed as much in the North and East as in the South. How, given this, can one pretend that it is a novel and distinctive phenomenon, originating as a creative reaction by those excluded from development, and that it may have, moreover, an almost redemptive mission?

In order to respond to these objections, which cast doubts on my whole vision of a new society, we have to go back to the meaning of the division between formal and informal. It is necessary also to lay out all the possible interpretations of this complex reality, showing how the usual economic interpretations *choose* to privilege certain characteristics so as to exclude possibly reading it another way. Saying this certainly does not allow me to assert that my analysis of the informal is the 'true' one, but simply that it is a legitimate interpretation, as legitimate as the others, and overall just as plausible in what it suggests.

The significance of the formal/informal division

An Algerian colleague, keen to see his country benefit from full development and annoyed to hear Western experts speaking condescendingly about the informal as though it were particularly a feature of the Third World, exclaimed at a conference:

How come the informal has been discovered particularly in the Third World, when it exists everywhere and always has? It's as though someone wanted to accuse developing countries of delinquency relative to economic rationality.

One can go on forever about the extent and first appearance of informal activities. It has, nevertheless, been established that the *expression* itself appeared in the 1970s with reference to Africa, before spreading to include Latin America and then the rest of the Third World. It would be surprising that it took so long to give the phenomenon a name if it were really as ancient and worldwide as is sometimes said. The 'discovery' was, in fact, rather belated given what could be observed in reality. This belatedness can in part be explained by the stranglehold of conceptual frameworks dictated by 'economic reason'; also, the fact that the 'discovery' took place first in Africa is perhaps not just an accident. Things like handicrafts and minor trades, often carried out somewhat illegally, have always existed. Illegal work and domestically based activities expand periodically in industrialised countries themselves, linked with cycles of formal economic activity. However, these phenomena remain relatively marginal. In the 1970s African context, informal activity was occurring on a massive scale, and for this reason acquired a new significance.

As use of the expression spread, along with others that were comparable or in competition, economists studying the phenomenon couldn't help feeling vaguely discomfited. The term *informal economy*, along with most other suggested labels, seemed inappropriate to them, not very well put, clumsy, unfortunate and unsatisfactory.

Out of the forty or fifty words used (in various languages) to designate this 'sector', most of them simply qualify – either directly or indirectly – whatever is meant, in a *negative* way. So the informal is *non*-structured, *non*-official, *non*-organised (hence spontaneous). It is *a*-normal (hence marginal). It is *a*-legal if not actually *il*legal (thus parallel, black); *non*-capitalist, *non*-exploiting of others, *non*-visible and *non*-readable (thus underground, phantom, ghostly, occult, submerged, or shadow; the German *Schattenwirtschaft* means work in the shadows). In short, it appears to the economist as *a*-typical, bereft of its own logic or identity other than can be indicated by this displacement away from, or even effacement of, the 'normal'.

Certainly the bringing together of elements excluded from a coherent whole does not of its own accord create a new coherent whole. The economists thus found themselves condemned to accumulate empirical observations, looking for landmarks with the aid of arbitrary criteria, often with fairly unconvincing results. The trouble stems from the fact that the expression 'informal economy' is properly speaking an antinomy, if not actually self-contradictory. The *formal* which functions as the norm against which the 'catch-all' category of the informal – an unnameable bric-à-brac – is considered, is precisely the paradigm of economic analysis, that is to say, the set of imaginary elements[4] which establishes economic life as an autonomous sphere within the social.

The term 'informal', however, does not designate just an atypical and invisible economic reality, but also and more fundamentally a *society* which is unreadable and delicately placed in relation to modernity, being neither legal nor illegal, literally *elsewhere*, outside the terms of reference and normative imperatives of the dominant society. Of course many aspects of the informal, especially the strictly economic aspects, end up clearly visible in conventional terms (in particular jobs, production of goods and services, money incomes). Also, there are many immediately visible social manifestations, such as the pavements cluttered up with people and stalls, and the veritable invasion of urban spaces by the 'informal'. But even where life in the informal has been subjected to bureaucratic intervention and police control, it still is not really legalised, because for the most part it operates outside the framework where legality has any meaning (that is, the framework of a modern liberal society). The Third World 'society' where the informal takes place floats in a kind of *non-being*. The uprooted peoples of the Third World have been dispossessed of their own way of seeing themselves. They exist, and are presented, in the words of one writer:

for what they are not (non-formal, not developed, unemployed, unwaged, illegal, untaxed, not taken into account in official statistics, not counted in GNP, not constituting a social class, non-central, not organised); or for their lack (lack of capital, lack of entrepreneurship, lack of organisation and political conscience, lack of education, of political participation, infrastructure, rationality, etc.).[5]

One can, therefore, form a coherent theoretical view of the concrete heterogeneity of the informal only if one has already understood the theoretical role played by the formal. The informal is truly a case of delinquency with regard to economic reason. It is *the other* of the grand society.

This is why the informal has uncontestably to do with legality, but a legality understood in a wider sense than the purely juridical. The informal does not reduce down to the non-legal, nor to the non-registered, nor to the unregisterable. Equally, its delinquency in relation to accounting rationality is a *consequence* of its basic nature, but not what defines it.

The widespread use in French of the adjective *informel*, notwithstanding the suggestion to translate *informal sector* by *'secteur non-structuré'* (non-structured sector) to avoid any Anglicism, is perhaps explained by the unconscious perception of this threat posed by the appearance of the informal, by putting in question the 'formal' as the norm of society and its mode of organisation. This menace had, indeed, appeared already in the 1950s, in relation to informal art. One can transpose to the economic domain what Georges Bataille wrote about *l'informe* (not having a form) in art, as:

> not only an adjective with a particular meaning, but a theme serving to induce a demarcation, a categorisation so that each thing has its particular form. But what *l'informe* designates has no status in itself, has no 'rights' in any sense, and is crushed everywhere like a spider or a worm. Yet it serves its role; for it is essential, in order to keep the academics happy, that the universe take on a form.[6]

The emergence of the informal as a manifestation of the value crisis in the West was therefore already in the air. The economists, in refusing to recognise that economics is precisely a representation of the *formal*, are condemned to apprehend in the nebula of the informal only those aspects that somehow 'look like' the formal economy – and as a consequence are faced with only one of the dislocated limbs of the social whole. Thus denuded of its unity, denied any historical specificity, there is no way of making the informal intelligible in its own right. Cut away from the social whole, what one calls the 'informal economy' has no rationality in itself. It then truly comes to appear as a case of delinquency.

There is no question of denying that the various activities that one can classify in the informal are to be found more or less everywhere, notably in the developed countries themselves.[7] In fact we are witnessing today, as an effect of the growing unemployment crisis, a strong resurgence of marginal activities (clandestine work, odd jobs, craft activity) throughout Europe and the United States. But simply to baptise, as some people do, 'the informal' as a *quarternary* sector (after the primary/agricultural, secondary/manufacturing and tertiary/services sectors) is merely an appropriation at the symbolic level which in no way changes its informality.

The successive crises which have taken place in the West – social crisis in 1968, economic crisis in 1974 – have shaken the foundations of what constituted the frontiers of the formal. This concerns work (crisis of productive work, rise of services, new technologies), the Western cultural identity and the nation-state. Through a ricochet effect, a shock wave rippling back from the Periphery to the Centre, it has been discovered that the informal existed at the very heart of our own societies, and that it threatens the most deeply entrenched bases of our social order. For this reason, the recognition of the informal is also very much an attempt at its 'co-option', to plug the holes, plaster over the cracks in the edifice of modernity, do up the façade. In countries on the Periphery there are, as we shall see, various attempts being made to *normalise* the informal. Ivan Illich has suggested that, in efforts to overcome the stagnancy of industrial economies, we are likely to see an intensive effort at co-option and exploitation of shadow work: 'the shadow economy will become the main growth sector' and the informal sector will become 'the main colony which sustains a last flurry of growth'.[8] This amounts to an attempt at safeguarding the grand society, which, although derisory in some ways, is dangerous for the future of those excluded from the forward march of development.

The historical emergence of the informal and its 'discovery' in the 1970s are due primarily to the failure of development – a failure which constitutes the specific form taken by the crisis of the *formal* in the Periphery. The schema of industrialisation and of the formal economy (sectors, firms, salaries, profit and loss ledgers, etc.) has been built up on the experience of the developed West, which is held up as the model. This schema, born of a long and complex history, has a whole host of social correlates. We can cite among others: the work ethic, individualistic society, economic (self-interested) rationality and cost/benefit calculation, the cult of performance. The formal economy implies also the framework and goal of *economic nationality*, that is, a coherent and dynamic industrial structure made up of a set of interdependent sectors implanted on the territory of a nation-state.[9]

These historical conjunctures, which have assured the fortune of the West, are felt by the rest of the world as a set of conceptual and institutional constraints to which they must align themselves. The West *makes* history; the rest have to *take* (and take up) this history. By force or seduction, the multiple dimensions of the model have been imposed, one way or another, throughout the Third World. *Development* signifies, on the economic level, the sought-after result, as does the nation-state at the political level. The grand society is envisaged as a society of prosperous nations. The massive and widespread, if not total, failure of this *mimesis* is what explains the emergence of the informal.

In terms of Western imaginary, its metaphysics and way of seeing things, this phenomenon – no longer transitory, but durable and even proliferating, which ensures the survival of the towns of the Third World – can be perceived only as *in*formal: informal economy, informal industry, informal work, informal society. This social totality, adjudged amorphous, after having originally been denied and repressed, ends up by becoming an object of fascination because of its vitality, the endogenous creativity visible within it, and some extraordinary successes which have cut right across Western business enterprises. At the same time, it continues to be considered by economists as basically irrational.

This emergence of the informal, that economists had wished to reduce to nothing more than odd jobs and hangovers from the past, something unimportant and transitory, takes on its proper meaning and historical significance only when looked at in the framework of this double crisis: of the formal at the Centre, and of development on the Periphery.

The paradoxical situation of the informal *vis-à-vis* the ethnocentrism of economics

Whether in the Cameroon with the Bamileke, in Rwanda with the artisans affiliated to the Kora association, at Ouagadougou, at Cotonou, or in Abidjan, everywhere within the nebulosity of the informal are found *comprehensive strategies* of response to the challenges that life poses for displaced and uprooted populations in peri-urban areas.

These are people torn between lost tradition and impossible modernity. The sphere of the informal has, incontestably, a major economic significance. It is characterised by a neo-artisanal activity that generates a lot of employment and produces incomes comparable to those of the modern sector. It satisfies an important part of the needs of urban populations, especially those of the 'have-nots' in the shantytowns. Resolving practical problems of living spaces and daily life has all sorts of economic ramifications, so much so that the practical importance of the 'informal economy' is no longer a matter of debate. Some 50-80% of the population in the urban areas of these countries live in and from the informal, one way or another. Moreover, the 'informal economy' and more generally the 'informal society' do not constitute a closed world. There are all sorts of bridges and ties into 'formal' national and international structures. At the same time, this 'fuzzy set' of activities possesses its own coherence and specificity.

Can one then speak of an *other* economy, demanding an *other* economic analysis, in conformity to an *other* economic rationality? For most economists, whether they are orthodox or dissident, the economy is *one,* and economic science is *unique,* since there is *one* economic rationality. And this economic rationality is pretty much identical to Western reason pure and simple. This comes down, as we have seen, to what we have called the *maximine* principle: to maximise outputs by mobilising all the means available and by organising them in the most efficient way; to minimise the energy expended to attain a given objective.[10]

The end result is that, looked at through these economistic eyes, social realities quite different from those of the 'formal' Western economy end up being 'economicised' – that is, interpreted exclusively in terms of modern norms. This has a close parallel with economistic analysis of the practices of so-called primitive societies. For example, the Trobriand *kula*, with its great sea expeditions to acquire bracelets and magic necklaces that are sources of privilege and glory, is brought down to the level of trade and commerce; and the Kwakiutl *potlatch* is reduced to a form of pre-capitalist accumulation. The link between 'formal' and the *particular form* of the 'market economy' is in fact axiomatic in economic method. In nineteenth-century political economy, the attempt was often made to distinguish between a 'substantive' economics whose subject matter is trans-historical, defined by an invariant content (that of material production, exchange and consumption in the process of social reproduction), and a 'formal' economics whose concern was to represent in a theoretically pure way the logic and workings of the market economy.[11] However, this distinction is misplaced. In reality the substantive and the 'formal' are strongly linked; the 'formal' analysis of the market economy represents a chosen emphasis (both methodological and ideological) in analysis of the substantive modern economy.

In this sense, the economists' reduction of traditional practices is formally legitimate but strongly ethnocentric. What happens is that these supposedly 'proto-economic' practices are considered to be *irrational*. All *departures* from modern norms are, in the eyes of the economists, reduced to a failure to conform with universal reason. Similarly, the informal in the contemporary world is considered *a priori* at the level of the substantive, then the theoretical filter of the 'formal' theoretical apparatus is applied. In many ways the substantive informal thus appears deviant. Yet it is difficult to condemn this informal economy *in toto* as irrational. It was so condemned early on. More recently, scrupulous experts have recognised the relative 'success' of certain informal enterprises under conditions where the modern economic logic has failed. One can cite, among other examples, the cases of urban transport and of shoes fabricated from old tyres in Dakar. In both instances, official or capitalist enterprises have had to give up when confronted with competition from the informal.

This sort of situation gives rise to a paradox which is difficult for the economist to resolve: the informal economy cannot be rejected or condemned, yet neither can it be admitted as an authentic 'alternative' founded on an *other* rationality. Its relative success therefore has to be considered as *only temporary* – its existence is possible (and, more particularly, *theoretically* permissible) only because of the peculiar prevailing circumstances (which themselves are temporary and irrational). In an aberrant environment, a rational system cannot succeed; whereas a system which is partly absurd becomes paradoxically more efficient. That is, in a social universe not dominated by economic values, and therefore irrational, it is reasonable not to be rational and it is reasonable to replace a formally rigorous optimising calculus with a prudent but somewhat 'fuzzy' assessment of advantages and disadvantages of different ways of proceeding. Hence the possibility of, but also the limited scope for, an *African-style management*.

The informal economy is therefore seen as *transitory,* as are the social circumstances onto which it grafts itself. It is to be 'normalised'.

This involves separating the 'progressive' part which is able to be modernised, from the 'regressive' part which is destined to disappear. So, for example, in research carried out by Philippe Hugon and his colleagues, it is considered that, in Madagascar, hat-making, hardware, ironmongery, metalwork, foundry casting, working in wood, basketry, buildings, car repairs and electrical repairs are all sectors with positive potential because they are induced by economic development. But the remaining informal activities are, according to them, engendered by underdevelopment and for this reason condemned as parasitic.[12] Or in the case of Zaire, Jean-Pierre Lachaud and Marc Penouil's research group consider the following as 'involutive' and therefore destined to disappear: clothing, small business, jewellery, shoe repairs and malachite workers. The 'evolving' and therefore 'formalisable' activities include: cabinet-making, ironmongery, boiler-making, ironsmithy, car mechanics, moped and motorbike repairs, radio and electronics servicing, fishing and bars/restaurants.[13]

Such an approach makes a mockery of all the complexity and all the extra-economic richness of the cloudy informal. This attempt at co-option of the 'healthy' part of the informal for development, however praiseworthy it may be compared with attitudes of negation and destruction pure and simple of the 'sectors', is still totally ethnocentric. The view we are proposing, of the informal as a laboratory of 'alternative' sociability, requires that we reject the universalist pretension of the economists (and no doubt, of Western people more widely). So our question is: Is it well founded to see in the informal, an *other* rationality at work? An *other* economy in gestation which would await its future theoreticians?

The informal certainly conforms to a 'rationality' other than Western economic rationality – that of 'productivism', of production for production's sake, and the law of the *maximine*. The surplus from artisanal activities, when indeed it exists, is usually not invested in enlarged reproduction. It is used to engender group solidarity, expended in festive activities. The scrap merchants of Kigali, for example, put together some of their earnings to have beer festivals, and through this they strengthen the links between association members. Boss-employee relationships can be situations of exploitation, but they rarely reduce to the form of a classical wage or salary system. In the Congo these relationships, regulated by custom, conform to a pattern of avuncular ties (uncle-nephew): the apprentice is considered as the nephew of the master craftsman.

The question whether this different 'rationality' underpins a whole *other economy* does not allow such a categorical response. The informal does have very important economic aspects, and this justifies completely its analysis in conventional economic terms. To speak, as does Jacques Bugnicourt, of a *popular* economy is quite tempting, as this corresponds well with the positive aspect of the whole phenomenon. The question is, what conceptual framework is pertinent? For economists, indeed for the mainstream of Western thought, there is a single science of economics applicable to all economic phenomena. Working in favour of this postulate of methodological and ontological unity is a fairly weighty historical and methodological tradition. 'The economic' is thought of as an autonomous and transcendent domain because it rests on an autoreferential sphere of representations, most of which are directly linked to the West. The key concepts of (natural) need, scarcity (meanness of nature), work (transformation of nature to satisfy natural needs), production, income and consumption, together delineate a semantic field that is perfectly self-sufficient, that is, perfectly *saturated* in its own terms, without any real need of an opening to the outside. These concepts, however, really have nothing obvious about them. Their operational significance is the result of a very long and specific history; and the hold that they have over reality is largely particular to our culture, even allowing that systems of demarcation exist in other cultures which are more or less comparable for partial domains.

The informal, properly understood, cannot be dissociated from the *whole of the social context* – that is to say, from all the neo-tribal structures and relationship patterns with a residual or newly reinvented cultural identity, the metaphysical or religious beliefs (such as syncretic cults), the very specific daily practices concerning food, clothing and everything else. The informal covers the whole ensemble of daily practices, from the removal of household refuse to the functioning of theatre groups. 'The economy' in the Western sense obtains its rationality only by the dissociation of the narrowly economic from the larger social context, and then the evacuation of the social of any content other than the economic. The artificial exclusion (if not negation pure and simple) of the social and cultural context of the informal economy, the methodological *dis-insertion* of it by outside analysts, is what makes the informal appear to involve deviant and irrational practices.

If one apprehends the informal in its totality, one sees that it has to do with a whole different *form of activity* which obeys a social rationality (or rationalities) not reducible to pure economic logic and hence not reducible to the terms of analysis emanating from the West. The informal follows a logic of 'maximisation' of social advantages, but in terms of power, prestige or influence either within the reference group or in the interplay of such groups. This is perfectly reasonable, but it does not reduce to a search for profit or growth of the production unit.[14]

In fact the economist apprehends only a part even of the economic dimension of this complex reality, because the greater bulk of it is so submerged within social life that it is not easily discernible. A sociologist from Dakar and the Chodak research team from the ENDA organisation (Environment and Development in the Third World), looking at unemployment in Dakar, became involved in studying how the populations of the greater Yoff district live.[15] This is one of the poorest districts in Dakar. The 'networking' structure makes it possible for families averaging twelve people to have access to a money income around seven times larger than the 'official' figures show. The informal 'economy' is at the origin of this. It is not a matter directly of *products* of the informal activity which explains the difference. The direct source of the supplementary income is the accumulation of 'drawing rights' on the various networks in which the family members participate, not the sale of goods and services as such. There is an intense circulation of gifts, money, investments, loans and advances, reimbursements, contributions, rotative credit associations *(tontines)*, and so on, which in turn relates back to a very substantial activity of goods production, furnishing of services, delivery of goods. All these materials, money, goods and services enter into complicated social circuits: gifts for births or marriages, presents, voluntary or forced loans, and so on. Calculating the real standard of living (or an average income per head) of the population for purposes of international comparison, under these conditions, would be a real headache; and one may well wonder about the meaningfulness of the result. Only goods and services coming from outside the local milieu, such as foodstuffs from the country or from abroad, and imported goods, are strictly constrained by the money returns obtained from outside for goods and services supplied. On the margins of the grand society, spheres of communal reciprocity develop in the cold waters of market calculation. This does not mean that, in these islets where the logics of the gift and of seduction, of ceremony and parade, are all in play, strategic manoeuvring, ambition and self-interested 'calculation' are not also employed. The point is that even the forms of management African-style are not reducible to economic rationality.

Conflicts in interpretation of the informal economy

Because of its lack of definite form (its amorphous state), the informal economy lends itself to many interpretations. Each tries to force it back into a particular mould, and so in a sense it becomes polymorphic (multiformed). This characteristic is incompatible with the 'economic myth'. The informal simply does not fit into the semantic field of economics. Economic logic defines as *formal* economic activity, a 'something' which has come to correspond less and less with actual reality. What is happening is that informal work and production are presumed to resemble what is, rightly or wrongly, still called 'formal' work and production. The economists studying the informal try, by every means they can, to assimilate it back within their established conceptual repertoire – even if this means finding a logic to the informal that it really doesn't have. Now, precisely because it is nebulous, the informal lends itself quite well to this operation, but at the cost of forgetting some essential features of the whole phenomenon, including some within the economic domain itself.

There are all sorts of *déjà vu* features of the informal 'sector'. And it is certainly true that identification of characteristics 'familiar' from somewhere else can tell us something, even though it is invalid to reduce the informal to *déjà vu* elements alone. So, for example, the *déjà vu* syndrome is at work in the various titles given to manifestations of the informal. 'Artisan' activity – production in small workshops by skilled craftsmen, handicrafts, etc. – is *déjà vu*. This artisanal activity is not really the paradigm for the informal sector. But historically, in Europe, the artisanal class, in its modes of work, its products, its particular social structures and logics, preceded large-scale commodity production and extended markets, the wage and salary system, standardisation/mechanisation of industry and the logic of profit. The identification of the informal sector with an old type of artisanal system – whether considered as surviving from the past, newly emerged, or even newly reinvented, allows the sector to be reabsorbed into the great evolutionist myth of modern society, and reduced to a phase of this evolution. The designation of the sector by some analysts as 'proto-industrial', i.e. as a type of activity which is not yet industrial but which contains the seeds of the industrial, is quite revealing on this point.[16]

Also *déjà vu* are the *'petits métiers'* or small-scale trading and service activities. Abdou Touré, a sociologist from the Ivory Coast, has made an in-depth study rich in earthy detail and vitality, with a sharp analysis of social structures and specific values.[17] But throughout he seeks constantly to furnish an interpretation referring back to Europe, particularly to seventeenth- and eighteenth-century France. References to Fernand Braudel, to Louis-Sébastien Mercier *(Le Tableau de Paris)*, Arlette Farge, Philippe Aries *(Vivre dans la rue à Paris au 18ème siècle)*, François Furet and Mona Ozouf, Jeffrey Kaplow *(Les Noms des rois; Les Pauvres de Paris à la veille de la Révolution)*, bear witness to this assimilation of the informal sector to an equivalent of small-scale trades in Europe. Touré does indeed show that in Europe the destruction of traditional society and the urban influx at the beginning of the Industrial Revolution gave rise to needs that the formal sector could not satisfy, and to a social class which could not be integrated within an insufficiently dynamic economy. And so small trades grew up: chimney sweeps from Savoie, sellers of wood from Auvergne, masons from Limousin, public writers, pedlars. The activities of these nomads and street people fall away or are transformed with the onrush of economic development. By transposing this analysis across to Africa in the late twentieth century, the idea of a unique model of social evolution is not challenged; indeed it is perpetuated. The informal 'sector' is again seen as transitory and marginal, either intermediary or residual in the larger scheme of things.

Also *déjà vu*, at the other end of the spectrum of possible interpretations, is the image of the black market. Illegal activity and uncontrolled exploitation respond, it is often argued, to the laws of supply and demand. This has been noted particularly in the former Soviet Union, with the parallel black-market economy – also called the second economy or unofficial economy. It is also seen in the West when the state tries to cut across so-called market forces too strongly: this leads to moonlighting, illegal work and outright criminal activity.

Paradoxically, the informal 'sector' here becomes held up as the ideal-type of economic behaviour. The rises and falls in clandestine activity correspond to the mythology of the market. In such situations, it is the official economy which becomes 'informal', in the guise of an irrational administered or command economy. By contrast, even when illegal (drug-dealing, for example), the informal sector obeys economic laws. The economist will generally concede that no economic 'form' can be accorded absolute legitimacy, and will concede also that productive activity and the system of wages and salaries relies on a framework of civil law. Walras himself argued for abolition of the slave trade notwithstanding the clearly evident supply and demand. However, this does not diminish the ideological hegemony of the *ideal-type* of activity, responsive to supply and demand.

In this light, it is hardly surprising that the emergence of the informal 'sector' in the Third World has also been hailed as the appearance or resurgence of the liberal economy. The Peruvian economist Hernando de Soto, an advisor to the unfortunate presidential candidate Mario Vargas Llosa, went so far as to speak of a 'popular capitalism' opening *another path,* as opposed to the 'shining path' of the Maoist left.[18] Guy Sorman, a journalist and free-market ideologue, sees in these 'barefoot entrepreneurs' the cutting edge of 'the new wealth of nations'.[19] The fact that the drug economy, developing in a rampant fashion over the ruins of development projects, is the example *par excellence* of this obedience to market laws, does not seem greatly to bother these ultra-liberal economists. The same interpretation is adopted by some Latin American commentators, and also by some Anglo-Saxons of neo-classical persuasion. When informal activity is perceived as a revolt against state-led, centrally planned, or anti-economic development, it is hailed as embodying a healthy reaction from the social body. In this case the informal 'sector' does not need to be reabsorbed into the formal. It is already *in essence* formal. Although illegal in relation to *official* society, it is *legitimate* in the eyes of economic reason.

Yet another form of *déjà vu* is that expressed in small-scale commodity production. More substantial and respectable than the *petits métiers*, more modern than handicrafts surviving from the past, this small-scale commodity production is capitalist in its dominant logic: it works for the market; it operates within the money economy; it requires inputs of raw materials and equipment obtained in the marketplace. All the same, it is not always capitalistic in its behaviour. The activities function with a bastardised salary system with many features deriving from traditional hierarchy patterns. It tends to amount more to simple reproduction than to the indefinite expanded reproduction of capitalistic enterprises. Finally, it is not 'modern' in size since it remains small. On the other hand, it does offer some analogies with the 'flexible workplace' that the crisis of Fordism has made popular.

All this makes this sort of activity into a transitional sector *'already seen'* in Europe in the guise of the small firm. This constitutes a part of the fabric of modern economies, seemingly with an indefinite lifetime given the observed persistence of small and medium enterprises alongside large industry. And if this means that the transition towards the supposed ideal-type of a normal production and normal wage system is no longer quite as sure, we enter the 'co-capitalist' sector – that is, a neighbour of capitalism, able to coexist with it, alongside it without being quite identical. These ambiguous activities none the less still point the way to development. The descriptive phrase, 'small-scale non-exploitative activity', used by some Algerians for their informal 'sector' illustrates quite well this sort of interpretation.

Déjà vu, also, are partial reductions along the following lines: informal 'sector' equals subcontracting or remote-controlled sector, a satellite or subordinate activity dependent on the modern sector or on foreign capital. In this case, either the informal sector structure permits underpayment of the proletariat that it employs, or it assures outlets for the modern sector (which supplies and provisions it), or it facilitates the reproduction of the workforce needed in the modern sector and approximates, in this respect, the domestic economy. Here the meaning of 'informal sector' is reduced to its *function* relative to capitalism. There is no real enquiry into what it may represent in itself.

Turning to the more subtle interpretations of Hugon and Penouil-Lachaud, we leave the immediate *déjà vu*. Philippe Hugon has been very cautious in arriving at his interpretations. Conscious of the polymorphous character of the informal economy, but keen to see in it a force for development, he acknowledges the atypical aspects in their diversity, and emphasises both the way it embodies resistance to proletarisation and the positive qualities of the whole phenomenon. From all this emerges his idea of a co-capitalist development.

According to Hugon, informal activities should be seen 'not as relics from the past, but as modern creations which reinterpret old social relationships while also inventing new ones'. He goes on:

> The question is, however, whether the proliferation of small market activities in Third World towns can be explained by the positive role that small producers play in relation to the dominant system, or, on the contrary, by the inability of the latter to integrate the former. ...
>
> According to anthropological work, small urban activities are typically the place where old relationships reappear, whether they are social, lineal, or ethnic. Small-scale producers are at the margins of capitalist systems even when they are at the heart of the social or urban system.[20]

Here, although the norm of actual activity is established by the mode of capitalist production, Hugon's ideal was rather that of socialist development. In a study of the informal sector in Madagascar, a collaborator of his put this quite naively: the artisanal workers in expanding sectors of activity should form cooperatives, thus participating in the construction of socialist development.[21] This, it was argued, might give some chance of success to a *non-capitalist path of development* for the 'progressive' (or, in Hugon's terminology, having a potential to evolve) fraction of the informal sector.

Leaving aside the capitalist/socialist preferences, what we see once again is the importance of the conceptual distinction between regressive (involutive) and progressive (evolutive) sectors. Hugon tries to relate this dichotomy, which in the first instance involves an *ad hoc* demarcation with a 'statistical' or 'descriptive' basis, back to some supposedly underlying economic logic of the productive versus the unproductive. Thus the personal services sector, which has been induced by underdevelopment, is considered to be involutive; these services are considered implicitly as parasitic. The material services sector (repairs, etc.), which has been induced by development, is by contrast evolutive.[22]

The thesis of 'spontaneous' development, articulated by the research group led by Marc Penouil and Jean-Pierre Lachaud, represents possibly the most audacious move forward in the economic analysis of the informal economy, as far as recognition of the difference and originality of the whole informal phenomenon is concerned. The latter is presented as a 'spontaneous' process which demonstrates the vitality and the creativity of new and different societies made up of traditional communities which have been transformed by the shock of modernity. Faced with the threat of destruction, destructuring and deculturation, and confronted with evidence of the failure of copycat development efforts initiated by public institutions lacking the technical, financial and human means to carry out such developments anyway, the 'civil societies' – or, more exactly, the actually existing social groups within national territories – proceed to invent novel solutions. They do this somehow spontaneously, thus demonstrating an authentic ability to resolve the problems of their survival – including technical matters (using, by definition, appropriate technology) – on the basis of different social relationships (with atypical wage systems, ethnic solidarity, new community relationships). According to these analyses, the informal 'constitutes the greatest reservoir of adaptive and inventive ability which exists in developing countries'.[23]

So in this perspective, the informal is not a case of *déjà vu*. The phenomenon, in its entirety, is not assimilable to the old artisanal production and trade form, nor to any of the other 'intermediary' forms. It amounts to a resistance to mimetic development. Nor does it have a function that can be co-opted by the modern foreign sector (through satellisation, etc.). It demonstrates a genuine originality. The economy and the social organisation that it puts in operation constitute a genuine 'alternative' path. But for doing what? To what end?

At this point Penouil and Lachaud hold on tight to the fact that they are, after all, economists. Their stratagem is to assess the informal as a case of an original path but with classical development still as its *telos*. In other words, this 'alternative' evolution conforms in the end to the sole model that can constitute a valid and conceivable horizon for an economist: the technological society and a unidimensional civilisation. This is why a whole section of this 'sector', which obviously has no place in this final state, must be rejected and condemned as 'involutive' and 'regressive' – for it is truly the ideology of progress which gives meaning to the economic project. The 'informal sector' thus is not transitory in itself, but its historical role is either transitory or non-existent.

The informal economy, under this sort of interpretation, would seem to represent the long-awaited reality of 'alternative' development, or 'the other form' of development.[24] The failure of endogenous technocratic development (as in Nyerere's Tanzania) had made it seem unlikely that this *other* development would ever be discovered.

But the informal does work, the informal is different from the *normal* economy, therefore the informal is this development which is other. Unfortunately for its advocates, this logic is specious and this 'other form' of development is a mystification. The argument plays on a confusion between ends and means. It is simply presumed that the goal remains that of classical development, which means that the difference is admissible only at the level of the means. As in all evolutionism, pluralism is at best recognised only for the past, never for the future.

However, there is no reason *a priori* to conclude that the informal carries within itself a developmentalist finality, characteristic of adherence to the grand society. On the contrary, it may be well and truly pregnant with an *other* society.

Thus the economistic interpretations of the informal range from pure and simple negation to an ambiguous reconnaissance. All in all, however, 'developmentalist' thinking, seeing the informal as a means or a route to development, is very problematical. It ends by legitimating the state as a formal entity in the Third World, making it into the prime mover in a 'normalisation' of the informal; whereas I would be tempted to say that it is rather up to informal society to give itself a real state, or more exactly an adequate institutional form, when the time comes. The existence of a sphere full of vitality and creativity, born in the rupture, developing on the margins and protected by its difference, constitutes the first outline and the hope of a genuine *'alternative' society* and not an *other* development.

Even when the specific nature of the informal has been recognised, along with its status as an *absolute social fact*, one final objection can be raised against the hope of seeing it as constituting a true alternative path. At an economic level, the informal lives in symbiosis with the 'modern' economy. Won't the shipwreck of the grand society – and therefore of the modern economy – entail *ipso facto* the foundering of the informal sphere that depends on it?

Not necessarily. Concretely speaking, the artisans who work in scrapmetal-recycling need car wrecks or food-tins to produce the many and various things that only they know how to make, just as the shoemakers need old tyres. If cars disappear, what will these artisans and repairers become, not to mention all those workers dependent on the modern sector for their raw materials and even for their outlets? The objection is both serious and ridiculous. For any follower of modernity, this constitutes a solid argument, because technical mastery is central in the modern economy, which is itself fundamental to the grand society. But the question makes those familiar with the informal society smile. Granted, the informal is a vast enterprise which recycles the rubbish of the grand society. However, society's rubbish is recycled because it is freely available and costs nothing; industrial production is used because it is there. It is in no way an indispensable part of the *modus operandi* of the informal, for the informal is constituted on a social, not a technical footing. If waste items are no longer available, they can be replaced by some comparable production; even sophisticated metallurgy can be carried out by some artisans in the 'informal'. Above all, there are almost unlimited possibilities of replacing one thing and activity by another.

On the other hand, when the informal starts to become *formalised*, it actually becomes more fragile. When workplaces take on the *form* of modern industrial workshops, the networks of solidarity give way to economic rationality. Businesses become more sensitive to cyclical and structural failures in the formal economy.

A French worker-priest together with local partners once founded a factory workshop in a *barriada* (shantytown) in a Lima suburb.[25] This workshop was on the dividing line between the formal and the informal, between economic rationality and *Indianness*. The experiment ended in collapse, in spite of support from the local church and substantial help from outside, because of the degradation of the official Peruvian economy, eaten away by spiralling inflation. Hyperinflation murders formal work and encourages all sorts of trafficking, from speculation to drugs; but it leaves the informal economy pretty much alone.

Artisan workers in the Sfax medina who woo the World Bank experts and work partly for external markets, are more critically affected by changes in supply and demand than those in Kumasi (Ghana) who make spare parts or equipment cobbled together for local activities, which are themselves mainly informal. And yet these people are, no doubt, still in a less secure position than their cousins in Techiman who have the wit to make their own electricity by re-using Diesel motors taken from tractors sent to the scrapheap.

A society of this sort in truth possesses infinitely more resilience than the grand society. Improvisation is the order of the day. Creativity and inventiveness are put to work to reconstruct a social life, and there is no difficulty finding or mastering the techniques needed by the new society. The alternative society will always perform well in relation to its own norms, as it doesn't have to challenge productivist society. The dangers that lie in wait for such a society come from elsewhere.

Notes

1. Serge Latouche, *L'Occidentalisation du monde*, op. cit., especially ch. 5: 'Au-delà ou ailleurs' (Beyond or elsewhere).

2. As stated in Jacques Charmes, 'Quelles politiques publiques face au secteur informel?', *Notes et études de la Caisse centrale de coopération économique*, no. 23, April 1989, p. 5.

3. See particularly Ivan Illich's analyses in *Shadow Work*, Marion Boyars, London, 1981.

4. In the French original, *éléments imaginaires*, meaning the ideological and symbolic dimensions of experience of the members of a society, from the key theoretical categories to the normative and affective. – *Translators' note*.

5. Arturo Escobar, *Celebration of Common Man*, photocopy, 1988, p. 11. The author adds: 'Not being seen was not very comfortable. But they can adjust to this social invisibility, and dispense with it when necessity demands.'

6. Georges Bataille, *La Part maudite*, Gallimard, Paris, 1930, p. 217. See also on this point Napoleon Constantin Biguma's thesis *L'Economie informelle ou la naissance d'une alternative: le cas de Rwanda*, Lille, June 1989, pp. 16-18.

7. On the interpretation of *petits métiers* (small-scale production, trade and service activities) of the eighteenth century, as a possible alternative sociality to industrial capitalism, see *L'Occidentalisation du monde*, op. cit., p. 123.

8. Ivan Illich, *Shadow Work*, op. cit., p. 2.

9. See *L'Occidentalisation du monde*, op. cit., pp. 97ff.

10. See Chapter 2 above.

11. This methodological dualism is found, for example, in much of the work of John Stuart Mill and Carl Menger. More recently, the idea of a substantive economics at the same time richer than and in opposition to the formal economics of the market was developed by Karl Polanyi in his efforts to identify the specificity of market societies and the incompleteness of a purely 'formal' economics. These themes have received much attention in the pages of the *Revue du MAUSS*, and several articles and debates there furnish a background to the very condensed argument given here. In translation we have rounded out the argumentation to some extent. – *Translators' note*.

12. Philippe Hugon, 'Secteur informel et petite production marchande dans les villes du tiers monde', *Revue Tiers Monde*, no. 82, April-June 1980, p. 409.

13. Marc Penouil and Jean-Pierre Lachaud (editors), *Le Développement spontané des activités informelles en Afrique*, Pedone, 1985.

14. That is, it is necessary to comprehend the group, its construction of relationships and meanings, what has symbolic weight, the codes of honour, the origins of success and shame (etc.), in order to understand how 'advantages' will be assessed. Only by reduction of these dimensions to a uni-dimensional category applicable to discrete entities, such as an individual's 'utility' or '$' (or a company's profit), can canonical economic science find application. – *Translators' note*.

15. Emmanuel Ndione, *Dynamique urbaine d'une société en grappe*, Enda, Dakar, 1987.

16. See the analyses by Pierre Judet, 'Quand la Rhur entre au musée', Claude Courlet, 'Les industrialisations endogènes', and their Grenoble colleagues, in the dossier 'Industrialisation rampante et diffuse dans les pays en développement: quelques-points de repère', *Revue Tiers Monde*, no. 118, April-June 1989, pp. 403-53.

17. Abdou Touré, *Les Petits Métiers d'Abidjan*, Karthala, Paris, 1985.

18. Marcel Niedergang, 'Un écrivain dans le Pérou de tous les dangers', *Le Monde*, 4 April 1990. Hernando de Soto has published a book called *El Otro Sendero: la revolucion informal* (*The Other Path: the informal revolution*), Ojeva Negra, Bogota, 1987.

19. Guy Sorman, *La Nouvelle Richesse des nations*, Fayard, Paris, 1987, pp. 319-20.

20. Isabelle Deble and Philippe Hugon, *Vivre et survivre dans les villes africaines*, Presses Universitaires de France, 1983, pp. 161-2.

21. Philippe Hugon, 'Les petites activités marchandes dans les espaces urbains', *Revue Tiers Monde*, no. 82, April-June 1980, pp. 406-27.

22. Hugon, ibid., p. 409.

23. Paul Harrison, *Inside the Third World*, Penguin Books, 1979, quoted in Penouil and Lachaud, op. cit., p. 92.

24. This argument is made explicitly in a key article by Pierre Mettelin, 'Les conflits d'interprétation', in Penouil & Lachaud, op. cit., pp. 70-103.

25. Daniel Gilbert, *Barriada Haute Espérance: récit d'une coopération au Pérou*, Karthala, 1990.

5

Siren Song: Perspectives in the Wake of Development

Development's castaways, washed up on the archipelago of the informal or trying to get there, are still tempted by the mirages of development. They may at any time abandon their wrecks and the refuges where they have found a footing in an effort to get back on board the sinking ship of modernity. The hope we place in informal societies and in the ability of those excluded from modernity to reinvent a new and different human life outside the logic of modernity, development and the West, may thus be short-circuited. In some respects we ought to abandon any such illusions. The temptation of development, and the desire of Western experts in the Third World, international organisations and official heads of the nation-states involved in aid and development, all to 'normalise' the informal sector, have a fair chance of winning the day. The most dangerous solicitations, the sirens with the most insidious song, are not those of 'true blue' and 'hard' development, but rather those of what is called 'alternative' development. This term can in effect encompass any hope or ideal that one might wish to project into the harsh realities of existence.

The fact that it presents a friendly exterior makes 'alternative' development all the more dangerous. It hides fatal traps and ambushes which are made even harder to sniff out and bring to light by the fact that those involved in 'alternative' development happily adopt all the criticisms made about non-alternative development, so-called 'mal-development'. So the analyst has to be very much on guard to avoid all the booby-traps; good intentions are, unfortunately, not enough.

As Ivan Illich notes, redefining development serves only to 'reinforce the Western economic domination over the shape of formal economics by the professional colonization of the informal sector, domestic and foreign'.[1]

Newly industrialised countries and the temptation of development[2]

Having ignored and repressed the informal sphere for decades, international organisations such as the ILO, foreign non-governmental organisations and domestic state authorities have all recently subjected it to paternal solicitude. This is mostly with regard to the narrowly economic aspects of work, production and income. Looking at the solely economic aspects of the informal, cutting these away from their social underpinnings, one sees in the most favourable cases a good example of 'diffuse industrialisation'. Here, the informal economy doesn't so much resemble cottage industry, as forms of budding industrialisation such as the 'industrial districts' of which the English economist Alfred Marshall spoke at the beginning of this century. A network of many little workshops which are both competitive and complementary, operating in the same social and cultural milieu, gives rise to a compact and resilient productive tissue with the potential to 'perform' – that is, to become competitive in exterior markets. By aiding the *healthy part* of the informal sector through appropriate *support* policies, one hopes to achieve just this result. One will thus arrive, to borrow Pierre Judet's useful phrase, at a 'fully-fledged industrialisation' of a sort likely to be self-propagating.[3]

This is a good example of the attempt at *normalisation*: at making the informal conform to the formal. The desire for normalisation is quite comprehensible, even if not entirely legitimate. The experience of the newly industrialised countries (NICs), especially South Korea, is enough to seduce any Third World country. Experts everywhere tend to hold South Korea up as a model. It is in fact quite plausible to analyse the Korean performance in terms of a successful passage from 'proto-industrialisation' and the informal, to 'fully fledged industrialisation'. With state encouragement, successive stages of sectoral development and gradual achievement of technical mastery have taken place. Why shouldn't this happen elsewhere tomorrow, in Thailand, in Tunisia, or even in the Cameroon?

Why not indeed. Nothing theoretically precludes such a possibility. However, it should be made clear what is implied by the successful passage. This pursuit of a *fully fledged* industry is aimed, obviously, at 'true' and classical development, in the sense of obtaining a solid purchase in modernity. The preservation of certain cultural specifics will, in this perspective, be analysed not as something important on its own terms, but as potentially an 'extra plus' – a possible advantage in the mastery and use of the Western techno-economic machine, in line with the example provided by the Japanese. As Dominique Perrot so nicely puts it, one pretends in this way to 'transform the grain of cultural sand clogging the cogs of development, into a lubricant which would absorb the shocks'.[4]

However, such a mutation of the informal, while in some specific instances not impossible, is none the less both paradoxical on the logical level and ambiguous in its actual implementation.

The logical paradox of the normalisation of the informal

State development projects have always taken the 'formal,' and 'official' way; and now when it is seen as desirable to find ways to encourage spontaneous initiatives, whose strength springs precisely from their 'informality' and lack of institutionalised recognition, one is confronted with the paradox 'be spontaneous!'.[5]

The logical paradox of the normalisation of the informal derives from this *double bind* or contradictory double imperative, studied in psychology by the Palo Alto School.[6] In parallel with a person with a weak psyche who, when confronted with an impossible choice of this sort, takes refuge in schizophrenia, societies at risk are plunged into crises which can take violent forms. The Shah of Iran's directive to 'modernise' – that is to say, both be yourself and be the other – engendered the revolution that is now part of history. The papal encyclical *Populorum Progressio* underlined the same bind in its own ways:

A tragic dilemma: either one keeps ancestral beliefs and institutions, but gives up progress; or one opens oneself to foreign techniques and civilisations, but throws away the traditions of the past and also all their human richness.[7]

In the case of the informal, the double imperative to 'modernise' is even more perverse, for the informal is already a synthesis of modernity and tradition. It becomes a question of somehow conserving the dynamic and original quality of this creative activity while simultaneously coming to take the form of a mimetic development. These are rather long odds!

Co-option of the informal sector under economistic, developmentalist or nationalist banners (the informal is usually ethnic or interethnic, regional and across regional boundaries), is contradictory. This co-option does not stop at a simple legalisation of activities which had remained undeclared officially while being fundamentally 'healthy'. Sometimes it goes as far as aiming to free-up the formal economy itself. The normalisation of the informal here becomes, at the limit, an *informalisation of the formal*. The informal becomes the prototype of the true market economy!

Now, the 'debureaucratisation' called for in the South and the North, as in the East, even in non-command economies, is very ambiguous. It is often necessary and justified to liberate initiative that has been suppressed by administrative red tape. But it can amount to a deregulation that, in the name of freedom, licenses brutal exploitation of workers. It also signals a weakening of national solidarity when, in the name of efficiency, there is a dismantling of the welfare state structure. Such changes also signify a shift away from a 'national' development perspective in favour of a transnational economy – the latter coinciding with various infra-state residual structures, but without there being any real vision of a desired form of social organisation.

The *co-option* of the informal, its ideological takeover through defining what is 'healthy' at the heart of the nebulosity, and furnishing recognition along with technical and financial support for diffuse industrialisation, has integration with the world economy as its goal. The requirement is to bring this selected part of the informal into the mould of the formal. The informal economy, which *ex ante* exists as a successful improvisation in the face of failed mimetic development, thus becomes, *after the event*, a true *'alternative' development*.

Given that endogenous development experiments, such as in Tanzania, have become bogged down in incoherence and bureaucratic inefficiency, the good samaritans in NGOs and elsewhere are only too glad to find this salvation path for their hopes. Thus, one can see the humanist development experts tenderly nourishing the hope that, after so many flops throughout the Third World, they hold at last the *real* recipe for development: this model of diffuse industrialisation. South Korea, previously seen as an unjust dictatorship, becomes the ideal for those who preach development of the whole person and all people! And this despite the harsh regimentation of the workforce ('bloody Taylorism') and the aggressiveness in exterior markets which have guaranteed its emergence.

But even when the bitter pill of 'economic *raison d'Etat*' is swallowed, and one agrees to renounce any moral scruples for realism's sake, the goal for which everything has been sacrificed is not necessarily attained. There is still a particularly difficult bend in the road to negotiate. This is the passage from defensive 'ethno-industrialisation' to fully fledged industry with a transnational vocation. Putting 'popular barefoot capitalism' into competition with multinational giants, suggests Alfredo De Romana, 'is like suggesting that an anaemic boxer be set up to "compete freely" with one that has been specially prepared and trained-up for months'.[8] Moreover, are efforts at initiating *national* development not perhaps becoming anachronistic, given the present crisis in economic nationality?

'Ethno-industrialisation' develops in the form of little cells that proliferate in a favourable milieu but hardly ever become large. Accumulation for its own sake just isn't the way they operate, even when they are flourishing. They are not fixated on making it on an international scale, even in cases where they benefit from a multi-ethnic clientèle. Although informal industry may often seem close to the 'stage' of fully fledged industrialisation, any hasty normalisation actually runs the risk of provoking collapse. According to Daniel Théry, this is what has happened with brickmaking in Tunisia. The allure of technological mimetism induced support for those businesses that chose large-scale operation and up-to-date technology, instead of allowing space for a distinctive locally inspired effort at 'endogenous technological gearshift'.[9]

In fact, substantial further success with the policy of normalisation may well be impossible. What was previously possible for Japan and, in some respects, more recently in the NICs, becomes less and less likely elsewhere, for three main reasons.

1. Overcoming the formal/informal contradiction implies imposing performance pressures not only for *standardised efficiency* at a national level, but in *international performance* as well. The informal society aims at *effectiveness*, not at efficiency. It aims at a result which is satisfying while maintaining decent conditions – not at a result

appearing brilliant in isolation but which takes no account of anything else. Reason rather than rationality is involved. Choices are not made by calculations based on quantifiable elements alone, but by a subjective working out of the many aspects to the problem. Because the economic is set within the social, the coherence of the whole – or *social reason* – takes priority over market reason. Putting such a system into competition with the techno-economic model poses a severe challenge. Although informal structures are almost indestructible on their own ground, they are weak and vulnerable when they venture into outside territory. Of course, there are zones in Africa where local dynamism is rooted in fairly well-established international networks (for example the Sfax medina and the Bamileke networks in the Cameroon). Nevertheless, it is hard to see how these regional economies could give rise to a national industrialisation. It would have to succeed in the face of an already-evident transnational technopole, which connects a *deterritorialised* (off-shore) Third World with local economics of both North and South, emerging in the midst of an ocean made up of second-rate economies at best and the 'Third World deteriorating into Fourth World' in total dereliction at worst.[10]

2. Nation-states are in a state of crisis, even of decomposition. In particular, the cornerstone of the nation-state order, economic nationality, seems definitely out of date. The whole rationale for a state policy of normalisation of the informal is linked to the objective of constructing an economic nationality. Does this not, then, amount to a nostalgic and not very realistic desire?

3. The normalisation of the informal tends to destroy the social ties existing at infra-national levels, on which the informal's dynamism rests. It introduces, indeed, the most destructive ingredients of outdated modernity: egoism, individualism and unchecked competition, which actually eat away at the social underpinnings of endogenous creativity, the tissues of social solidarity and networks with clients. This corrosion would tend to compromise any hopes placed on the informal as a way through to some sort of *post-modernity*.[11]

This leaves the question of where the informal may be headed anyway. It is often repeated that the informal is a veritable laboratory. But why, if this is so, should it be a laboratory where the results of social experiments always fit a model taken from the past? Why should there not be radically novel results, not just in the sense of new products or techniques, but new *social forms?* Surely, if the present crisis is really a sign of a profound crisis in modernity, the relative success of the *irrationalities* of the informal is a reason *not* to despair at the failure of utilitarian reason, considered in the light of non-performance of the West and the wreck of the grand society.

The ambiguity of 'assistance policies' in the informal sector

For some years now, international organisations and NGOs have taken an active interest in the 'informal sector' in Africa. Their interventions have generally taken the form of support policies along three planes: social, technological and financial. These policies are very ambiguous: their motivation is mostly praiseworthy, but the results can be disturbing.

Under the aegis of the ILO, a support programme of this sort, covering the three aspects, was undertaken in Rwanda (Kigali), Mali (Bamako), Mauritania (Nouakchott) and Togo (Lomé). The Rwanda experiment was clearly the most 'successful', yet even it raised some questions. It was aimed at bringing the Kigali informal artisans into a social and urban structure and providing them with technical and financial support. Obvious improvements were brought about in the living conditions of these artisans, thanks to their obtaining social recognition (a professional card). A good level of cooperation was established among participants, and with popular banks. Access to more efficient equipment on a self-managed basis was made possible.

Some other aspects, though, were more problematical. International paternalism has a tendency to create a mentality in which people expect to be helped. Policy choices are, in turn, biased by *transfers of desires* between the helped and the helpers.[12] This showed up clearly in *training programmes*. The training that artisanal people in the informal really need is not necessarily what is offered to them. On the other hand, what they themselves would like, influenced by the blandishments of modernity, is not necessarily on the right track either. Technologies introduced from outside present several dangers. First, they can discourage local creativity and reintroduce technological dependence. Secondly, they may bring about a rise in capital intensity to the detriment of job creation. They can also lead to over-capitalisation. Pressured by manufacturers and salesmen, and often badly advised, the budding artisans may choose over-sophisticated equipment. Cabinet-makers, for example, buy machinery capable of six distinct operations when in practice they only need two.[13] Finally, at the level of *urban land-use controls*, paternalism has had frankly negative effects. Instead of allowing space for dynamic processes to create an original urban space appropriated by the participants, the mimetic obsession of the public powers and foreign experts has led them to *normalise* artisanal activity in separate zones for industries and crafts. This holds terrible dangers for the vitality of the whole 'sector', since it is far more than a simple economic entity. Life and profession are coextensive with each other, the links are not merely instrumental.

The same experiment, on a similar scale, was tried in other African countries. The results from the ILO's point of view were much more mediocre. The actors did not fully cooperate in the effort – not, at any rate, in the same proportion as in Rwanda. The social and cultural context, very favourable in Rwanda, was much less so in these other places. The intervention remained alien and was experienced as externally imposed. A principal reason for the success in Kigali, undoubtedly, was the role played by the Catholic Church, which is very well implanted in Rwanda. It has a major place in social life, where it has replaced earlier religious practices. This is a good case of *cultural filiation*: Christianity has become a truly local religion, the substitution being possible. Organisations with a religious motivation were involved from the outset in the development of the Rwanda informal sector. Such circumstances were not found in Mali, which is an Islamic country, or even in other Christianised countries.

Another experiment which has been somewhat ambiguous in its outcomes is that of the SIDI (Society for International Development and Investment). The SIDI is an offshoot of the CCFD (Catholic Committee against Famine and for Development). It was founded in 1963 and is made up of various members: associations, banks, religious congregations, tax-deductible investment schemes, individuals and ordinary businesses. Subscribers agree to put back in all revenue which exceeds inflation in order to increase capital and allow activities to expand. Numerous other groups of the same sort can be identified, such as the Ecumenical Cooperative Development Society of Dutch origin. There are comparable financial cooperatives in the West itself, for the financing of 'alternative' economic projects. HEF-Boomlan in

Flemish Belgium is one interesting case of providing assistance to businesses which do not have exclusively market goals. The SIDI is an NGO specialising in financial support for projects judged to be both 'interesting' and *viable*. Through loan guarantees, it allows artisans in the informal sector to turn themselves into fully fledged small and medium-scale businesses. The conditions the SIDI attaches to its intervention are laudable:

> The business being helped must somehow, either by its production or its functioning, respond to a local need, and must use local labour while respecting social laws, and if possible work with primary products produced on the spot.[14]

This amounts, however, to the search for the golden goose. One has to wonder whether all these conditions are often met – especially given the fact that the 'formal' businesses of the Third World are meanwhile trying more and more to insert themselves into the informal.

This sort of intervention, very probably beneficial for the lucky ones, *normalises* part of the informal. It doesn't really try to change the rules of the development game, and the hoped-for development is only 'alternative' at its departure point. Under normal economic conditions, the normalised business will in due course have to face national and international competition. The objective, in looking to a generalisation of this strategy, is to multiply the number of businesses *normalised* in this way, thus stimulating 'development' from the bottom up. This involves a sort of theory of 'micro-projects'. Development comes about by energising the milieu through seeding initiatives which, though limited in number, spread like an oil-slick by virtue of their very success.

We return at this point to all our previous questions. First, is 'development' possible? And if so, why has it not already happened? Decades of diverse experiments in this arena suggest that this dynamic of micro-project multiplication simply does not take place. Blockages arise beyond a certain size threshold. Micro-level activities would, by now, have to be counted in their millions, and yet the 'least advanced countries' which benefit from them are still reportedly drifting deeper into underdevelopment.

Secondly, in this view of informal enterprise, the paradigm of development itself is not queried; at the most there is a cultural *dimension* being added as spice. According to conventional economic wisdom, the success of the normalised business enterprise must be largely at the expense of other participants in the formal or informal sector. The argument is that, by playing on the double field of the formal and the informal, the unit receiving assistance manages to find a niche in the market better than others. But this diagnosis considers only the economic aspect of the informal. No attention is paid to the fact that it involves a different social structure, nor to the potentialities and peculiarities deriving from this. This misconception can result in rapid failure of assistance policies on their own terms, as happened in the Haute-Espérance *barriada* experiment in Peru, discussed at the end of the preceding chapter. Also, the successes of this type of normalisation policy can mean the non-pursuit of other forms of social experimentation. The reaction of some Turkish banks to SIDI proposals is eloquent testimony to the interest the informal has for them: 'We have wanted to get into this sector which we know very little about but which is clearly important.' No comment.

Development based on the informal, with which the partisans of 'alternative' endogenous development nourish their hopes, is a contradiction in terms. *The paradigm (concept and model) of development is profoundly unidimensional*; it excludes cultural pluralism and difference, whereas the informal rests on their existence and is nourished by them. *The paradox of the normalisation of the informal* and equally of the 'alternative' development whose very name is suggestive of its difficulties, stems from the following double bind: *either one is in the different dynamism characteristic of the informal, or one sacrifices this dynamism for normalisation.* Formalising the informal boils down to asphyxiating it.

'Alternative development' and alternatives to development

As Ivan Illich has noted, 'up to now, economic development has always meant that people, instead of doing something, are instead enabled to buy it'.[15] The castaways from the development misadventure are not able to buy anything at all. They are *condemned* to make everything. Their survival thereafter depends on how good they are at sorting things out for themselves. It is not a case of an *other* development, rather of a *beyond* (at the same time as being *within*). They are literally *elsewhere*, outside development; and in certain respects *be-*

fore, as there is a linking back to what existed previously, stretching across the break caused by modernity. They are also *after*. We can speak of a situation of *post-development* for two reasons. First, because the informal dynamic emerges *after* the passage of modernity and *after* the tidal wave of development; and secondly, because the planet of the castaways will expand to its true size only *after* the grand society has gone down.

At the same time, a wide range of the initiatives and practices which belong to this 'alternative' space are easily taken over by 'alternative development' ideology, even though their inspiration mostly comes from elsewhere – from outside the universe of development, outside the West and its logic, at a distance from modernity and its myths. This is the case with almost all 'autonomous' or 'convivial' visions and activities. The prefix 'auto-' and even more its Anglo-Saxon form, *self*, lend themselves to this ambivalence. 'Do it yourself' relates just as easily to an individualistic concept of the subject – even if a group – in isolation and concerned with itself, as it does to a rupture with individualism and the high-performance rat-race.

The themes of 'basic needs', of food self-sufficiency and of 'appropriate technologies', are situated at the meeting-point of divergent paths, and it is a treacherous intersection. The opposition between 'alternative development' and *alternative to* development is radical, irreconcilable and one of essence, both in the abstract and in theoretical analysis. To say this is not Manicheeism or dogmatism, rather it follows as a consequence of employing minimal rigour so as to avoid confusion and the dangers that may arise. It is a case of avoiding falling into the traps that one has denounced. Since both pathways can start off together, with a common trunk as it were, and since historically these matters have been very muddled in the discourses of NGOs, welfare agencies and alternative movements, it is far from easy – although undoubtedly necessary – to show clearly where the two paths diverge.[16]

Under the heading of 'alternative development', a wide range of 'anti-productivist' and anti-capitalist platforms are put forward, all of which aim at eliminating the sore spots of underdevelopment and the excesses of maldevelopment. However, these visions of a society truly convivial for its members – for all men and women and the entire man or woman – often have no more relationship with development than did the Age of Abundance of primitive societies,[17] or the remarkable human and aesthetic achievements of some pre-industrial societies which knew nothing of *development*, not even the word itself. The debate over the word 'development' is not merely a question of words. Whether one likes it or not, one can't make development different from what it has been. Development has been and still is the *Westernisation of the world*.

Words are rooted in history; they are linked to ways of seeing and entire cosmologies which very often escape the speaker's consciousness, but which have a hold over our feelings. There are gentle words, words which act as balm to the heart and soul, and words which hurt. There are words which move a whole people and turn everything upside down. Words like liberty and democracy have been such, and still are. And then there are poisonous words which infiltrate into the blood like a drug, perverting desire and blurring judgement. Development is one of these *toxic* words. One can of course proclaim that from now on, *development* means the opposite of what it used to. The papal encyclical *Populorum Progressio* tried to do just this, by appropriating development into a theology which was traditionally hostile to the ideology of Enlightenment and progress. Similarly, if one proclaims that 'good development is primarily putting value on what one's forebears did and being rooted in a culture',[18] it amounts to defining a word by its opposite. Development has been and still is primarily an *uprooting*. One might, similarly, decree that the bloodiest dictatorship be called a democracy, even a popular democracy. This wouldn't prevent the people from clamouring for the *reality* of a democracy. By the same token, enunciating 'good development' will unfortunately not prevent the techno-economic dynamism relayed by the national authorities and by most NGOs from uprooting people and plunging them into the dereliction of shantytowns.

The authentic alternative to underdevelopment is, possibly, in the process of being invented by Third World *civil societies*, but it certainly is not initiated by development ministries even if the latter, like the road to hell, are paved with good intentions. By placing itself under the banner of development, the alternative movement dons the opposition's colours, hoping perhaps to seduce rather than combat it – but more likely to fall into the abyss itself.

In order to avoid misunderstandings and show the oppositions between 'alternative development' and *alternatives to* development at the level of concrete practice, it is necessary to deal one by one with the main issues and highlight their ambiguities. I shall examine in turn the three principal planks of 'alternative development': food self-sufficiency; basic needs; and appropriate technologies.

The ambiguities of food self-sufficiency policies[19]

It seems obvious to advocate a policy of food self-sufficiency. With food scarcity looming as a threat almost everywhere in the Third World, from the Sahel to North-East Brazil and Bangladesh, it seems urgent to do something about it and not to get bogged down in agonising about why it has happened. One can be satisfied by an explanation in terms of natural drought or population explosion without noticing the contradictions that exist between a policy of subsistence agriculture and the logic of world economic integration, or the conflict between self-sufficiency ideals and the pervasive impact of transnational economic and cultural evolution.

Self-sufficiency is a magic word which brings hope; it seems an obvious response to problems that, only too evidently, are genuine, concrete and dramatic. Yet this simple pragmatism hides all sorts of ambiguities, some carried by the concept itself and some relating to the policy – or rather policies – that may be inspired by it. Who puts self-sufficiency policies into practice? How are they defined and carried out? Like all successful concepts, it can come to mean just about anything; one can pin anything one likes on it. There is therefore great danger involved in fixing such a goal for oneself without due care.

The ambiguities of the concept derive from its origins and from its fashionableness. The result is a wide range of possible meanings and intentions. A bit of history is necessary here. We can pinpoint several stages in the implementation of the concept. The idea, if not the theory itself, has a complex Eastern and Western origin with movement in both directions and simultaneous mistranslation. As significant inputs, we can discern a Chinese influence, Indian sources, French equivocations, and the trendiness of marginality in the 1960s.

The Chinese influence comes from one of President Mao's slogans: 'Rely on your own strength.' The Chinese conception of socialist autarchy was widely admired, benefiting from the aura of *tiers-mondiste* (Third-Worldist) mythology in the 1960s and from the personal charisma of the 'great helmsman'.

The Indian source flows from Mahatma Gandhi's ideas. Gandhi

popularised the term *self-reliance*. The Hindu word *swadeshi*, used to express the idea of self-sufficiency, certainly has distinctive Indian connotations; but in fact Gandhi borrowed the English word from Emerson's Puritan philosophy and linked it to the term *swaraj* (self-domination, autonomy) which is more deeply rooted in Indian thought. Gandhi was furthermore influenced by the ideas and practice of Tolstoy, who made his own shoes and personally aimed at frugal 'self-sufficiency'. Strongly against wholesale industrialisation, Gandhi favoured autonomy at village level, with a measured evolution of crafts and small industries based on agriculture. Even though this heritage was wiped out in India itself by Nehru and his successors, *self-reliance* as a Third World strategy was subsequently popularised by President Julius Nyerere in Tanzania. The theme was adopted by the Group of 77 in 1979 with the initiation of the Arusha programme.[20] The concept's high profile has been maintained ever since. In 1980, at the 7th Congress of the PDCI-RDA, the official political party in the Ivory Coast, food self-sufficiency was adopted as the guiding principle;[21] in 1989 in Burkina Faso it was the keynote of the policy agenda. Numerous further examples could be given. Non-government aid and development organisations took up the theme quite naturally. The right to self-sufficiency in food is, for example, written into the charter of the Frères des Hommes (Brotherhood of Man), and this organisation's 1980 campaign centred around 'the right of peoples to feed themselves'. ORSTOM, the French Scientific Research Centre for the Third World, even established a whole research division on this subject from 1982 to 1987.

The French contribution comes through the translation of the English self-reliance as *'auto-centré'* in French, and from the linking of this term with a tradition of French thought about economic independence based on the interdependency of different sectors of economic activity. 'Auto-centred development' in this sense (especially industrial development) had its base in ideas disseminated by François Perroux. This line of analysis then links up to certain *tiers-mondiste* analyses, such as those of Raoul Prebish and later Samir Amin, contrasting autocentrism to extraversion.

Finally, the fourth influence comes from a way of thinking in vogue since the 1968 political crisis in France, juxtaposed with various anti-industrial and anti-growth sentiments. Along with the discovery of ecological threats, zero growth, the Club of Rome report, and so on, came a fascination for the theme of *self/auto*-everything – autonomy, self-organisation, the endogenous, 'do-it-yourself', self-instruction. Autonomy is set in opposition to heteronomy (the law of the other). This is the era of Ivan Illich's *Conviviality*.[22]

This whole self-sufficiency movement, deep-rooted and trendy at the same time, is basically a reaction to an evolution and politics which was starving the South and poisoning the North. It has its clearest expression in the rise to popularity of Green politics and alternative lifestyles. Over-industrialisation, including that of the agro-food sectors, is denounced at every turn. To produce one kilocalorie of beef in countries of the North, an average of 80 kilocalories of fossil energy are needed, and in some cases more than 200 kcal! We are eating not wheat but fuel!

The definitive 'co-option' which gave the concept political clout occurred in the early 1970s when the World Bank, under the impetus of Robert McNamara, advanced its *basic needs* programme. This amounted to a complete reversal of the Bank's previous approach, which had relied on encouraging free play of markets (laws of supply and demand), and which had meant replacing self-supporting agriculture with marketable export crops. After the about-face, the aim for the least developed countries was to help them survive through assuring for themselves the covering of essential needs. Between 1975 and 1980 many LDCs took up this discourse enthusiastically.

As one can see, the vogue for the concept does not free it of ambiguities. Self-sufficiency, as one agronomist complains, 'remains a vague concept not linked to any precise geographic or historical concept, and often one drifts away from it towards related notions, under the influence of other arguments and ideologies'. These related notions include, in particular: food autarky, food security, and the struggle against a food deficit.[23]

Going beyond the ambiguities inherent in the origins of the concept and leaving aside those that inevitably arise with actual implementation of self-sufficiency policies, there remains a fair uncertainty about what exactly is intended by self-sufficiency. How do we distinguish self-sufficiency from auto-subsistence (surviving on one's own)? In part this raises the problem of the model of society being used and of the target unit. If the targeted entity is an individual or a family, then self-sufficiency is identical to auto-subsistence, but if the self-sufficiency in question is at the level of a village, a region or, *a fortiori*, a whole nation, then peasant auto-subsistence may condemn city dwellers to die of hunger.

Auto-subsistence implies turning one's back on the market and relying on a polyculture of survival (along the lines of post-1968 ecological naturism), or, at the very least, a shift away from major markets and international exchange circuits. City dwellers can try, in cases of crisis, to reach self-sufficiency through cultivating vegetable gardens and peri-urban plots of land. The programme called *Boia-fria* (literally 'cold meal', from the name given to seasonal workers without personal resources) in Sao Paulo State, has in these terms had a certain degree of success in some towns. In this case, local self-sufficiency served as a substitute for agrarian reform.

At the other extreme, self-sufficiency can aim to go beyond covering the needs of farmers alone to the creation of a basis for nationwide industrial development. Then it becomes a strategy of agrarian dynamism: providing surplus crops necessary to supply towns with food staples through controlled 'progress' of agrarian techniques, along with restoration of community structures and price policies favourable to the peasantry.[24] This strategy contrasts with another that is more 'classical': that of providing financial surpluses through the export of cash-crops. Self-sufficiency will usually connote autarky – even if the latter is a curiously unfashionable word these days, the vogue for self-sufficiency does at bottom have strong similarities.

Self-sufficiency in the first sense of survival implies recourse to 'appropriate technologies'; in the second sense of nourishing industrial development it is premised on the 'green revolution' or even industrialisation of agriculture. The former aims at limiting and putting brakes on rural exodus by separating the small-scale farming activities *(micro-fundia)* from the logic of world market competition. It aims at preserving and reconstructing a coherent agrarian system which will not only make survival possible, but also permit revival of the rural communities. The latter option of funding industrialisation through agricultural surpluses means going beyond mere 'self-sufficiency' levels so as to finance the 'inputs' needed for this strategy. This policy, however, takes as its benchmark the global market, even at the risk of provoking crisis in agrarian systems. But conversely, auto-subsistence can also compromise national self-sufficiency when the country refuses to feed the town, as happened in 1918 in Russia. Overemphasis on the micro-social and the ambition of making sure each cell is responsible for its own means of reproduction – a very strong version of 'autonomous' which sometimes finds favour with NGOs – is closer to auto-subsistence than to self-sufficiency, and has a strongly romantic flavour. But the self-sufficiency concept is not free from this ambivalence: does such a strategy amount to seeking a refuge in the past, or to a solution for the future?

This question is not unconnected to the preceding debate on auto-subsistence versus self-sufficiency. Even those Third World countries now counted among the poorest were self-sufficient in the past. Pre-independence Algeria was a good example, as was Morocco until the 1960s, as well as Iran and many others. The Sahel countries were almost self-sufficient in cereals at the beginning of the 1960s, but food subsidies and imports now represent more than 20% of cereals consumed.[25] Some countries (Algeria, Morocco and Iran, for example) currently have to import between one- and two-thirds of their food needs. According to the FAO's statistics, overall imports of agricultural products for human food consumption in developing countries have doubled between 1974 and 1984.[26]

Western colonisation and influence have, one way or another, led to a retreat from many self-sufficient crop types and cultivation methods. Such is the case with high altitude cereals and quinoa (a legume) in the Andes, amaranthus (a sort of spinach with remarkable qualities) in South America and millet in Africa. One can object that this 'ancient' self-sufficiency bordered on auto-subsistence; and it is true that a very high proportion of the population in those times worked in agriculture. It has also been maintained that the present problem of hunger is a result of demographic growth, and that a quantitative and qualitative change has occurred in food consumption norms. This last point is debatable. It is certainly hard to prove that higher calorie consumption has occurred, as traditional diets are not well known and changes in diet towards a more 'Western' type (meat, sugar, fats) are not necessarily advantageous. In any case, one has to acknowledge that, for the Third World, the advent of modernity and the entry into modernity have not, apart from exceptional cases, brought about an evolution of traditional agrarian systems – more often their destruction.

Certainly the concept of self-sufficiency goes beyond peasant auto-subsistence, since it implies surpluses and qualitative improvement in nutrition. But it is still at odds with commercial

industrialisation of agriculture, although not excluding regional specialisation in order to bring about the self-sufficiency goal at the
national level alone. In Burkina Faso citrus fruits rot in some regions
low in cereals, while they are sorely lacking in zones with likely grain
surpluses. Means of communication, the organisation of distribution
and transportation networks, and the setting up of cereal banks, would
seem likely to help the achievement of self-sufficiency. NGOs such
as Frères des Hommes and Terre des Hommes are supporting *triangular* operations in the South in an effort to make it possible for regions
with short supply to buy what they need in over-stocked regions of
their own country or a neighbouring one.

In sum, food self-sufficiency is a policy which, even if it neither
obeys liberal logic nor conforms to the international free-exchange
game, is coherent with some strategies against underdevelopment, and
is also defensible from the point of view of protecting the environment.
Yet such a policy is not self-evident, and its exact content is yet to be
established – or, at least, to be chosen and made more precise.

When it comes to putting self-sufficiency policies into practice,
contradictions appear at several levels, including both international
organisations and the national agencies which are the prime movers
behind the policy. I shall look at each in turn.

International organisations

In his famous novel, *Dr Jekyll and Mr Hyde*, Robert Louis Stevenson
presents us with a hero who has a double identity. By day he is a kindly
doctor and by night a criminal. The partnership of the International
Monetary Fund and the World Bank somewhat resembles this tale.
Whereas the World Bank sees the only hope of salvation for the least
advanced countries to be in slowing down the deterioration of the
population/food relationship by a policy of self-sufficiency (or even
of auto-subsistence), the IMF continues to work from liberal analysis,
preaching financial orthodoxy and encouraging the development of
export crops to guarantee the equilibrium of the balance of payments
and the budget. So-called 'structural adjustment' policies are a new
illustration of this phenomenon.

This does not mean to say that there is necessarily antagonism
between the two goals. Some cash-crops are compatible with the
development of subsistence agriculture. Staple food plants can grow

under the shade of oil palms. In fact cocoa needs a protective leafy cover, such as is provided by coconut trees in New Britain and bananas in the Ivory Coast. The requirements of crop rotation can facilitate the alternation of staple crops with plantings destined for export. A rise in the level of peasant money incomes through the sale of export crops can contribute to improving the yield of staple agricultures by allowing the purchase of equipment, fertilisers, and so on. In Africa, staple crops are often looked after by women, whereas cash-crops are most often grown by men. This specialisation by sex does not necessarily cause any conflict in work. Growth in export crops can go hand in hand with that of staple crops. In the Ivory Coast, for example, plots of land are now given to workers for their food needs before future plantations are set out.[27]

On the other hand, cash-cropping is often incompatible with the cultivation of staple crops (this is the case with coffee and peanut oil), and sometimes compromises definitively their future cultivation by destroying the soil. The various inducements to produce cash-crops (finance, resettlement assistance), can add up to a real politics of dissuasion for the cultivation of staple crops and lead to massive imports of substitutes at very low prices.

The ILO, FAO and NGOs tend to favour the auto-subsistence path. International public assistance to needy states tends more in the direction favoured by the IMF. The latter's thrust is reinforced by the GATT (General Agreement on Tariffs and Trade) which pushes for the opening of frontiers and the freeing-up of world agricultural commerce.

The arguments of these latter institutions are simple, often simplistic: the comparative advantages and relative production costs, especially where the poorest countries are concerned, justify recourse to huge imports of cheap cereals. This makes it possible to feed towns cheaply and also to reduce famine in rural areas. In the nineteenth century the industrial development of agriculture speeded up thanks to just such a politics. Even if there are some glaring failures from specialisation evident in some Third World countries, no proof has been given that, from an economic point of view, there was any advantage to be gained for these countries by their depriving themselves of the advantages of cheap provisioning of food through imports. With uncontrolled population growth, pursuit of the policy of self-sufficiency in food often entails industrial 'inputs' anyway, such as miracle seeds, chemical fertilisers, pesticides and agricultural machinery. As Requier-Desjardins notes:

> Under these conditions, the cost of a policy of food self-sufficiency in terms of imports of industrial products and technology, is likely to be higher than the cost of the food imports that it is aiming to reduce.[28]

All these reasons militate in favour of developing agricultural exports and modernising agriculture. Yet still this does not mean that attempts at self-sufficiency are necessarily irrational. It means only that, as things stand, they have been justified only on ideological grounds (e.g. nationalism, eco-naturism) or by strategic considerations outside economics.[29] Working against such a policy are orthodox economic methods of evaluation and the dominant technocratic logic. Nevertheless, the fact that experts in orthodoxy come from countries which all practise protectionist agricultural policies and engage in dumping onto the world market may make these logics seem a bit suspect. Why do they promote the opposite of what is done in their own countries?

National politics

At the level of individual countries' policies relating to the problem of food self-sufficiency, a very wide range of situations is to be found. It is interesting briefly to review something of this range, choosing a very contrasted sample of the real socialist countries, Algeria, the newly industrialised countries, India, and the least developed countries.

1. The 'real socialist' countries. Socialist countries have always claimed to have broken away from the world market in order not to submit to its laws. They tried policies of food self-sufficiency long before the word was fashionable, indeed when the term 'autarky' still had currency. Their intention was usually to subordinate agriculture to the needs of fast-track industrial development. This policy, which initially was attempted in a brutal bureaucratic way by collectivising land, has generally produced negative results. The Soviet Union and Hungary, which had been agricultural exporters, saw their production diminish. However, in countries where large-scale drainage and irrigation programmes were carried out, and in those where considerable autonomy was left in the hands of the production units themselves, self-sufficiency was attained and even exceeded. Albania and North Korea are examples of the first instance, and post-1956 Hungary an illustration of the second. Roumania is a good counter-example of failed bureaucratic management of agriculture. The Ceausescu regime didn't even honour its own food coupons, condemning the population to the 'Romanian Sandwich': a cheese coupon between two bread tickets. The rigidity of the policies of agrarian 'systemisation' had led to a situation of quasi-famine. Centrally planned 'modernisation/industrialisation' has failed in general (see, for example, the former USSR), with perhaps the exception of the former East Germany, where large-scale exploitation gave moderately good results.

2. Algeria. This country envisaged both food and industrial self-sufficiency through an auto-centric development. Agriculture and industry, and each sector within these two domains, were to play their part in the equilibrium and dynamism of the whole. The result was a very cute experiment in extroverted industrialisation accompanied by massive food dependence! The reasons for this failure stem, no doubt, from the contradictions between the macro-economic goals defined for agriculture by bureaucrats and technocrats in Algiers, and the agents' motives at the level of production units. Agricultural workers and local management were not interested in carrying out plans which were in any case not suited to local conditions. The subsequent choices favouring industrialisation led to those in charge becoming less and less interested in agriculture. Then, after the death of President Boumediene, Algeria attempted, through a policy of liberalisation, to lessen the penury of staple products that had arisen from the limits on imports imposed by the slump in oil export revenues. The results, however, were only modest, and the continuing food shortages led to riots in 1988.

3. The South-East Asian NICs: Taiwan and South Korea. Taiwan and South Korea launched a policy of industrial development and modernisation of agriculture following an original plan of action. After a realistic and effective agrarian reform, they chose a Japanese-style 'modernisation' of agriculture, i.e. an approach based primarily on rigorous selection of seeds, use of appropriate fertilisers, better water control and more frequent harvests. The increase in inputs per unit of the intensively farmed plots permitted a substantial increase in productivity per hectare and per worker. This agriculture is closer to intensive gardening than to American-style extensive mechanisation. Sophisticated tools are introduced after adaptation and miniaturisation as required. The result has been that the agricultural sectors have become net exporters. They are now running up against problems of disposing of surpluses much like those faced by the EEC producers with whom they compete for Third World markets.

4. India. This country tried to attain food self-sufficiency through a *green revolution* characterised by the modern agronomist's 'holy trinity' of miracle seeds, fertilisers and pesticides.[30] It succeeded 'quantitatively' in regions where the importation of the agro-industrial model with machines and irrigation could succeed, that is to say, on the big cereal plains. The Punjab thus became a big producer region with considerable surpluses. However, there has been a heavy price to pay: increase in social inequality, elimination of poor farmers as well as of small-scale peasant farmers and dependence on imports of machinery (tractors) and other sophisticated products. Imports of chemical fertilisers exceed previous imports of cereals and are counted in millions of tonnes. In less favoured regions which couldn't or wouldn't import the 'technical package', such as the mountain areas of the Deccan, ecological and human catastrophe has occurred: destruction of the forest and of the Dravidians who lived in and from it, soil exhaustion, and indebtedness of the peasant farmers. As the agronomist Marc Dufumier observed:

> The early varieties to come out of the Green Revolution proved to be very demanding on fertilisers, prone to diseases and various parasites, vulnerable to adverse climatic conditions (drought, flooding) and rigid in their cultural requirements.[31]

5. The LDCs. For the least developed countries, the agro-industrial model is out of the question unless they have financial means; and it is unclear whether it is applicable or profitable anyway, owing to problems with soils and tropical climate. Famine in Ethiopia is partly explained by the thoughtless use of miracle strains which, unlike the less productive traditional ones, could not stand up to drought. The significant niches in world markets are still those cash-crops for which there is no substitute: coffee, cocoa, cotton – when the soil constitution allows them – and out-of-season crops such as strawberries and green beans. Results have been satisfying in countries where the introduction of market-gardening for export has brought about diversification and enrichment of the local diet. In most cases, though, achievement of self-sufficiency would require the construction of coherent agrarian systems. A policy which genuinely advantages peasants would have to be put into effect, first of all price-wise, which runs up against the problem of supplying towns cheaply. Yet if the right conditions are fulfilled, 'traditional' agrarian systems are perfectly capable of adapting and evolving to respond to new needs.

The fuzziness of policy objectives

These examples are sufficient to highlight several ambiguities in the targets and implementation of food policies. For example, if the goal is to restore rural self-subsistency, this may conflict with general food self-sufficiency. The recent examples of Peru, Morocco and Tunisia show that reliable and cheap supplies of food to the towns are vital to keeping order. Therefore a lot of political courage is needed to maintain a policy of paying peasants for produce at a price far above the world price. Under particular conditions this may be feasible. Zimbabwe instituted a policy of high agricultural prices since it could not carry out extensive agrarian reform or import the means of modernisation. The leap in production was spectacular and the whole initiative was a clear success. Before independence, declare the leaders of the National Farmers' Association in Zimbabwe, the traditional sector had never succeeded in producing more than 3% of the maize sold in the market. In 1983-84, in spite of two years of drought, the production from the traditional sector reached 30% of maize sold and in 1985 more than 50%.[32]

The non-price determinants of food output levels are complex, and for this reason the effect of price levels on consumption and production of agricultural products in the Third World is by no means as simple or mechanical as the textbook supply-demand economic model might lead one to imagine. A drop in prices does not necessarily cause a drop in production or an increase in consumption. A rise does not always have the opposite effect either. Eating habits, limited money incomes, or simply routine, all have an important part to play. For national products that are *commercialised*, a rise in prices is usually followed by a leap in production. This was seen in the Ivory Coast for rice in 1974, 1982 and 1984. Tanzania, by contrast, often given as an example of endogenous development, failed miserably in the same terms. The probable reason there, however, was that President Nyerere's communal villages were set up in a bureaucratic way, and technological mimetism was much stronger than the programme managers let on.[33]

Overall, we can see that a self-sufficiency policy can be put into practice in very different ways, as diametrically opposed as development of agro-industrial methods in the food goods sector, and reconstruction of autonomous agrarian systems. But whatever the policy proclaimed, the way it is put into practice can lead to results that are the opposite of what was intended.

The ambiguities of self-sufficiency exist not only on the economic plane, but also on the cultural. For the most part, it is Western countries that enunciate the problems and decree what the Third World needs – imposing their vision and judgement as if they were obvious and unquestionable. The idea of food self-sufficiency thus appears closely linked to that of *basic needs*: both concepts arise out of the Western imagination.

Doubtless all these economic, technical, political and cultural ambiguities are what account for the almost unanimous success of the concept of self-sufficiency in Western countries, in the divergent milieux of the big international financial organisations as much as in NGOs. Meanwhile, for many Third World countries, increasing food supply problems make it understandable that people cling to this ray of hope. The variable and often disappointing results recorded almost everywhere are the simple corollary of these disparities and misunderstandings.

The partisans of 'alternative' development have not paid attention to these difficulties, nor have they clearly sorted out their own positions. Self-sufficiency in food matters is most often considered to be obviously a positive step in the *right direction*, without any real critical appraisal.

The trap of basic needs

The debate over basic needs is just as ambiguous. The underlying reason is that the notion of basic need rests on a perfectly debatable

naturalist vision, and the very notion of *need* relates to a charac-
teristically Western way of functioning in society. In this domain, the
Good Samaritan sentiment, which motivates the strategies of so many
NGOs, can misguide with resulting disillusionment. It is easy to
perceive the ideological *coup de force* inherent in such statements as
the following by Hugues Puel:

> Even if essential needs cannot be the object of an exact scientific determina-
> tion, because they are a mixture of nature and culture and they vary as a
> function of the type of civilisation, it is none the less true that the distinction
> between essential need and secondary need is well-founded.[34]

The fact that we will never know on what this 'well-founded' distinc-
tion is based, authorises us not to rely too heavily on these humanists.
Past humanists have, no doubt unwittingly, led the people of the Third
World along the road of ethnocide, i.e. of cultural extinction.[35]

Paternalism is, indeed, at the heart of the issue. 'Essential' needs
are those required to cover an individual's *costs*, meaning a Western-
type individual. In the non-exhaustive list which includes nutrition,
health, education, etc., nutrition is the only one which really seems to
amount to a 'natural' need, in the sense of being shared by all living
beings. Moreover, this humanism-naturalism is politically treacherous
ground, for, even once the so-called basic needs are satisfied ('food,
clothing, housing'), the *true* Third World demands for dignity, recognition, status and identity need not at all be satisfied.[36] One can
perfectly well imagine a world just as inhuman and unequal as the
present world even though everyone is fed, clothed, lodged and looked
after. Oppression, injustice and humiliation would simply be effected
through other means.[37] It is no doubt *technically* possible to feed the
human flock in the undernourished South of the planet. The ample
ingenuity of Western scientists shows up in some crazy ideas, for
example, going as far as to imagine inducing genetic mutation of the
human species to allow the starving masses to digest grass and the
leaves of wild plants. Human engineering will thus contribute to
planetary conflict resolution![38] What makes this the *more* sordid is that
already, in some tips in Brazilian shantytowns, such mutations have
spontaneously been produced; children manage to digest normally
inedible spoiled scraps of food.

The idea that human needs are a mixture of nature and culture in
fact belongs to a received wisdom which is probably false. Insofar as

it is *human*, need is *entirely* cultural. There is nothing *natural* in the way that people normally eat and even less in the ways they dress and house themselves. The do-good attitude that emanates from the Centre and insists on cores of *basic needs* smacks of the old practice of alms-giving and has some hypocritical aspects that tend to cloud the whole debate.

'What is necessary in anything always has something revolting about it,' wrote Madame de Staël in the nineteenth century, 'when it is those with more than enough who are doing the measuring.'[39] The ambiguity of the theme of basic needs surfaced recently in the offensive led by UNICEF under the banner of adjustment with a human face. The sub-title of the version of the work published in France is very revealing: *Protéger les groupes vulnérables et favoriser la croissance* (Protecting vulnerable groups while encouraging growth).[40] The Good Samaritans want to achieve a more equitable situation, but do not give up in the slightest on the idea of development. Dominique Perrot unmasks the paradoxes of this approach rather well:

> The reasoning is as follows: development is economic growth but the latter doesn't ensure coverage of basic needs for everyone (in fact, it is an obstacle to getting coverage); so another dimension has to be added, that of essential needs; but the international economic order being what it is (in fact, a disorder), it is necessary to impose or propose adjustment policies for some countries, and, as those who have to suffer from these politics are precisely the most vulnerable, it is appropriate to add another dimension to the adjustment, that of humanity towards the poor to lighten their burden.[41]

The paternalism expressed here is grotesque, but this caricature of alternative development is not of our doing. The speciality of this 'Red Cross type' of approach (as Dominique Perrot terms it) is to reconcile what would seem unreconcilable: humanitarian concern and hard economic goals. Here, this reconciliation is achieved by simple assertion. In the long term, say the authors of the UNICEF work, 'the level of growth attained would be *at least as high* (through the adjustment with a human face) as that achieved through direct growth-oriented policies'.[42]

Such paternalism on the part of the Western humanist is rooted not just in a supposedly *fundamental* dimension of needs, but in the idea of *need* itself. Need as a category is linked directly to Western naturalism, and also derives from of a way of organising the social that is characteristic of modernity. According to the persuasive analysis by Ivan Illich, the idea of need first appears in Christian Europe in the Carolingian period. It emerges in the religious domain to support the division at that time being imposed between the mass of the faithful and the clergy. For the proper conduct of their spiritual life, the people *need* experts to guide their practices. No salvation is assured without aid from 'the individual acts of service provided by professionals in the name of the Mother Church'. The cleric becomes the first figure of technocracy, the one who knows how, whose power reposes on the *technical* knowledge of the ways to salvation. *Need* thus appears as the sign of a dispossession of the knowledge of oneself and of the external management of one's existence. From the ninth to the eleventh centuries, writes Illich,

> the idea took shape that there are some needs common to all human beings that can be satisfied only through service from professional agents. Thus the definition of needs in terms of professionally defined commodities in the services sector precedes by a millennium the industrial production of universally needed basic goods.[43]

The idea of a basic need is well and truly inscribed in Western ideology, whether this be in the form of naturalism, technocracy or humanism. One can find a parable in the fact that the person who has worked hardest to spread the idea of fundamental needs is one Robert McNamara, the President of the World Bank in 1973. This great humanist technocrat had in fact conscientiously and effectively managed the military intervention in Vietnam, with the bombing of Hanoi and the use of defoliants and napalm. This coincidence has a moral to it, for it suggests clearly the lack of contradiction between these two attitudes. As far as we know, Robert McNamara has never publicly questioned his earlier role; indeed, no one has asked him to. His professional conscience, his undeniable competence and uncontestable honesty were enough to serve as a guarantee to all the NGOs and alternative development offices which greeted enthusiastically his recognition of *their* vision of things. They preserve their scepticism, their criticism and their vigilance for on-the-ground operations, in connection with the *putting into effect* of the good intentions. And it is only fair to recognise that Robert McNamara merely took up an idea of Paul Streeten's, a humanist expert in the World Bank. Streeten, having examined a wide range of the development experiments in the

Third World, concluded that it was the success and not the failure of these strategies which was causing the hunger and poverty. From there he was led to suggest alternative strategies based on essential needs.

These so-called basic needs call rather obviously for 'appropriate technologies' to satisfy them. The needs are, in fact, likely to be better satisfied by specifically chosen means than through the offer of standardised products issuing from an uniform process of transnational production. So the critique of the ideology of fundamental needs is, inevitably, completed by that of the notion of appropriate technology.

Appropriate technologies: to what end?

All the same ambiguities weigh on what is called, in the specialist literature, 'appropriate technology'. The failure of development in the Third World often takes the form of failure in the transfer of modern techniques – rejection of the 'technological graft'. From the critical appraisal of technology, although often limited in scope to a denunciation of the mismatch between the most modern and advanced techniques and the conditions in developing countries where they are introduced, has come the argument for a recourse to appropriate technologies.[44]

What does this term refer to? To machines and factory processes better adapted to the economic, social and cultural context, often to so-called *intermediate* technologies. These are so designated because they are intermediate between traditional technologies and the most advanced ones. Intermediate from the point of view of the complexity of concept or manipulation; they contain fewer 'black boxes' or elements that are hard to understand. They are less 'sophisticated'. Because of this, the machines linked to them can more easily be repaired, produced or reproduced on the spot. They are appropriate in the sense that they can be appropriated by the Third World countries, meaning they can be mastered. They are also intermediate on the financial level. They are more expensive than the simple tools used by craftspeople, yet much less expensive than the latest inventions. Between the old hand-loom and the totally automated ensemble there is room for a whole range of intermediate techniques. It has been possible, similarly, to propose the appropriateness of purchase and use of second-hand equipment by the Third World. Finally, these techniques are intermediate as regards the number of jobs they create. It is well known that modern capital-intensive technologies do not create many jobs, whereas traditional tools provide work for a large work-force in a not very productive way. There is, therefore, a balance to be found between the degree of productivity and the number of unem-ployed.

Appropriate technologies are often traditional technologies that have been improved. Indigenous (autochthonous) technologies are, evidently, adapted to the local culture and environment. Improvement in productivity and profitability can, however, allow the introduction of innovations within the stream of local production methods, rather than upsetting them altogether.

Furthermore, these technologies are in general *soft technologies*, meaning that they show respect for the environment due to their small scale and manner of conception, and also because – in the case of indigenous technologies – they have stood the test of time. Adaptation to the environment may even constitute a necessary precondition for their choice.

All this does not, in itself, get rid of the inherent ambiguities. That these sorts of technologies may better suit the users in the Third World, well and good; but to what end? The implicit reply of a better adaptation to *their need* encapsulates the whole ambiguity. Is this need identifiable? Is it a case of the need of the state powers? Or of the dominant social classes? Of the oppressed? Is it a case of a survival need, satisfied through reappropriating the production of basic prod-ucts, or of some sort of construction of an industrial and technological society? Once again one encounters the two conceptions of possible futures of Third World societies: that of an 'alternative' development, and that of an *alternative to* development. And the same impasses are met as previously with food self-sufficiency and basic needs.

The inherent ambiguity is clearly present in the history of the idea of appropriate technology, and accounts for the difficulties with the concept – its seductiveness, its failures as well as its successes. Because the debate on *technological pluralism* was born in connection with the Indian economy, the appropriate technology idea has often been linked to Gandhi's thought. But in fact appropriate technology is less an outcome of Gandhi's critique of industrialisation (a critique which is itself ambiguous), than it is a taking charge by Western *engineers* of the problem of the failure of mimetic development. It proceeds primarily from a *Western* critique of modernity. Although clearly there is a moral dimension underpinning the whole approach, there is no question of renouncing either technocratic logic or economic reason. At bottom, it is an attempt to create a *technology with a human face*.

Ernst Friedrich Schumacher, a German economist who was the father of this concept, can be taken as representative of the appropriate technology partisans. Having fled the Nazi regime, he followed a career as a bureaucrat in Great Britain and carried out advisory missions for the United Nations. He had been influenced by German romanticism and German Youth movements between 1900 and 1930 which were very critical of modernity *(Wandervogel, Jugend Kultur)*. The rise around 1968 of the American *counter-culture* – particularly in California – and the search for soft technologies which went hand-in-hand with the realisation of ecological limits to growth, all contributed to the vogue for these ideas in the West and later to their export to the Third World. Once again the same motif: the West will save the Third World and resolve the problems that its intrusions have stirred up.

The engineers' view of things remains very technocratic. They seek to put their competence to the service of the Third World, through inventing and diffusing *other* techniques useful for resolving their problems. But by limiting the analysis of the Third World's problems to their technical aspects alone, even if understood very broadly as the totality of the problems implied in the triangular relation between human being, tool and nature, the goal remains one of development – even if one thinks of it as an *other* or *alternative* development. A critical analysis of the technological society, of its complexity and its logics is not undertaken, nor is a real enquiry into the causes of the failure of development. They go no further than the appearances of the technical problems. Development takes place through technology, but the latter has to be suitably acclimatised and progressively domesticated. Success in development comes about, at the limit, from the simple fact of having effected a *good choice* of technologies, not letting oneself be caught by the siren song of ready-made factories, nor misled by the mirage of a *technological catch-up strategy* (i.e. jumping directly from traditional tools to the latest space-age techniques).

The recognition, in the appropriate technology concept, of indigenous technological creativity, and of the ingenuity of local people, does lead to the possibility of countering some of the effects of planetary uniformisation. However, this potential is only rarely allowed to unfold according to its own logic. The whole approach runs into a lot of difficulties, notwithstanding the undeniable aptness in many cases of the proposed machines, the competence and commitment of the experts, and the exactness of the theoretical calculations of efficiency and profitability. Typically the success is only temporary, or else leads towards a development that is no longer really in any way alternative.

'Technological' improvements to indigenous procedures and tools, and even inventions of new imported intermediate technologies, can turn out to be 'profitable' – or at least more effective or profitable than the pre-existing solutions, and more effective or profitable than the most advanced technologies would be in the local context. One can cite many successful examples: small-scale sugar refineries, village cement works, handmade brick works, shoe workshops, textile factories, small dams. It is always handy to be able to cite these successes and contrast them with the glaring failure of some big projects, ready-made factories, or 'tech-fixes' that have failed lamentably due to lack of adaptation to the context. Thus in Benin, near Ouidah, a rather sophisticated irrigation system with a droplet system had been installed with pressurised water impulsion through PVC tubing, driven by an electric motor. Within a few hours the installation was completely unusable, as the palm tree rats feasted on the PVC. In Mauritania, the German motors which equipped pumps for deep-drawing wells were sensitive to the abrasive effects of the wind and sand. There are many other examples to be found. Most modern business enterprises in Africa that are still functioning have become costly millstones for the states in question. The 'project cemetery' is populated with 'white elephants' and 'desert cathedrals' – 'safari projects', as they call them in Africa.

It must be said, however, that the success of micro-level development and of appropriate machinery remains fragile, temporary, or opening onto development with no alternative. Undeniably many micro-projects also bite the dust. The energy spent introducing all sorts of improved stoves into Africa, with the aim of economising on wood, was finally not very successful. Most often people have returned to old traditional practices – because they are more convivial, because the wastage actually has positive spin-offs (heating, smoking of food items, elimination of insects, lighting of the home, impermeability of the thatch, etc.).[45] Furthermore, when it comes to protection of trees or replanting, the general rule has been misunderstanding of their role and ignorance of the many benefits they have in rural societies. In the same way, people pretend to be unaware of the destructive role of charcoal businesses, which operate with the complicity of the powers that be. Their impact is much more serious than the shape of the stoves.[46]

'Small projects' must, like any others, fit into bureaucratic norms of financing even if these are the norms of the little NGO bureaucracies. Because of this, they are rarely a reflection of a deep desire of the 'target' population, and they often miss their intended target. (In Chad, wells intended to lighten women's work have been dug near mosques, where they ended up being used by men for their ritual ablutions.) What is more, alternative technologies only cover certain limited sectors of production. Frequently there is not a very wide technological choice (although interesting less-capitalist avenues do often exist, at least potentially); and even less is there any appropriate technology in the car industry, aeronautics, electronics, nuclear energy, the space industry, robotics, and generally speaking any sectors that were not already represented in traditional activity. The appropriate technologies are able to develop largely thanks to a *de facto* protection due to distance, weight (e.g. cement, bricks), partition of markets (e.g. in agricultural products), differences in eating habits, cultural specificities. It is not by chance that one finds here all the elements that contribute to the success of the informal.

Still, insofar as they aim at development, and leaving aside any concrete difficulties of implementation, appropriate technologies come up against a whole series of objections that are hard to push aside. In truth there is no decisive argument to show the superiority or inferiority *in the abstract* of 'intermediate' techniques compared with latest technologies. But the logic of the technological society condemns them immediately. They are not in tune with the spirit of the age – rather they contradict the law of the dynamics of modernity: 'Whatever can be done, must be done.'

The arguments against the mimetic transfer of up-to-the-minute technologies – technical and financial dependence, low job creation, etc. – can easily be turned back the other way. Development is, after all, a facet of the society which makes *efficiency* the supreme value. Will anyone believe that the stone adze is more efficient than the chainsaw? Or the spinning-wheel better than the automatic spinner? Supporters of technological catch-up strategies will maintain, plausibly, that all the misfunctions related to high-level technologies can be *compensated for* through a judicious use of the very fruits of this sophistication. Difficulties in adapting such techniques should be resolved by an extra step in line with the same technocratic logic. The rewards that can be expected will make up for any difficulties along the way. Maximisation of production and therefore of surpluses, and the subsequent rise in incomes and investment levels which makes possible the entry into the 'virtuous cycle' of development, wipe out any other consideration.

So appropriate technologies are indefensible in theoretical terms and in the abstract, from the standpoints of both economic and technological reasoning. They can be tolerated only in very precisely delimited situations of penury, where it is materially or financially impossible to have recourse to the very latest technologies. The very argument of the *scarcity of capital* which seemed to Gandhi and Schumacher to be the best justification for the choice of low-capital-intensity (and inexpensive) choices, is perfectly easily reversed. They argued that since capital is scarce, it ought to be thinly spread over the whole workforce so as to provide a *productive* job for each person and thus improve the lot of everyone. Lack of capital, Schumacher argues, can explain a low level of productivity but not the lack of jobs. To which supporters of technological catch-up, and equally Nehru and the Indian planners, respond: 'Since capital is scarce, one must concentrate its use on investments which produce machinery.' Nicholas Kaldor recapitulates these arguments perfectly:

Research has shown that the most modern machinery produces much more output per unit of capital invested than less sophisticated machinery which employs more people. ... If we can employ only a limited number of people in wage labour, then let us employ them in the most productive way, so that they make the biggest possible contribution to the national output, because that will also give the quickest rate of economic growth. You should not go deliberately out of your way to reduce productivity in order to reduce the amount of capital per worker. This seems to me nonsense because you may find that by increasing capital per worker tenfold you increase the output per worker twentyfold. There is no question from every point of view of the superiority of the latest and more capitalistic technologies.[47]

The fact that the great majority of sophisticated ready-to-roll plants set up in the Third World don't work, does not shake this conviction. If an ultra-modern Nigerian steelworks operates at only 30% of its production capacity, it will be shown that the site was badly chosen and the operating units are not properly integrated. There are always *technical* causes for the failures of technology. The same goes for Ivory Coast sugar refineries, for oil refineries in Togo, the Cameroon and Gabon, for the Safi chemical complex in Morocco, and so on.

So technological considerations can justify intermediate technologies only *very provisionally*. On occasions where technicians become aware that ecological, soil, climatic and medical conditions are unsuitable for big dams in tropical regions, they can then on 'technical grounds' choose small dams. If the country has bad roads, ports that are too small, a hilly terrain and too few specialists, then the construction of housing with heavy prefabricated components in big factories will be 'technically' inadvisable, since the components will be damaged in transit, the factory will have to slow down production for lack of parts, and the erection of housing on-site will be badly done. Algeria is still suffering the consequences of this sort of bad technological choice. All these technical constraints, to which the technician pays attention *only after* many failures and when he can't avoid acknowledging them, are none the less seen as momentary – and technology prides itself on being able to resolve them. The blindness of the technician, the deafness of the economist, even when they are almost systematic, remain at the level of 'accidents'. These 'accidents' have their origins in the limits of technical and economic reason. But to take them properly into account one would have to have deconstructed this reason which is the West's very own.

Failure to question the technocratic logic and the supposed destiny of development perpetuates the complications and ambiguities. Underdevelopment is defined as a situation of penury and constraints. The struggle against the very real negative effects of this situation justifies, so the argument goes, using *realistic* means within the reach of those concerned, without encumbering them with theoretical rigour. For the partisans of 'alternative' development, this situation is only temporary: penury and constraints will be relieved by successful development. Consequently, the 'appropriate technologies' will themselves be only as temporary as the situation that justifies them. And this sense of the temporariness of the situation is heightened because of the tendency to take one's desires for realities. So in spite of the often glaring failures of mimetic industrialisation, appropriate technologies, in theory very well-judged, end up being very little used. As long as one remains inside the 'system', the solicitations of technology are very persuasive. The inevitable engineers prefer sophisticated machines which show off their competence. Company heads prefer factories which operate with very few workers to avoid conflicts in the workplace. Governments prefer big centralised units, which are easier to control, and which act as a shop-window. Transnational firms prefer implanting techniques which they have already tried out elsewhere and for which they have equipment, spare parts and specialists available, rather than throwing themselves into long, costly research to adapt to the terrain. Financial controllers prefer simple transparent arrangements, rather than complex operations which necessitate buying second-hand materials or more dispersed investments. Even if one takes no account of the fact that technological decisions have big commercial implications for prospective suppliers – and that such questions are dealt with bribes and inducements suggested over a glass of wine between dessert and cheese, and not simply in the clinical propriety of the air-conditioned research centres or the offices of humanist militants – it is easy to see that the alternative technological path in development has few chances and even fewer prospects.

The technological alternative acquires its proper meaning only in an *other* context. The whole of social reality is at stake here. Through the medium of technology, culture itself is in question. It is only a small step from the operational category of 'technology' to the question of the conception of knowledge. Posing this question can lead to the rehabilitation of 'ethnoscience'. From there, we move to the education system, and to re-evaluating the complex initation procedures of traditional societies. Little by little, the whole way of being social and the whole ensemble of values enter the picture. It is then not a case of a *different* way of maximising the GNP, but rather a question of ways of preserving or reconstructing a truly different society.

The questioning of the evolutionism which underpins developmentalist positions is only very partial in the approach of the supporters of appropriate technologies. The pluralism they espouse remains very limited. Any rejection of naturalism is far from being evident, as the discussion on basic needs shows. There is no clear repudiation of hedonism or even of individualism. Symptoms of the evil are being attacked, rather than the roots. An anti-utilitarianism of real consequence can only lead one to a rejection of development. From the point of view of an *alternative to* development, the invention of an *other* conception of technique takes on its full meaning and interest. Gandhi no doubt aspired to such an alternative. 'Every human being,' he used to say, 'has the right to live and consequently to have the means to feed, clothe and house himself. But to reach such a plain result, we have absolutely no need to call upon economists and their laws.'[48] This rejection of economics is manifestly a rejection of development. But even so, with the references to basic needs and to the right to life, perfectly valid in their own terms, this discourse still has a Western connotation which permits the assimilation of Gandhi's thought by Western logic (or at least a certain type of logic).

Appropriate technology remains in a state of *weightlessness* if it is left languishing within the framework of any sort of development. Undoubtedly this is the reason that informal activity is the true demander and user of appropriate techniques. This activity is not dictated by mimetism, but by a survival constraint; it doesn't conform exclusively to economic reason, but is grounded in another culture; it partly escapes the sirens' seduction and can be a departure point for a new society within which the aspirations emerging from the critique of development take on their full meaning.

Notes

1. Ivan Illich, *Shadow Work*, op. cit., p. 18.

2. An earlier version of the following pages, under the title 'Les paradoxes de la "normalisation" de l'économie informelle', was published in the *Revue Tiers Monde*, no. 117, January-March 1989, pp. 227-33.

3. See the dossier edited by Claude Courlet, 'Industrialisation rampante et diffuse dans les pays en développement', op. cit.

4. Dominique Perrot, 'La "dimension culturelle du développement": un nouveau gadget', *Cahiers lillois d'économie et de sociologie (Clés)*, no. 14, Lille, 2nd semester 1989, p. 48.

5. Nicolas Bricas & José Muchnik, 'Indigenous technologies and urban cottage industry in the food sector', in *Nourrir les villes* (edited by Philippe Hugon), L'Harmattan, Paris, 1985, p. 304.

6. Gregory Bateson, 'Toward a theory of schizophrenia', in *Behavioural Sciences*, vol. 1, no. 4, 1956, reprinted in *Steps to an Ecology of Mind: collected essays in anthropology, psychiatry, evolution, and epistemology*, Chandler, San Francisco, 1972, pp. 201-27; and 'Double bind', in *Steps to an Ecology of Mind*, pp. 271-8.

7. Pope Paul VI, *Populorum Progressio*, French edition, Editions du Centurian et Editions Ouvrières, Paris, 1967, as cited by Madeleine Ramaholimihaso, *Quand la route est longue, la réflexion s'enrichit*, Madagascar Publishing Society, 1989, p. 4.

8. Alfredo De Romana, 'L'économie autonome', op. cit., p. 129.

9. Daniel Théry, 'La brique en Tunisie: une occasion manquée d'embrayage technologique endogène', *Bulletin NEED*, no. 6, CIRED, Paris, December 1987.

10. Jean Chesneaux, 'Tiers monde offshore ou tiers monde quart-mondisé et libération du troisième type', *Revue Tiers Monde*, no. 100, October-December 1984, pp. 817-26.

11. See Michel Carton's plausible analysis, 'Les marginaux informels préhistoriques et post-modernes?', *Entwicklung/Development*, no. 24, 1987.

12. Dominique Perrot, 'Transferts de concepts et développement', *Bulletin du MAUSS*, no. 20, December 1986, pp. 103-20.

13. Jacques Charmes, 'Quelles politiques publiques face au secteur informel?, *Notes et études de la Caisse centrale de coopération économique*, no. 23, April 1989, p. 5.

14. Fréderic Prouteau, 'Le capitalisme intelligent de la SIDI', *CFDT Magazine*, no. 158, March 1991, p. 28.

15. Ivan Illich, *Shadow Work*, op. cit., p. 4.

16. At a meeting with Samir Amin and Alain Lipietz, discussing our recent respective positions (1986-87), my presentation of *alternatives to* development as opposed to their developmentalist ones came up against a total lack of understanding. 'But all that,' exclaimed Alain Lipietz, 'is exactly what is called "alternative" development.' See 'Trois auteurs en quête d'un tiers monde', *Cosmopolitiques*, June 1988, p. 83.

17. The reference is to Marshall Sahlins' work, *Stone Age Economics*, Aldine Atherton, Chicago, 1972, translated into French under the title *Age de pierre, âge d'abondance* (Age of stone, age of abundance). – *Translators' note.*

18. See, for example, Alidou Sawadogo, quoted by Pierre Pradervand, *Une Afrique en marche*, Plon, Paris, 1989, p. 109.

19. An earlier version of this section was published under the title 'Les ambiguïtés de l'autosuffisance alimentaire', in *Clés*, no. 16, Lille, 2nd semester 1990.

20. See Thierry Verhelst, *No Life without Roots*, Zed Books, London.

21. Denis Requier-Desjardins, *L'Alimentation en Afrique: manger ce qu'on peut produire*, Karthala, PUSAF, 1989.

22. Ivan Illich, *Tools for Conviviality*, Calder & Boyars, London, 1973.

23. Michel Labonne, 'L'autosuffisance alimentaire en question', in Philippe Hugon (editor), *Nourrir les villes*, L'Harmattan, Paris, 1985, p. 358.

24. These ideas are put forward by, among others, Guy Belloncle; see particularly *La Question paysanne en Afrique noire*, Karthala, Paris, 1982.

25. Pierre Dockes & Bernard Rosier, *L'Histoire ambiguë*, Presses Universitaires de France, Paris, 1988, p. 282.

26. FAO, *Rapport sur la situation mondiale de l'alimentation et de l'agriculture de 1984*, Geneva.

27. Denis Requier-Desjardins, *L'Alimentation en Afrique*, op. cit., p. 49.

28. Ibid., p. 40.

29. See for example Francis Kern, 'La dynamique du marché intérieur comme stratégie de développement autonome', presented to an Alsace-Third World Conference in Strasbourg, 12-13 December 1986.

30. François de Ravignan, 'Les mythes de l'autosuffisance alimentaire', *Le Monde Diplomatique*, June 1987.

31. In *Les Politiques agraires*, Presses Universitaires de France, Series 'Que sais-je?', Paris 1986, p. 33.

32. Pierre Pradervand, *Une Afrique en marche*, op. cit., p. 27.

33. See Daniel Théry, 'Le biais mimétique dans le choix des techniques: un facteur d'asphyxie du développement autocentré de Tanzania', *Revue Tiers Monde*, no. 100, October-December 1984, pp. 787-800.

34. Hugues Puel, 'Peut-on connaître les besoins?', *Economie et humanisme*, no. 210, March-April 1973.

35. See Robert Jaulin, 'Ethnocide, tiers monde, et ethno-développement', *Revue Tiers Monde*, no. 100, October-December 1984, pp. 913-27.

36. See Serge Latouche, 'Si la misère n'existait pas, il faudrait l'inventer', in G. Rist & F. Sabelli (editors), *Il était une fois le développement*, Editions d'En-Bas, Lausanne, 1986.

37. An expansion on this hypothesis is given in Serge Latouche, *Faut-il refuser le développement?*, op. cit., ch. 7.

38. See Jean Chesneaux, *Modernité-monde*, op. cit., p. 124.

39. Germaine de Staël, *De l'Allemagne*, Editions Charpentier, 1839, p. 9.

40. *L'Ajustement à visage humain: protéger les groupes vulnérables et favoriser la croissance*, Economica, Paris, 1987.

41. Dominique Perrot, 'La "dimension culturelle du développement" ', op. cit., p. 51.

42. *Ajustement à visage humain*, op. cit., p. 171.

43. Ivan Illich, *Shadow Work*, op. cit., p. 60.

44. The English 'appropriate technology' should, properly, be rendered in French as 'technique appropriée'. However, most French specialists have adopted the franglais 'technologie appropriée'. In translation we have the inverse problem. In French, 'technique' is a generic and abstract term, whereas technique in English does not have the same global connotations. We choose to employ 'technology' (singular) as the abstract category, and then refer to technologies (plural) and technique(s) for connotations of particular methods and procedures. – *Translators' note*.

45. Pierre Pradervand, *Une Afrique en marche*, op. cit., p. 287.

46. See Anne Bergeret, *L'Arbre nourricier en pays sahélien*, Maison des Sciences de l'Homme, Paris, 1990.

47. Nicholas Kaldor, verbal remarks quoted by Ronald Robinson in 'The argument of the conference', pp. 28-9, in Ronald Robinson (editor), *Industrialisation in Developing Countries: proceedings of conference, September 1964*, Cambridge University Overseas Studies Committee, Cambridge, 1965.

48. Gandhi, *Tous les hommes sont frères*, Gallimard, in the Collection 'Idées', Paris, 1969, p. 229.

6

The Standard of Living

'I beg your pardon,' said Yuan Hien, 'if you lack goods then you're poor, but being miserable means being unable to make use of the knowledge that you've got. I am poor, but not miserable.'

Chuang-Tzu[1]

In order to grasp even the *possibility* of a *human* life outside the confines of modernity with its pomps and values, a fantastic effort of *decentring* is required. The attempt must be made to tear oneself away from the familiar framework and reference points of modern life in order to conceive of a way of living on the planet Earth entirely different from the one which the last four centuries have made familiar to us. This is not a matter of looking ahead to new gadgets, nor even to new types of social organisation, as science-fiction novels tend to do. The admirable series by the likes of Isaac Asimov and Van Vogt offer us perfectly plausible techno-historical perspectives, but only among an infinity of other possibilities. In fact, these imaginative works do not really question the underlying *values* of modernity, or if they do, only in a partial and marginal way. As to what human beings will actually produce in a century, what they will love and hate, we really know *nothing* and we have no means of knowing. How will social relationships be constructed? What 'political' or cultural forms will serve to structure people's lives? What will be the divisions between the irreducibly personal (the experience of pain, if nothing else) and collective life, the nature of relationships between the sexes, between generations, questions of proximity, group relationships, and so on? We don't have the slightest clue; there again, we simply have no means of knowing.

This imaginative blind-spot is due to what is, properly speaking, a sort of *totalitarianism* of the grand society. The latter, as we have seen, excludes any mode of social life other than itself, on the grounds that it and it alone is rational. Even so, we ought to admit that various other societies, quite unacquainted with the belief in progress, which did not even think about development, have existed for thousands of years and, sometimes under the most severe conditions, have dealt success- fully with economic matters without knowing it and almost without caring about it. In the icy solitude of the Great North, as under tropical heat, people have succeeded in living in harmony with their environment and in creating humane and convivial societies. Under other skies, other people have been able to devote most of their lives to the creation of beauty, or to play, or to living a splendid or heroic life. We cannot judge in advance the choices and the eventualities of post-development society. But we can put forward some plausible hypotheses starting from the interpretation of how those excluded at the present time organise themselves.

The analysis proceeds on the hypothesis that if, say in a century, there is still human life, it will not be founded so much in continuity with our own way of life (that is, in the manner of modernity), as in *rupture* with it. All the arguments of preceding chapters have sought to explore this rupture, to trace its causes and effects. Any possibility of survival beyond the crisis of modernity presupposes that the contradictions provoking its death might indeed be surmounted. This means that we can sketch certain *characteristics* of the society that may be created by development's survivors, through considering the movement through this rupture and beyond – keeping in mind that this movement does not constitute a terminal state, just another departure point for new adventures; at which point so many other elements come into play that it becomes impossible to say any more.

The point at which the decentring, the uprooting, is most difficult to achieve, is undoubtedly *economicity*, that is, the tendency to reduce our life to its economic dimension. Technology permeates modernity to such an extent that it may seem the heart of it. Yet it is probably easier to imagine a world where technology has stopped than a world in which the economy is no longer the *raison d'être*, a world without wealth and poverty, or at least without wealth and poverty as *we* understand them. A reflection on the idea of *standard of living* is a very good way to get a feel for what is distinctive about the society of the castaways.

It may seem strange to speak of *rupture* when the sole concrete evidence furnished of this, the informal, is so much linked with modernity. The informal is, indeed, a byproduct of modernity. In many respects there is an undeniable continuity. But at the same time it introduces a weakness into the heart of technocratic society's scheme of things, through the *re-embedding* of the economic within the social totality. Fragile as this may be, it constitutes a seed with the potential to subvert the stability of the grand society and to bring about a total reorganisation of the scattered elements that once constituted the modern world.

Standardisation of life[2]

When, on 24 June 1949, in his message to Congress on Point 4 of his inaugural address, President Truman announced the necessity 'to assist the people of economically underdeveloped areas to raise their standard of living',[3] he aligned himself with an objective already accepted as obvious and indisputable for all modern states. The Charter of the United Nations had a few years before, in 1945, affirmed in its Article 55, the global objective 'to promote higher standards of living'.

According to both popular opinion and scientific usage, 'standard of living' refers to material well-being and is a measurable thing, similar to per capita Gross National Product. 'The standard of living,' wrote Jean Fourastier, 'is measured by the quantity of goods and services which may be purchased by the average national income.'[4] Increase in the level of this indicator is the result of economic development, which in turn supposedly derives from the improved exploitation of natural resources through rational utilisation of science and technology in the form of industrial machinery. Equalisation and uniformisation of this standard across the globe becomes the ideal towards which organisations strive the world over. Although perhaps in 1949 things were not articulated quite as explicitly as this, no one really questioned the objective or the reasoning underlying this ideal. As Bertrand de Jouvenel put it in 1964: 'The improvement of the material condition of the greatest number is, in our times, fact, hope and desire.'[5]

Yet, if concern for survival is as old as the world itself, and moreover not peculiar to the human species, the obsession with *this particular* 'standard of living' is very recent. The latter is inscribed within modernity, which operates on the proposition that a man is 'worth what he is worth', as measured in good hard cash. This is the bourgeois vision of social value. As G.H. Radkowski writes, 'contrary to the peasant, the artisan, the noble, or the cleric, the bourgeois is a being defined socially only by what he has, because he is worth something'.[6] The triumph of the bourgeois world will be complete with the universalisation of the weekly pay-packet. From that point, everyone will know what they are worth, their standing in dollars. The greater number of people will know by this that they are not worth very much, but will be able to console themselves knowing that there are others worth even less than they.

Interest in salary levels, on the part of wage-earners themselves but also as a general social preoccupation, dates from the industrial era. As more and more people were turned into wage-earners, the wage became the basic component of the standard of living. Even so, when the founding proclamation of the League of Nations was made on 28 June 1919, according to which 'the well-being and the development of people form a sacred mission of civilization',[7] the concept did not yet translate into a measurable index. The ambitious planning in the USSR under Stalin and Khrushchev for catching up and overtaking the Americans was still not expressed with the straightforward simplicity of a goal of equality in GNP per capita. Although there was widespread use of the term 'standard of living', the concept did not yet have its technical meaning of a precise and statistically determined economic datum, but remained a general notion that was vague, eclectic and subjective. In particular, the concept was still far from being used as a categorical imperative to the exclusion of all others. Over a long period, human geographers have studied different modes of living around the world, attempting to describe the ways of life specific to a given region or a given social milieu. Quantitative (and implicitly normative) measures were largely absent from this sort of work, in favour of the concern for the qualitatively different features of each people or region. Economists today can get away with using the standard of living concept to quantify the differences, partly because ways of living have become increasingly uniform, with the result that differences in *modes* of living can more and more easily be translated into differences in *levels* of living.

Attainment of the self-evident character of the standard-of-living concept has, in fact, been possible only by virtue of a whole series of recent circumstances and events, and a process of social change whose roots go back far further. Examination of these recent circumstances, and of their origins, can shed light on the implications and significance of the new concept. It turns out that its much-vaunted universal applicability is still far from self-evident. Looking at the world in terms of 'standard of living' is a bit like looking through dark glasses:

it screens out the colour and richness of life itself. Perhaps, therefore, it is necessary to get rid of the theoretical and practical obsession with this index of well-being, to find (or reacquaint ourselves with) other less reductive modes of evaluation, and through this to rediscover the full spectrum of human experience.

The recent invasion of GNP per head

For the Anglo-Saxon reader, it may seem a travesty to date the emergence of the preoccupation with the standard of living from the period following the Second World War. The expression itself is in fact very old. However, its meaning has evolved very considerably through time. Originally it indicated an *irreducible minimum income,* a subsistence level of living, the cost of the reproduction of the workforce, in the classical political economy tradition of Malthus, Ricardo and Marx. It was still defined in this sense as late as 1934 in the *Encyclopedia of the Social Sciences*.[8] Since then, while not totally losing this connotation, but affected by improvements in living conditions, the expression came to indicate more a *desired* manner of living (level of living), or normal living conditions (contents of living). This was the usage on which economist Joseph Davis insisted in his February 1945 presidential speech to the American Economic Association.[9]

It is clear that it becomes more and more difficult to dissociate the connotation of goal from the question of fact. The actual average level is always going to be situated somewhere between the two notions of the norm: the irreducible minimum and the desired level. The progressive absorption of the descriptive (the actual level) into the normative (setting the standard) is very revealing of the gradual degeneration from a concern with issues of quality to the preoccupation with quantity alone that has come to dominate the Western perspective.[10]

Among the specific circumstances that have led the standard of living to become the daily obsession of our contemporaries and the dominant reference point in economic policy, three phenomena appear to merit particular discussion. These are: the general spread of the concept of national accounts, the growth of mass consumerism in the major industrial countries during the 'thirty glorious years' (1945 to 1975), and the universalisation of the myth of development.

In the absence of any system of accounting, however imprecise, for the measurement of social conditions, it is vain to endow the concept of standard of living with any sort of quantitative meaning or to give it a generalised usage. *One cannot truly enjoy one's standard of living unless one is conscious of what it is!* Today, however, this consciousness is pushed to the extreme for most of our contemporaries, engendering a veritable fetishism for the *amount* of income. Making up for the lack of time to enjoy the fruits of our labour, the greatest satisfaction can at least be drawn from the contemplation of the amount one has earned in comparison with those lower down on the scale. This can lead to all sorts of manipulation of statistics for political purposes. Indeed, the citizenry are really so far from being little *Homines oeconomici* that they attach primarily symbolic value to their incomes!

Following the Great Depression, with the vogue for Keynesian ideas and the interest in macro-economics, the major industrial countries equipped themselves for the first time with statistical research institutes. Quantitative data began to adorn economic concepts and to subvert them from within. As early as 1940, Colin Clark made a comparison between the incomes of different countries. International organisations proceeded to propagate the new cult of figures. Though some Third World states were still living pretty much in the Neolithic Age, without any sort of market integration, they were adorned with statistical apparatus as part of the trappings of a nation-state. The attribution of standardised measurements became a categorical imperative. Living standards could at last be quantified and thus compared. The ideal of global equality of standard of living was no longer utopian; now it translated as a specific quantum of dollars which could at least be referred to, even if not achieved. The utilitarian objective of the greatest happiness for the greatest number had found its scientific formulation.

The Universal Declaration of Human Rights of 1948 proclaimed the equality of all human beings. This abstract universalism necessitated theoretical indices of happiness which would be applicable everywhere. GNP per head provided a convenient measuring rod, one that could claim equal relevance all over the world. Before the War, under the conditions of colonialism, such a preoccupation would have been impossible. It would clearly have been meaningless, for example, to calculate the average standard of living for citizens of the British Empire by adding together English and Indian incomes. Decolonisation, however, brought the rise to pre-eminence of the 'natural' unit of the nation-state, on which basis the idea of equality between nations' standards of living – for example English and Indian – could plausibly be espoused. Imperialism was the last rampart to be stormed in the triumph of economism and the universalisation of the grand society.

The unprecedented growth of the developed economies during the thirty years after the Second World War had some spectacular effects on the standard of living for the general mass of people. The centuries-old poverty in industrialised societies virtually disappeared. Work for all in a free society resulted in the general improvement of well-being under the guardianship of the welfare state. The expectation took root that universal affluence was just around the corner. Each person, once conscious of his or her place on the ladder, scrambled to catch up with those who were ahead. The existing disparities – which were less and less tolerable the narrower they became – were seen as destined to disappear, as they lacked any democratic legitimacy.

The myth of development was thus born. What had taken place in the industrialised countries would generalise itself across the planet. A difference between countries was seen as a delay or backwardness, condemned as unjust and unacceptable. The elimination of these gaps became the definitive planning objective. GNP per head, the basic indicator of the standard of living, became the fundamental criterion for measuring the level of development. Other indices of living standard were also established, non-monetary but still quantitative, ranging from life expectancy to the number of doctors per square kilometre. In all respects, the compilation of a database required national accounts. The different indices were most often strongly correlated, so GNP per head has ended up with a virtual monopoly in official reports.

Periodically, there have been reactions against this savage reductionism. The World Bank, in the wake of Robert McNamara's famous speech in 1973, called for the use of other indicators. The Bank drew attention to the growing income distribution disparities which, in most of the developing countries, were camouflaged behind statistics measuring growth in average per capita income. It called for the inclusion of other objectives besides the increase in the GNP, such as reductions in unemployment and increases in the incomes of the poor. Eventually, the World Bank approved the adoption of 'a socially oriented measure of economic performance'.[11] The United Nations has, more recently, managed to establish an index of 'human development', taking into account life expectancy, education and the access of people to resources. Application of these new criteria results in a higher ranking for some poor peoples who have preserved their resource base, and pushes down the wealthy ones who have squandered theirs.[12]

These changes are only superficial corrective measures, somewhat arbitrary and expensive to implement, which are unlikely to knock the good old GNP per capita off its throne. In any case, these sorts of responses are by no means new. Concern with the need to take into account the multiple aspects of reality was already evident in the work of the earliest statisticians of development. A United Nations report in 1954 on the definition and measure of 'standards' and 'levels of living' called attention to twelve possible components of the standard of living for international comparison. These were: (1) health, including demographic conditions; (2) food and nutrition; (3) education including literacy and skills; (4) conditions of work; (5) employment situation; (6) aggregate consumption and saving; (7) transportation; (8) housing, including household facilities; (9) clothing; (10) recreation and entertainment; (11) social security; (12) human freedom.[13]

The practical import of such attempts remains largely symbolic. Even where they have led to concrete action in the direction of meeting basic needs, self-sufficiency in food production, or appropriate technologies, their overall impact has been questionable. The results of applying such criteria have not been without ambiguities, and such policies have not had sufficient impact to bring about changes in the dominant GNP-based perspective. In short, they have contributed to further emptying the development concept of any precise content, while underlining the paradoxes and impasses of the grand society. Thus development today ends up meaning fighting against growth; the grand society can keep its promises only through destroying its foundations, especially at the ecological level; and so on.

The battle against misery has been declared, and indeed has been pursued with great violence. Who really has been concerned about the underlying ambiguities of the whole campaign? A few isolated voices, at times prestigious ones like Gunnar Myrdal's, have made themselves heard, but to little effect. The struggle, daggers drawn, for the highest standard of living per head, has become an obsession in the international arena, while the reduction of the gap between the well-off and the wretched remains declared as the priority objective. Each country, by any means still compatible with maintenance of world peace (and sometimes not restricted by that), endeavours to gain over its neighbours and to carve out a slice of the market for itself at the expense of others. Tariff and non-tariff protection, subsidies and fiscal policies, industrial politics (that of MITI, the Ministry of Industry in Japan, for example), the dismantling of social security systems, deregulation, and the most cynical marketing and wage-bargaining ploys, are among the gamut of the obvious stratagems in this mad scramble. With a sometimes unconscious hypocrisy, the winners then lend a helping hand to the laggards so that they may catch up. The experts possess miracle prescriptions for any problem, guaranteed to work as long as they are given free play at both state and private enterprise levels. They hope to succeed (though nobody knows how) in squaring the circle.

The notion of the standard of living carries in itself the demand for equality at the same time as a competitive spirit. By this miraculous conjunction everyone will be saved, and everyone will be a winner.

The ancient origins and significance of 'standard of living'

'Standard of living' encapsulates all the dimensions of the dominant paradigm of the West, of modernity and of development. This paradigm constitutes a perfectly auto-referential sphere made up of only a very limited number of elements. The interaction of these elements is auto-dynamic; the system as a whole works supposedly to provoke unlimited growth of material wealth.

The standard of living concept thus has the same historical origins as the general economic paradigm itself, and it is possible to make out the tortuous genesis of the modern usage. Everything revolves around the reduction of the *good* to the question of *how much*. This transition simultaneously eliminated the possibility of admitting a plurality of social values, and allowed the quantification of the sole dimension retained.

Life, if it is a question of its level, is in itself a multiform effervescence. It is a 'melting-pot of passions' rather than a cold and calculating reasoning. The standard of living can become an objective in life only through an inhibition of perception, a limitation of ambition, and an outright repression of emotional impulses.

The objective of a 'good life' can manifest itself in a whole host of different ways, from the warrior's heroism to asceticism, from Epicurean enjoyment to aesthetic toil. However, the insertion of the good life within a larger framework of the presumed *common good* requires reduction of the manifold personal arts of living and diverse ways of knowing, down somehow to a single collective project. This can easily come to imply, as regards ends and even means, a homogenisation of individual pursuits and purposes. It is not by chance that Truman as well as Kennedy referred to the 'common good'.[14] The old Aristotelian and Thomist term evokes much more the ideal of the just and responsible city-state than it does a rich and individualist society. But in the modern world, the only good that appears as common to all people, leaving aside cultural differences, is life as a physiological property – and, *ipso facto*, human life to the detriment of other living species.

This modern cult of life is very different from what can be found in other cultures. In Brahman India, for example, life is also given a pre-eminent value; however, it is envisaged as a cosmic whole. The earthly life of the human individual does not have great meaning and counts for little. Animals and the natural world have as much right to live as man. Since the death of some individuals is the condition of life for others, what is glorified is the dynamic flux that assures the order of the cosmos. Death is not excluded from life.

The West, on the other hand, has long since declared war on death in all its forms, whether through poverty, violence or natural causes. This campaign reduces the 'great life' to a concern with survival. Whereas for the Romans, life without good health wasn't worth living, the quantitative modern cult pushes on to life's artificial extension. Suicide, the abandonment of deformed babies, euthanasia – are all proscribed.[15] What matters is to live more, and not well or better. This selection of the quantum of life as the sole objective comes to be expressed on a double level, physiological and social: on the one hand prolongation of the duration of life, on the other hand elevation of the standard of living. Then these two levels tend to become merged in a naturalist metaphysics, where the concept of 'need' serves as the lynch-pin joining the two levels together.

If we accept the analysis of Illich, the concept of 'need' first arose in application to an individual's spiritual condition. The Middle Ages saw the emergence of a privileged class, the religious professionals, defined as uniquely capable of satisfying the need each individual had for ensuring his or her soul's salvation.[16] In its transposition into the secular sphere, the concept of needs retains this double structure: every individual has needs; the satisfaction of these is dependent on an outside expertise. At the physiological level, need now refers to the number of calories per head, with various correlates like the amount of protein, fat and carbohydrate. At the social level, it is the number of dollars. Survival for everyone also becomes a political end; this was a purpose of the Leviathan, the great technocrat of the seventeenth century; similarly, on the eve of the French Revolution, the welfare or happiness of everybody ('a new idea in Europe', according to Saint-Just) became the objective of the 'enlightened despot'.

The emergence in ideology and practice of the utilitarian individual seeking to maximise his or her pleasure and to minimise his or her pain, did not translate immediately into triumph for the pursuit of the highest standard of living for one and all. It is useful to repeat this point, which was discussed at length in Chapters 2 and 3, in view of the overly pregnant mythology of the harmony of interests. The logical consequence of the arrival of the calculating subject is, rather, a wild unleashing of *passions*. In England, Puritan inhibition permitted a channelling of these passions into a search for material accumulation. This reduction of the drama of life to a spectacle of transactions in the marketplace was much more difficult to achieve in France. The Marquis de Sade showed with implacable logic the type of anarchy to which calculating individualism could lead when the passions were not suitably throttled. Economic reductionism has succeeded in imposing this repression, funnelling anguishes and desires down onto a single plane, leading to the one-dimensional perspective of the marketplace.

When human happiness comes to be interpreted as merely material well-being, the differences between after-life, worldly happiness and physical survival become blurred. Survival was promised, in the West as in other societies, first of all in the after-life.[17] Loss of a rapport with the dead in the West resulted in the resurrection of the body being given a more and more abstract connotation. An abstract *eternity* in the great beyond took the place of the more concrete sense of *immortality* held by earlier generations. Later, with the proclamation that 'God is Dead', this eternity transposes to the pursuit of a purely secular objective, mere physiological survival. The chasm between the physical and metaphysical is then rebridged when the ideology of economic growth lifts up physical survival to the sacred heights of a general *'well-having'* incarnated in the level of national consumption.

Well-having aims at the maximisation of *'objects'*, i.e. at maximal material throughput. But the 'value' of these objects of consumption remains quite ambiguous. As regards social objects destined for consumption, the accumulation of physical products lacking much practical use has little meaning beyond a certain point. The accumulation of machinery to be used as inputs in production of other goods does have a practical meaning, which consumer goods in themselves lack. The standard of living strictly speaking measures the level of consumption, which means the amount of waste produced. Our gadget-culture is the inevitable end-product of the whole process. Abundance brings with it the loss of meaning of what is consumed. In the deluge of objects, it has become almost impossible to desire something on one's own account rather than because it is an object possessed or desired by others. Advertising plays to the full on this mimetic logic of desire. And ultimately the anguish of having nothing more to desire adds to the distress of desire unsatisfied.

The basis for evaluating both physiological and psychological need is *utility*. The triumph of utilitarianism is thus the necessary condition for the twin sports of maximisation and equalisation of living standards. The reduction of the multiple dimensions of life to what is quantifiable finds its definitive expression in money, and its locus of realisation is the market. Generalisation of the market system accelerates the process of money reductionism, and this in turn facilitates the market's extension. Utilitarian reductionism and the obsession with consumption drive the expansion of markets; and the consumerist logic of increasingly large sectors of social life reinforces the calculating and utilitarian perspective. The secret of the market is to reveal the *'preferences'* of buyers and sellers, and through this to furnish the otherwise impossible measure of usefulness. The market works *well* and brings *good*, under the economists' theory, ensuring that the best use will be made of available factors of production. The citizens, having become agents of the economic machine, end up believing in it. In this way the great myth of modernity is implanted, with its promise that each and every person will be enriched through advances in labour management, science and technology, and that, moreover, there is no end to this accumulation of riches.

The American amassing of riches has become, observes Bertrand de Jouvenel, 'the fairy tale of the modern age'. He points out that with an annual increase in GNP of 3.5 per cent, which was typically a minimum for France in the 1950s, one ends up with a 31-fold increase in a century, and nearly a thousandfold in two centuries – which, obviously, makes no sense.[18]

The incongruity of 'standard of living' in the Third World

The Westernisation of the world has by no means brought about a universal equalising of real living standards. Rather, what has resulted is the imposition of the *concept* of standard of living as the dominant category for perceiving social reality (and therefore underdevelopment), so that achieving an increase in living standards becomes a moral obligation for the leaders of emerging nations.

Attention has often been drawn to the problems associated with transposition of statistical measurement techniques from industrial societies into the Third World. Jean Chesneaux observes:

> The unemployed worker in the slums of Caracas is amazed to discover that he enjoys a standard of living, defined in terms of GDP, which is quite enviable. No less flabbergasted, the fisherman in Samoa who lives quite at ease in relative self-sufficiency, learns that, in terms of GNP, he is one of the poorest inhabitants of the planet.[19]

The first case illustrates how an unequal distribution of wealth removes all meaning from an average figure, while the second reveals the absurdity of international comparison of indices when lifestyles are very different and in fact *non-comparable*. Political economy has not been able to construct a satisfactory theory of the objective value of all things, which means it is impossible to proceed in terms of evaluation and summation of objective *utilities*. These are subjective and by nature mutually incommunicable (the *no-bridge* problem). There is no choice but to be content with a bastard calculus on a basis of *arbitrary conventions*. With careful application this can be useful. But often the attempt is made to give to this empirical 'do-it-yourself' procedure a status that it doesn't properly have, by linking it back in more or less mythical fashion to the neo-classical theory of relative price. The essentially arbitrary and conventional character of the statistical 'cuisine' is often forgotten even by those who do know. Constant reminders about the limitations of national accounting do not go far enough. Arbitrary as the inter-sectoral demarcations used for construction of the social accounting matrices are for the industrialised societies, it borders on the absurd to transpose them outside these developed societies into the Third World.

Competent statisticians have always emphasised the limitations of their methods.[20] In practice these words of caution have gone for nothing, since quantitative reductionism has become so entrenched in the logic of modernity and the spirit of the times cannot be held at bay by ritual precautions. Nevertheless it is useful to recall some of the absurdities involved.

Standard of living is assessed by the volume of goods and services consumed by the inhabitants of a country. However, only the goods and services regularly exchanged on the market enter into this calculation, and these do so even if they are not the object of a genuine exchange. As a result, important aspects of the quality of life are not taken into account; and inversely, those things we 'consume' which imply a degradation in the quality of life are valued and counted as positive contributions. As Bertrand de Jouvenel writes:

> The measure of consumption is simply a measure of goods and services which are obtained from enterprises by private individuals and which are subject to payment. It is apparent that this measure omits: (1) many services rendered by public authorities; (2) free goods and services; (3) external costs inflicted by transformations in the course of economic activity.[21]

Among the things escaping measure are the entirely unpaid services rendered by mothers to their children, without which, of course, there would be no economy at all; and unpaid domestic work in the home, which in the developed countries constitutes a part of the 'hidden' economy. These are aspects of what Illich has called shadow work. For Great Britain, Colin Clark in 1968 estimated the value of unpaid housework as being of the same order as official GNP in 1871, and still amounting to about 50% of the GNP of 1956.[22]

At the other extreme, an increased consumption of fuel due to traffic congestion and longer travel distances between home and work translates into an increase in our consumption of transportation and, therefore, into a rise in the standard of living. As de Jouvenel observes:

In the United States, food consumption per head measured in constant prices, increased by 75% from 1909 to 1957. However, according to the calculations of the Department of Agriculture, the increase in physiological consumption was at most 12 to 15%. This means, as Kuznets suggests, that at least four-fifths of the apparent growth in food consumption is due, in fact, to an increase in transport costs and the distribution of foodstuffs to the urban centres.[23]

Further, the exclusion from valuation of environmental goods in limited quantity, and the inverse practice of taking into account the enormous expenses needed to repair degradations to environmental conditions of life, recreation and work, or to compensate for them, introduces additional distortions. 'According to our way of counting,' de Jouvenel observes ironically, 'we would enrich ourselves by making the Tuileries into a parking lot and by turning the Cathedral of Notre Dame into an office building.'[24]

Using this particular notion of national accounts, reflecting a particular Western interpretation of reality, the underdeveloped countries appear poor in ways that we think ourselves rich; but conversely they are (and were) infinitely richer in some things in which we are now poor. They have at their disposal goods and services which are non-measurable or undervalued – and fragile – such as open space, the warmth of the tropics, leisure, solidarity, and so on. By the prevailing standards of the world system, their purchasing power, which comes more and more to signify their power in any terms, is infinitely smaller. But this measures only the *Westernised portion* of their socio-economic reality.

The paternalism of the international agencies dealing with the Third World is premised on a terrifying ethnocentrism. If we were to pursue a true and genuine internationalism, or universalism, the proper approach would be to invite 'experts' from the last remaining 'primitive' regions of the world to draw up a list of the 'lacks' from which we, the people of the *developed* countries, suffer: loneliness, depression, stress, neuroses, insecurity, violence, crime rates, and so on.

Yet all these considerations, however cogent, still do not challenge at its roots the logic of economic reductionism. They amount to words of warning, little heeded in most cases even though on some occasions they are given weight. Similarly, for some years now, well-intentioned statisticians have been providing estimates of negative externalities, such as pollution, and trying to suggest corrective measures. While these efforts are significant and make an important contribution to policy debate, they are inevitably limited in practical effect and do not question the underlying valuation logic.

Things would change if one were to reconsider radically the question of the basis for drawing the boundaries around the 'economic' domain – i.e. how the basic categories such as production, consumptiona and work are defined. The early economists, when they were searching to find the essence of economic activity behind the appearances of the market process, actually struggled at length with this problem. Thomas Malthus, for example, wrote at length of his perplexity:

> If the exertion which produces a song, whether paid for or not, be productive labour, why should the exertion which produces the more valuable result of instructive and agreeable conversation be excluded? Why should we exclude the efforts necessary to discipline our passions, and become obedient to all the laws of God and man, the most valuable of all labours? Why, indeed, should we exclude any exertion, the object of which is to obtain happiness or avoid pain, either present or future? And yet under this description may be comprehended the exertions of every human being during every moment of his existence.[25]

Indeed, why shouldn't a dance staged to ask the spirits for a rich harvest be considered as work? Why shouldn't the tom-tom played next to the campfire be considered as the production of leisure services, or the caresses of a wife as part of national consumption? Is not the use of a personal vehicle the production of a transport service? Its purchase an investment? Isn't the work expended by the labourer at a factory the consumption of accumulated energy, i.e. of capital?

At this point all the boundaries break down, and traditional reference points fade away as soon as one throws off the shackles of the taboos governing habitual practice in the tribe of economists and their supporting statisticians. Malthus and the economists after him, threatened with vertigo, had no choice but to take refuge in common sense. In practice, this 'common sense' serves to keep non-sense at bay. It interprets the practices of the European marketplace on the basis of well-established prejudices. But it is the Western consciousness alone that has established this system of classification. There is no 'work' in the modern sense without the 'Protestant ethic';[26] no production (in the modern goods and services sense) without the myths of nature, need, scarcity and a conception of matter borrowed from eighteenth-century physics; no commodity consumption without the generalised market. What may separate, in the infinite variety of human activity, playful gestures from productive acts, the object produced from the object consumed, is entirely dependent upon particular cultural norms and values. Rearing an animal, a dog or a cow for example, could be considered as investment, production, or consumption, depending on the animal's habitat and whether it is intended to hunt, plough, provide meat, parade, or show affection. *The currently dominant accounting categories represent a radical form of cultural imperialism.* It is not only that happiness and the joy of living in countries of the Third World are reduced to some paltry level of GNP per head by this world-scale statistical butchery, but also that the very substance of this life in its richness and potential is scorned and misunderstood. As Ivan Illich has said: 'Up to now, all efforts to substitute a universal commodity for a local value have resulted not in equality, but in a hierarchical modernisation of poverty'[27] – in other words, in misery and dereliction.

Paradoxically, the fascination with a rising standard of living is often even greater among the populations of the Third World than in the West. The reason is easy to understand. Neophytes to the cult of the gods of modernity as they are, the social classes uprooted by change in their societies give themselves over with frenzied urgency to the prospects held out by modern life. They see increase in monetary income as their only means of regaining some sort of social status. Those in the West, or at least some of them, are by now a bit blasé, and have acquired a certain reserve and maybe some new wisdom. The West has become attuned to criticisms of the growth concept and aware of the so-called 'limits to growth'; people are holding onto traditional values (or a nostalgia for them), or inventing anti-utilitarian 'post-modernities'. All the same, this paradox does not much alter the general drift of the story: post-modernity for the rich remains a somewhat abstract, whimsical, utopian affair compared with the concrete solidity of life for the castaways in the informal sphere.

The denied richness of the other and the rediscovery of the plurality of life

In the effort to measure the standard of living in the Third World, with the laudable goal of raising it, a tragic farce has been perpetrated. The attempt to increase well-being has contributed more and more to the negation of being itself. Not only has the wealth of the 'other' been occulted (even lost in the others' own estimation of their worth), but the very basis for its survival is threatened. Wealth and poverty are eminently relative. Not only do they depend on the reference points adopted, they also depend on the view of reality employed. So for instance, as the ethno-geographer Joël Bonnemaison has put it, the island of Tanna in the New Hebrides

> is rich and poor simultaneously, according to the interpretation which is adopted. Its people live in a certain abundance if looked at in their traditional terms, but they look 'proletarian' if seen from the imported socio-economic perspective.[28]

All the values which fail to pass through the filter of quantifiable utility, which are foreign to a 'dollarised' life, tend to be downgraded. Their practices, excluded from the defined standard of living, tend as a result to disappear. This is the case with heroic action, which in warrior societies is more highly cherished than any riches. It is also true of communal solidarity, which is a veritable treasurehouse by which much of the Third World continues to live in defiance of all economic logic. Such practices as ostentatious display, colourful parades, ritual challenges and various forms of sensual enjoyment which enrich social life, are all now beginning to lose meaning. Yet what sense does a rise in the standard of living have for a nomad society in the desert which aspires to lightness and frugality? One can apply to most traditional societies what Evans-Pritchard observed of the Nuer in Africa: quite simply, accumulating wealth is not a priority and it has no significance in defining social status: 'Wealth makes no difference.'[29]

In practical fact, the obsession with the standard of living and its increase has brought about an unprecedented impoverishment of life through neglect of its principal dimensions. Death, for one, is shunned, devalued. It is viewed as the insolvency of the human enterprise, the inevitable loss posted on the bottom line whatever the credits entered on the balance sheet.

In many previous societies, wealth was considered a gift left behind by the dead and had meaning in its 'material' or accumulative form only as a proof of recognition by the living of their debt to the dead. Death and the dead are, however, completely expelled from the realm of economics and deleted from the inventory of stocks made by the living. This loss of meaning of death is perhaps the greatest source of 'impoverishment' of modern man. There is no longer any price that can buy reconciliation. Western man is condemned to live his death as a failure, and to kill his own life in order to ease the pain and forget the final absurdity.

Illness and ageing are likewise seen as flaws and failings. One part of the hidden treasure of Third World societies is the way in which they relate to the old and the sick. Illness and ageing are not considered as maledictions of nature which separate the individual from the world of the living and which must be treated in isolation, the victim ashamed and guilty. Illness may be a source of tragic conflict if the cause is attributed to sorcery, but it is also a source of personal and social enrichment. Suffering has become unbearable and intolerable in the West only because it no longer has meaning. The fact that pain is inherent in the human condition, and perhaps necessary, highlights to what extent its refusal and trivialisation contribute to our impoverishment. Similarly, old age is honoured in non-Western societies because it is the elders who transmit the knowledge gained through their experience and familiarity with tradition. It is also true that they are not very numerous. In the West, by contrast, the combination of lower birth rates and longer average lifespan has led to the old becoming an 'encumbrance' on our societies, devalued because of their artificial exclusion from active life, often abandoned and in some cases frankly mistreated.

Our impoverishment culminates in contempt for poverty. Most cultures honour their poor. The ancient Greeks that we admire so much, found great enjoyment in their leisure and their meagre resources; it was in these conditions that their culture most flourished. Even in the West until the eighteenth century, poverty was not necessarily seen as a disgrace. 'The poor,' writes Alain Caillé, 'were not necessarily to be looked down on, in principle at least.' But he adds:

'Who today could be made to believe that a man without a shirt can be happy? Nobody. And for good reason, because someone without a shirt today must be a rank failure.'[30]

Frugality and austerity are neither defects nor misfortunes. They express socially recognised values and are even at times considered signs of divine choice. The vow of poverty testifies to a desire for holiness. One can even see in this act a utilitarian calculation, inasmuch as one is a believer! As Jacques Austruy says:

> Supposing God's existence, and the world here and now to be a world of ephemeral tests, renunciation of the goods of this world in order to 'gain' eternal life in paradise is a form of saving, the interest payable being infinitely more than anything hitherto known, in the management of the valley of tears.[31]

The trouble is that once one postulates, as Pascal did, this connection with the beyond in terms of calculation and reasoned bet, faith no longer comes into it. The introduction of Western reason into morality has killed the wisdom that nourished earlier societies. According to the Stoics, true richness consists in limiting desires. Most schools of wisdom, and in particular Buddhism, which continues to prosper, define the acquisition of self-mastery as the goal of existence, and see the secret of a happy life in moderation in pleasure and preservation of an equilibrium between different values, never unlimited accumulation on a single plane. Material deprivation, which we take as the sole criterion defining a disreputable poverty, was in traditional societies often no more than a minor aspect alongside *other* purifications. For the Serere in Senegal, as for many others, the *true* misery is loneliness. According to a Serere proverb, 'Poverty is not a matter of having no clothes, the truly poor person is one who has no one.'[32]

All societies have their own concept of 'wealth', and this concept is expressed most often with tangible indicators. It includes all the natural or man-made objects and all the cultural gestures and creations (names, dances, chants) that are individually or collectively available. Possession of these values confers a status, a prestige and a power in society. Moreover, even the most 'primitive' of non-Western societies are acquainted with some sort of 'paleo-monetary' goods. These often serve as a sort of measure of wealth. Some social rituals centre around the concentration or the consumption of what Bataille calls *'la part maudite'*, the accursed share, the surplus to be disposed of. These

'riches', incarnated in material objects, and to some extent autonomous from general social *values*, are not identifiable with wealth as
in the West. The modes of production, circulation, exchange, accumulation, and destruction of these ritual riches differ; their 'purchasing
power' is particular to the situation; and the 'games' involving such
wealth do not usually have the power totally to disrupt society. But
when the West's 'general equivalent' – the dollar – and the sophisticated gadgetry that accompanies it are introduced, all this specific
'wealth' is delegitimated. Cowrie shells, Amerindian wampum, the
sacred stones of the Lapps, the beaten copper kettles of the North-West
American Kwakiutl, all these have no place in the world economy.

Conversely, in making the material necessities of life enter into the
circulation of wealth, modern affluent society creates true penury.
This is what puts the poor at risk of dying from hunger: they cannot
afford to buy what they need to live. Thus the poor become the
miserable. Péguy, long ago, contrasted poverty to misery. According
to Paul Dumouchel, 'misery, whether material or spiritual, always
takes the form of exclusion and isolation'. He further states:

> Misery never occurred in primitive societies, because the obligations of
> solidarity prevented it from existing just as they forestalled scarcity. ...
> Even if the primitives are poor, tremendously poor, they are not ac-
> quainted with this alteration of character and life that misery induces.[33]

It often happens that these 'wealths' of primitive people are trans-
muted into money on contact with the West. This arises because the
primitive people realise that money in our world takes the place of
their riches; but there remains one difference: their own riches engender neither disreputable poverty nor absolute destitution.

The concept of the standard of living has imposed itself with the
force of a truth beyond all dispute because it is inscribed in the logic
of modernity itself. But the universality of the concept is as fallacious
as that of the West. Its promises are as illusory as those of development. It stands as the symbol of the grand society. By the same token,
the evident failure of development, of modernity and of Westernisation, gives us a chance to recognise the phantasmagorical character
of the standard-of-living fetish and to rediscover the multidimension-
ality of life.

A grand society of beggars

Is it better to be poor than rich? It is well-known that Aristotle, like most of the sages in antiquity, considered material riches in an unfavourable light. The preoccupation with acquisition and management of personal wealth and property was not conducive, he thought, to the practice of virtue. It is recounted none the less that he replied to a disciple questioning him on this point: 'It is better to be rich than to have to beg at the rich man's table.' Frugality and material poverty are not vices, it is dependency that is dishonourable. In Xenophon's *Memoirs*, Socrates is supposed to have suggested to Euthero, who was obliged to till his own land to the detriment of his health, that he should hire himself out to a better-off citizen. Euthero retorted with pride that he would never accept *servitude* any more than he would be a beggar.[34]

For a long time after that in the West, and in some places until very recently, to 'work for someone else' indicated a *fallen state*, not much less degrading than begging. It was not dishonourable to sponge off a parent, a friend, or a protector, but it *was* to earn one's living through dependent employment. Although the degree of disrepute in which the hired worker or beggar was held could vary, the common point was that poor people, if reduced to one or other of these states, became shameful in their poverty. Contempt for the destitute in their wretched state contrasts with the respect accorded to dignified poverty. Until the industrial age, the norm was not so much to *create employment* as a way of providing incomes for the poor, as to offer them plots of land and thereby provide them with resources. Heteronomy, meaning simple dependency on others, was an indignity that one did not dare to impose even on the indigent.

Our rise in per capita standard of living, of which we are so proud, has been obtained only at the price of submission to wage-labour, that is, the loss of independence and autonomy. This reaches its height with the richest, who lower themselves to the point of becoming gilt-edged 'beggars'. For G.H. Radkowski, the whole of advertising, and all of what G.K. Chesterton called beggary by the rich, is part of the fall from grace of our 'elites' – door-to-door canvassers, sales representatives, marketing activity, sales promotions, market research, commercial delegations, and so on, up to high-level trade missions seeking to pull off the 'deal of the century', or indeed fraud and duplicity in the attempt to 'buy' potential clients (as in the recent Euro-Japanese scandal revealed by the 'Lockheed Affair').[35]

It is impossible even to watch a television drama without being importuned by the scandalous irruption of this *new beggar class*. Television films are sliced up by 'ads'; classical music concerts are 'sponsored' by oil companies and the like. The loss by the propertied classes of their traditional pride, and the disappearance of any sense of honour in the chase after money, brings about a confusion of values and a degradation of moral sense.

This 'demoralisation' is tending to spread throughout society. Sporting individuals first, but also artists go 'door-to-door' seeking sponsors. Intellectuals, including some of the most brilliant, have their hearts set on 'selling themselves' and go off in search of 'juicy' contracts. Honoré de Balzac, in lauding Stendhal, stigmatised the shameless pursuit of success:

> I like that proudness of character or that sense of self-worth. While one might be able to excuse begging, nothing pleads in favour of this seeking after flatteries and articles that modern authors give themselves over to. This is a beggary, a pauperism of the spirit.[36]

The patronage of yesterday did not always do honour to the talent thus purchased, unless the princes in question gained no other profit than a bit of incense. These days, the 'sponsors' get benefits through promotion of sales. By contrast with a patron, writes Wladmir Andreff, 'a sponsor considers his investment in sport as a professional activity, whose likely publicity and financial returns are carefully assessed, and to which he devotes the last of his efforts and all his negotiating skills'.[37] As to those who are 'sold', they glory in this display of servility and bootlicking. It is a no-holds-barred race, a competition to see who can carry depravity the furthest. Drawing attention to oneself through the crassest come-ons, flattery of the authorities, glowing overtures to the powers-that-be about the services that one could offer, all this has become a 'must', as the vile idiom has it. The 'me me me' is no longer detestable, one is learning how to put it to work: there are even specialist schools teaching the art of self-adulation. The ancients ran after 'honours' in order to reach immortality. The moderns do business in reputation without the slightest concern for the lifetime of the product.

Most of our contemporaries do not in any way feel this as a spiritual degradation or as a humiliation to the soul. Under the banner of communication techniques and lobbying, the debasement of thought becomes an art in itself. Anything goes in the effort to heap blame on the antisocial intellectual who baulks at courting media attention, or the academic who refuses to prostitute himself incessantly before the moneylenders. Observing this general complicity in vacuity is rather distressing. It suggests a disturbing corruption of values. Is not this attitude of indifference to abject behaviour a sign of wretchedness within our society as a whole? The 'true misery' perhaps lies in this across-the-board obligation to earn one's salary by begging it from someone else through flattery of their basic instincts, rather than appealing to the nobility of their sentiments.

Of course, one might consider this point of view as nostalgia for a dead world and attachment to the values of a long-gone age. It is clear that I am speaking of another time. What I am trying to convey here is that business morality, this ethic of autonomous individuals, free and strong, gets perverted into a generalised corruption and solicitation of people's interests (often the basest ones), simply because consumers, users, agents and managers are all to greater or lesser extent human, and thus subject to psychological weaknesses. Everyone strives to *manipulate* everyone else, and all are more or less manipulated. The exaltation of the autonomy of the individual leads, in fact, to the triumph of a depersonalising heteronomy. More generally, we are seeing the 'prostitution of speech' denounced by Illich: 'the dollars spent to power any nation's motors pale before those that are now expended on prostituting speech in the mouths of paid speakers'.[38]

Goaded by ambition, idleness, or perhaps simply in an attempt to get out of the red, many colleagues, with an admirable show of enterprise, are inventing new disciplines that will be 'saleable' to the authorities or wealthy institutions. The number of *niches* grows and grows. In this way we get an economics of health, an economics of education, an economics of culture. But these domains are in turn infinitely divisible; one can specialise in the economics of mental health or the economics of Aids, in the economics of fashion, of music, of sport, of the cinema. One might go a lot further; and the same is true in psychology, sociology, anthropology, even geography and psychoanalysis.[39]

It is difficult to know what to say to all this. After all, it is *useful* for the authorities to be informed; in modern society, large sums of money are at stake in all these fields, and these ought not to be spent irresponsibly, above all when it involves the taxpayers' money. The decision-makers' options have to be made as clear as possible through a good knowledge of the facts. If possible the choices should be rational.

Empiricists, survey-makers, field-economists, data-collectors, statisticians and the like provide the factual knowledge. The 'formalisers' (who erroneously take themselves for theoreticians), makers of mathematical models, furnish the instruments for rational decisions. The institutions are willingly persuaded of the necessity of these propositions and of their legitimacy; they may even be the instigators of them. They 'cough up' without much need for arm-twisting. The sums that fatten the researchers, or at least ensure them a mediocre survival, are usually modest compared with the overall budgets for the projects in question.

Secondarily, these disciplinary creations permit a multiplication in the supply of thesis topics, which thus responds to the growing demand. Or indeed this might be the starting point of the whole process. Thesis candidates are interested in finding some financial support, and their supervisors will encourage them in this quest if they haven't headed off in that direction already. From this point, a research team will quickly be established, growing in accordance with Parkinson's Law. It will need more detailed data. This makes necessary a centre for statistics-gathering in the area, staffed full-time. In the space of a generation, I have observed this process at work and watched offices of all sorts, big and small, prosperous and insolvent, sprout up before my eyes. Some die, but most often just to be reborn under another form and grow up again. The process is far from reaching an end. It just goes on and on. The possible territories to be claimed are endless. And anyway, it is hard to mount an effective criticism: for not only is it difficult to avoid being compromised oneself, more importantly one is confronted with the evident utility of it all, and to speak against utility is a crime against reason.

The trouble is that if we follow this process through, we end up with the paradox of planning denounced by the Hungarian economist Janos Kornai. To satisfy the need for knowledge, the whole population will soon find itself engaged in finding out what it is doing. As long as machines produce for us the 'necessary' goods, there is virtually no limit to the process. One might imagine an economics of the economics of health, and why not an economics of the economics of the economics of health?

Is it really useful for the 'leisure society' to sacrifice its *joie de vivre* to an obsessional quest for knowledge of its obsession for knowledge? The more leisure appears possible, the further away it gets. Women find themselves condemned to the bind of work – even if this is sometimes experienced as a sort of 'liberation' given how intolerable housework has become, and given also the extent to which a second income has become a necessity. This shadow work which grows along with industrialisation has now reached such proportions that to speak of leisure for non-salaried hours becomes a bit of a joke: the time spent organising one's living space, 'reconstructing' one's body, not to say the many hours per week for commuting to the distant suburbs.

Knowledge produced in these conditions is not innocent, rather it is technocratic and calculating. It works to reinforce the economisation of life and the technification of attitudes and ways of doing things.

Such is the outcome of the fight for life among intellectuals: beggary with ever-increasing perverse effects. Most often, the process is described on the assumption of innocence and honesty on the part of the actors in it. It would require a fair heroism and lucidity not to succumb – two qualities that are extremely rare in contemporary society and certainly not encouraged, since they bring no tangible gain.

The society of the castaways can function only on some other logic, with some *other* wealth, and an *other* poverty.

Notes

1. From *Chuang-Tzu*, ch. xxviii. Here rendered from the French in Lie-Tsu et al., *Philosophes taoïstes*, op. cit., p. 312. A rather different translation is offered by A.C. Graham, from the Chinese to English, in *Chuang-Tzu: the inner chapters*, Mandala, London, 1991, p. 228: 'As I have heard it, lack of means is called "poverty", proving incapable of living by the Way one was taught is called "deteriorating". The trouble with me now is poverty, not deterioration.' Cf. also *Chuang-Tzu*, ch. xx (in Graham's translation, ibid., p. 120),where Chuang-Tzu replies to the King of Wei: 'A man having the Way and the Power but being unable to act on them, that's sinking low. Having tattered clothes and holes in your shoes is poverty, it isn't sinking low. This is what they call being born in unlucky times.'
2. The several sections following are a reworking of the essay 'Standard of living',

pp. 250-63 in Wolfgang Sachs (editor), *The Development Dictionary*, Zed Books, London, 1992.

3. Harry S. Truman, 'Address on Point 4', op. cit., p. 105.

4. Jean Fourastier, in 'Niveau de vie' (Standard of living), in Jean Romoeuf's *Dictionnaire des Sciences Economiques*, Presses Universitaires de France, Paris, 1958, p. 800.

5. Bertrand de Jouvenel, *Arcadie*, op. cit., p. 170.

6. Georges Hubert Radkowski, *Métamorphoses de la valeur: essai d'anthropologie économique*, Presses Universitaires de Grenoble, Grenoble, 1987.

7. Covenant of the League of Nations, 28 June 1919, Article 22.

8. Carl Brinkmann, 'Standards of living', in *Encyclopedia of the Social Sciences*, London, 1934, pp. 322-4. See also the entry under 'standard' in the *Oxford English Dictionary*, 2nd edition, p. 505.

9. J. Davis, 'Standards and contents of living', *American Economic Review*, vol. 35, no. 1 (March 1945), pp. 1-15.

10. For once at least, the French language is less ambiguous than English: the expression *niveau de vie* clearly indicates a positively established fact, and its recent appearance has prevented any semantic ambiguity. The merit of this expression derives partly from the fact that it condenses together a whole series of related notions – subsistence level, income level, average per capita income, living conditions, consumption expenditures, cost of living, minimum wage, and so on. – *Translators' note*.

11. Robert McNamara, 'Address to the Board of Governors', World Bank, Nairobi, 24 September 1973. In Report WBI 3/2: G14, 1973, p. 12.

12. See the report 'L'ONU dresse le palmarès du "développement humain"', in *Libération*, 25 May 1990.

13. United Nations, *Report on International Definition and Measurement of Standard Levels of Living*, Document E.CN 5/299, 1954.

14. Truman, 'Inaugural Address' and 'Address on Point 4', op. cit.; J.F. Kennedy, 'Inaugural Address to Congress', given on 20 January 1961.

15. The callous disregard for life of the Nazis and of fascism is only an apparent exception. Death is exalted in the service of the state (eugenics, extermination, etc.). The phrase '*viva la muerte!*' of the Francoist General Quepo de Llano expresses the mistrust of the joys of life, not a recognition of Nietzsche's 'great life'. There is a kind of inversion of equivalent values taking place: modern life is death, let us therefore exalt death in order to try to give meaning again to life.

16. Ivan Illich, *Shadow Work*, op. cit., p. 61.

17. This is a play on the French 'la survie' which can mean both survival and after-life. – *Translators' note*.

18. Bertrand de Jouvenel, *Arcadie*, op. cit., pp. 132-3.

19. J. Chesneaux, *Modernité-monde*, op. cit., p. 64.

20. See, in particular, NBER, *Studies in Income and Wealth* of the US National Bureau of Economic Research (*Problems in the International Comparison of Economic Accounts*, vol. XX).

21. Bernard de Jouvenel, *Arcadie*, op. cit., p. 178.

22. Colin Clark, 'The economics of housework', *Bulletin of the Oxford Institute of Statistics*, vol. XX, no. 2, May 1958; cited by Bernard de Jouvenel, *Arcadie*, op. cit., pp. 178ff.

23. Bertrand de Jouvenel, *Arcadie*, op. cit., p. 170.

24. Ibid., p. 267.

25. Thomas Malthus, *Principles of Political Economy*, 1st edition, London, 1820, p. 42. In the 2nd edition (1836, reprinted by Augustus Kelly, New York, 1968), the same theme is traversed at greater length, the entire chapter 1 (pp. 21-49) being devoted to discussion of the question 'Of the definitions of wealth and of productive labour'. He complains, for instance (ibid., p. 23), that it is unhelpful to make a broad definition of wealth that 'includes every thing whether material or intellectual, whether tangible or otherwise, which contributes to the advantage or pleasure of mankind, and of course includes the benefits and gratifications derived from religion, from morals, from political and civil liberty, from oratory, from instructive and agreeable conversation, from music, dancing, acting, and all personal qualities and services.' So finally, in the name of workable definitions, he concerns himself primarily with 'the labour which is realised on material objects [which] is the only kind that is at once susceptible of accumulation and definite valuation' (ibid., p. 46).

26. As in the works of Max Weber, this convenient expression relates less to the Reformation religions than to certain secular forms of puritanism that are found as well in some Catholic traditions like Jansenism and Pietism.

27. Ivan Illich, *Shadow Work*, op. cit., p. 4.

28. Joël Bonnemaison, *La Dernière Ile*, Arlea/Orstom, Paris, 1986, p. 157.

29. Edward E. Evans-Pritchard, *The Nuer: a description of the modes of livelihood and political institutions of a Nilotic people*, Clarendon Press, Oxford, 1940, p. 181.

30. Alain Caillé, *Critique de la raison utilitaire*, op. cit., p. 118.

31. Jacques Austruy, *Marginalia*, June 1969; cited by Claude Albagli in *L'Economie des dieux céréaliers*, op. cit., p. 72.

32. 'Rafle, du nâkk, yërë, waaye ki rafle movy ki annul nit', cited by Emmanuel Ndione, *Dynamique urbaine d'une société en grappe*, op. cit., p. 154.

33. Paul Dumouchel & Jean-Pierre Dupuy, *L'Enfer des choses*, op. cit., pp. 206-7.

34. Xenophon, *Memoirs of Socrates*, Penguin, 1970, bk. II, ch. 8, pp. 110-11. See also Hannah Arendt, *The Human Condition*, op. cit., p. 82.

35. Georges Hubert Radkowski, *Métamorphoses de la valeur*, op. cit., p. 72.

36. Honoré de Balzac, *Etude sur la Chartreuse de Parme de Monsieur Beyle*, Climats, 1989.

37. Wladimir Andreff, *La Diversité des pratiques sportives et la 'marchandisation' du sport*, op. cit., p. 39.

38. Ivan Illich, *Shadow Work*, op. cit., p. 65.

39. All these examples really exist. One could furnish authors and titles. I have even seen the birth of a semiotics of ice-hockey.

7

The New Society of the Castaways

The island of the non-Crusoes

Daniel Defoe's *Robinson Crusoe*, whose pages have enraptured every Western adolescent, is one of the true founding myths of the grand society. This castaway is the individual *par excellence:* a true WASP (White Anglo-Saxon Protestant). Crusoe is a child of the Enlightenment, Faustian and Promethean; he makes rational use of the scarce means available to him in order to obtain from nature all that she can give him. This is *Homo oeconomicus*. Friday, servant and brother, benefits from the Declaration of Human Rights *without* being a citizen. Collaborating with the victor, he thus avoids being vanquished, and participates in his master's victory like any loyal employee of a capitalist firm. Crusoe, the *natural* individual, is the prototype of the capitalist proprietor and patron, and the representative of the rich developed countries. Friday, the *denatured animal*, emancipated thanks to Robinson, is the prototype of the proletariat and representative of the LDCs (less developed countries). The Robinson Crusoe myth retells our own history.

Development's castaways do not resemble Robinson Crusoe at all. They are more like betrayed Fridays, misled and abandoned by their master. Having embarked by choice or duress on the good ship of development, the storm has thrown them into the sea in proximity to some desert islands. They can attempt to cling desperately to the wreckage, trying, against all odds, to regain the vessel as it goes down. Or they may set foot on these new shores and sort out a way to survive. Crusoe was set up on his island with a double endowment, his puritan education and a tool box, that is, Western culture and industrial technology. Development's castaways also have a double techno-cultural heritage: the residue of their irremediably lost former identity, and the aborted passage through an inaccessible modernity. This double bastard allotment is undoubtedly an encumbrance, and the paradoxes and contradictions inherent in it may lead to madness, paranoia and death. How can the tensions be resolved between the incompatible cultures, or between the unlimited promises of the Western dream and the frightful denudation of harsh reality?

The message from the informal sector provides, on this point, a glimmer of hope. Even if theoreticians, scientists and philosophers cannot see how to achieve a synthesis between tradition and modernity, between the West and its other, development's castaways may succeed in practice in inventing a life, in reconstructing a *sociality* through a more or less happy fusing together of the different elements.

The spectre of misery is certainly not the most dangerous threat facing the castaways' society. The informal domain already demonstrates that solidarity is a form of true wealth. To put one's 'poverty' in common in the hope of obtaining abundance is not entirely unrealistic. The social functioning of the neo-tribal networks *produces* the equivalent of new services and even new material goods. The economy of reciprocity, with its complex obligations, is not merely a mode of *circulation* of previously existing goods produced outside the networks; it is in itself productive, without this being taken account of, and *without the society itself knowing it* – which indicates the extent to which the re-embedding of the economic within the social effaces any trace of its presence. These loans and borrowings, whether within familial networks, revolving credit unions, or along other lines, have the role that banking services do elsewhere. The collective preparation of meals, or various repair, maintenance and installation services, undertaken *naturally*, have the worth of housebuilding, plumbing or interior decorating enterprises. This applies equally to shoe-making, metalworking, cabinet-making, baking, and also education and health. The communal organisation of the outcasts brings with it a *production* of collective goods, from refuse collection to cultural activities (theatre and festivals), which never appears as such, because it is immersed within the sociality. The poor are far richer than they are said to be, or than they believe themselves. The incredible *joie de vivre* that strikes many observers in African suburbs misleads less than the depressing objective evaluations using statistical apparatus which discern only the Westernised part of wealth and poverty.

Prophetic cults and syntheses

This concrete synthesis achieved in informal production is augmented by the synthesis at the symbolic level effected by 'prophets'. Among the false prophets, the demagogues who exploit the frustrations of the castaways to obtain power or wealth, there are more substantial attempts at making sense in a new way of what modernity's irruption has spawned, while drawing on currents of traditional metaphysics. Prophets are found everywhere in the Third World. The global triumph of science has not expelled religious sentiment. New cults flourish which seek to give some sense to the tension born from the loss of reference points and the heightening of frustrations.[1]

The rejection of Christianity on the island of Tanna (Vanuatu) and the resurrection of *custom* by the 'John Frum' movement is an interesting example. According to Joël Bonnemaison,

> the Tanna custom represents a lot more than just a formalised replication of the traditional society, it may well one day appear, paradoxically, as the prefiguring of an abruptly 'new' style.[2]

In the whole of Melanesia, the *kastom* (custom in the local pidgin) furnishes the 'alternative' to the West. 'The Whites have money, we have custom,' say the natives. Two systems of values are involved, with two different modes of representation. In the *kastom* as reinterpreted by the prophets, bedazzling modernity is exorcised as being a dangerous mirage. In resuscitating custom, the John Frum movement has given renewed life to a view and experience of the world as an enchanted garden. Custom is linked back to the very foundations of what gives meaning to life, to the land, to the roots, whereas the Whites' custom, money, touches only the surface.

The words of John Frum, as told in the founding myth, reveal the effort to re-establish the proper order of things:

> The Whites have the power of knowledge. The Blacks have the power of life. Knowledge without life, is nothing. The Whites possess pencil and paper, you possess the rocks and plants. The pencil and book make possible the manufacture of airplanes and submarines, but the rocks and plants allow foods to ripen, pigs to grow large and to return when they get lost, allow the sun to rise, the rain-charged clouds to come to the island and refill the springs and creeks, the thunder to growl, the tides to rise and fall, the turtles to come up to the island.[3]

The informal economy that the Melanesians are trying to establish on a primarily rural base is designed to avoid accumulation by an individual entrepreneur; it seeks to put into operation particular modern techniques in a collective way. It should not be inferred from this example, however, that rural and urban forms are necessarily antagonistic. They can often be complementary and mutually nourishing. Contact with rural origins strengthens resistance to the fascination of the West, helping keep alive the founding beliefs for an other *sociality*. The urban environment, by contrast, condemns the have-nots to adoption of modernity's heritage, both on the economic plane and in terms of so-called emancipation. We can see this complementarity in Black Africa and to some extent in Latin America. We also find there varieties of prophetism anchored in tradition and taking hold over modernity. Informal society spreads most of all in the urban periphery, but this is mainly a function of constraints and circumstances. Nothing of its underlying logic, its organisation, or its values is generally hostile to the rural world. In contrast to industrial civilisation, which is built *in opposition to* the country, subordinating and destroying it, the informal society rediscovers the necessity of being rooted in the local region, and of maintaining a peaceful and amicable relationship with nature. The success of the castaways' society is dependent, without doubt, on the achievement of this synthesis of values.[4]

On the other hand, urban prophetism which channels the frustrations of the young, those brought up in not only material but also moral squalor, is a far more aggressive and disquieting phenomenon. Islamic fundamentalist movements are of this type. They derive their support from generations of people who have already lost their roots through mimetic industrialisation and uncontrolled urbanisation. The popular Islam of the traditional countrysides contrasts sharply with the abstract, intellectual and therefore radical urban religion. Born of despair at the impasse of modernity, this messianic movement feeds on the desire for power. It is not really part of the informal society that runs alongside it. It reproduces the domination of town over country. It represents perhaps less a synthesis than an antithesis. As much as it is disconcerting for the West that it destabilises, it is also internally problematical.

Thus, in these reactive creations, there can be found some hopes for success but no certainty. The new haven for the survivors is still to be discovered. A lot of people will, undoubtedly, never get there. Even if the hopes that it fosters make it a desirable goal, the price of the passage should not be ignored. There are plenty of deserts to cross before reaching this promised land.

The Hindu novelist V.S. Naipaul sees the future of India as hopeless. The degeneracy of the civilisation there, he thinks, goes back too far and is irremediable. What remains of it, such as the caste structure and the resignation, is a source of misery, of injustice, of suffocation. Neither mimetism, nor a return to the past, nor a synthesis of tradition with modernity find favour in his eyes. So-called appropriate technologies are costly and ineffective imports; Gandhi and his followers have been able only to comfort the Indians within an apathy that gives no salvation. The culture of poverty is only an illusion or a fraud which masks oppression. And for all that, at the gateways to Bombay,

> the most important discovery was the extent and nature of the Shiv Sena's control. A squatters' settlement, a low huddle of mud and tin and tile and old boards, might suggest a random drift of human debris in a vacant city space; but the chances now were that it would be tightly organized. The settlement ... was full of Sena 'committees' and these committees were dedicated as much to municipal self-regulation as to the Sena's politics.[5]

Do these self-organised Maharashtrian squatters at the heart of the Shiv Sena movement (named after the Marath warrior Shivaji of the seventeenth century, who fought against the Mongol Empire) constitute a ray of hope? For Naipaul, nothing is less certain, since the Shiv Sena is a xenophobic movement which aims to expel the other Indians from the Maharashtra, and because the informal communities reproduce the caste structure: there are 'pariahs of the pariahs'.[6]

An extreme example of dereliction and impasse is given by the Iks, as viewed by Colin Turnbull.[7] As a result of being deprived of its hunting territories, this collection of hunters in the north of Uganda has been transformed into an extreme case of individualistic society. The law of the jungle and the fight for survival are there pushed to a point unknown in the West, putting at risk any maintenance of social relations. By contrast with the many ethnic groups who have preferred to disappear rather than renounce their culture, the Iks have put survival above everything. The result is a surreal form of *post-modern* society, a monstrous parody of our own society, a return to our own mythical origins of a 'state of nature'. This extreme situation is a risk for all the survivors from the grand society, both of the North and of the South.

The town mouse and the country mouse

Speaking of Tanna, we evoked a rural *informality*, that is, an agrarian continent in this planet of survivors we are attempting to explore. The archipelago of the informal hardly makes any appearance in the countryside. The most astonishing examples of the synthesis between inaccessible modernity and lost tradition are encountered in those shantytowns where the outcasts invent for themselves a new culture with its imaginary or symbolic dimension (prophetism), its social structure (neo-tribal relations), and its *economy* (the informal). The time has come, however, to emphasise that not all countrysides stay turned in on their traditions and routines. Alongside the heroic example of the Lobi in Burkina Faso, mentioned at the beginning of this book, enclosed in their ancestral way of thinking and living and voluntarily cut off from the external world through rejection of the White way, alongside the impasse of the Iks just mentioned, there is an *Africa on the move*.[8] The choice made by the Lobi is not unusual; the rejection of change coming from outside and the re-enshrouding inside internal values, erected into certitudes, is found to some extent everywhere in the Third World. It may be sterile for the societies concerned, but there is something grand about it all the same. It has, perhaps, something to offer for the future, which should preserve us from the temptation to condemn it and to intervene to 'make it evolve'. Are past forms ever truly outgrown? This role of *conservatory* warrants great respect even if we do not always understand it.

But the Africa of the villages is not restricted to these extreme forms. There is agreement from many knowledgeable observers, not to say those directly involved, that behind the façade of an undernourished Africa that one sees through the media, there is village life of astonishing vitality. Social movements in the villages also effect the daily synthesis of bastard modernity with elements of a tradition that is in crisis if not lost already. Here also, solidarity and 'neo-tribal' organisation are at the heart of the dynamic. There is a resurgence of associations with traditional sources, for example the *kombi-naam* of Burkina Faso, the *nimbe* of the Shona in Zimbabwe, the *mywethya* of the Kamba in Kenya, the *tons* of the Bambaba in Mali, the *m'botay* of the Ouolofs in Senegal; or new associations like the Six Ss.[9] When they are not overly oppressed, African peasants are perfectly capable of adaptation and innovation. The successful adoption of manioc in the seventeenth and eighteenth centuries, which revolutionised agriculture and food supply, is one example. On comparable soils, with an identical rainfall pattern, certain people such as the Kirdes in North Cameroon obtain a decent living for a population forty times greater than the inhabitants of Tiogo (in Burkina), without recourse to agro-industrial methods. Examples of this sort are not unusual. As Tanganuiwa Kusema, the Vice-President of the Zimbabwe National Association of Farmers, has declared:

> We want to recreate African solidarity on a new basis. We want to reunite people so that they can find their own solutions to their problems. If we get ourselves together, we can find solutions to all our problems.[10]

What matters is precisely this reappropriation of the problems. The Third World has been dispossessed of the management of its destiny and of its crises. When the African peasants are left in charge of their own fate, they demonstrate, like the artisans of the shantytowns, a creativity nothing short of miraculous. Peasant *self-advancement* is here and now a reality. Certainly, even at this level, the insidious Westernisation through the NGOs can lead to some deviations. The humanists in their *moralism* cannot avoid condemning expenditure on intoxicants (kola nuts, millet beer, and worse yet, foreign tobacco and alcohol) as a waste of potential savings, frowning upon the feasts and festivals where the surpluses all go up in smoke (which indeed was often the primary *raison d'être* for the peasant associations such as the *kombi-naam*), and advocate a work-ethic, and of course a 'democratic' form of organisation for the natives.[11] This teaching is dangerous because it is underpinned by money. There are always some schemers around who know how to dress things up to respond to the desires of the generous donor.

It is clear that the synthesis taking place in these sorts of movements introduces new elements. The new associations no longer necessarily have a tribal base; and as in the urban networks, people of different ethnicities can be linked together. The authoritative role of the chief and the power of the elders are no longer what they once were. The most important change, though, is perhaps the emergence, or re-emergence, of a voice for women – who are, in Black Africa especially, key economic actors. One of the causes of failure of policies for peasant settlement and restructuring was the fact that the organisers and designated group leaders were men, whereas the actual cultivation of the land was done by women. Women are traditionally very active in agriculture, but they are no less so in other economic enterprises. One can think of the Mama-Benz, who control the supply and distribution of a range of products in the Gulf of Benin, or the *dolotières* (the women who manufacture and distribute the *dolo*, millet beer) in Burkina Faso. The development of women's networks and the participation of women in mixed networks is, even in the Islamic countries, certainly a key element for the future. One can see here a return of the sorts of 'civil society' which in Black Africa used to accord a major place to women, in the wake of the colonial and post-colonial forms with their official masculine power which was at least partly alien to the local customs.

The population question

The West has placed a time-bomb in the baggage of the castaways: population growth.

The population explosion is not solely the result of the benefits of medicine; it stems equally from deculturation and Westernisation. Deculturation destroys the social structures which, in the past, worked to limit new births. Westernisation removes all the cultural rationale for these limitations. It is undeniable that self-interest pushes the wealthy to restrict their families so as not to compromise their comfort levels, and conversely can encourage the poor to multiply their children so as to increase their security and possibilities. But more fundamentally, the problem is that the key precept of utilitarian morality – the greatest good for the greatest number – works in fact to favour numbers and not happiness. The quantitative valuation of life, on which the Western vision is based, results in life itself, even reduced to mere survival, being regarded as a good to be produced. The proliferation of the human species, even if in a condition of mediocre well-being, is the usual result of pursuing the objective of greatest well-being. The achievement of greatest happiness translates, in effect, into the imperative of maximising the *quantity* of life. Perversely, one can find a justification for this in the Benthamite and neo-classical assumption of decreasing marginal utility of wealth: the accumulation of quantitative wealth in the hands of a particular group results in lower total happiness than its redistribution across a larger number of people.

The dynamic of economic growth also tends to encourage the increase in numbers, because then the responsibilities for support of the non-productive members of society are better spread over a larger young population. This is true even if in the long run it leads to a vicious circle: that one must have an ever-increasing young active population to support the growing numbers of aged people and children. Rich societies are therefore running the risk of seeing the inversion of the age pyramid as a result of their low birth rate. Some demographers, basing their arguments on abstract results from techno-science in agronomy and food biotechnology, argue that the Earth can support 50 to 100 billion human beings. But it is by no means clear whether the tolerance threshold for living a *really human life* has not already been exceeded. If it is not to be a case of feeding human rabbits crowded into hutches in degraded conditions, then numbers are a threat to quality. The greatest number will not be attaining the highest well-being. The rich countries, which have succeeded in reining in their population growth to the point of threatening their reproduction, offer to a growing mass of human beings the vision of survival only at the price of an intolerable degradation of the quality of life, through technical progress whose crazy trajectory is in danger of heading straight to catastrophe. By a kind of historical sleight of hand, the West, which has *destabilised* the rest of the world by its imperialistic expansion, becomes destabilised in its turn. The North, having invaded the South, is under threat of invasion by the sheer fact of numbers. Its wealth, acquired by virtue of global integration, is threatened in turn by this same integration. The pressure of the poor crowded at our doors is becoming intolerable. Our universalist values are in opposition to a closure of borders. Equality and respect for human rights make it imperative that we accept a sharing of opportunities, if not of wealth. We cannot expel the illegal immigrants and refugees without going back on what we ourselves stand for. The objective of the greatest happiness works always in favour of the greatest number.

When Margaret Thatcher sent the Vietnamese boat-people back to their country of origin, even the most xenophobic were made uncomfortable. Bernard Kouchner, the French Secretary of State responsible for humanitarian affairs, wrote: 'I was ashamed by this Western lack of spine, which denies its own values at just the moment when they are triumphing elsewhere.'[12] Of course no one actually offered to welcome them, but very few people find any moral justification for this sacred self-interest.

The exclusion of development's castaways opens up for them the scenario of constructing another society, outside the values of the West. Yet the very possibility of feeding a population in unchecked growth seems ruled out by the exclusion of the technological route, and control over population growth seems distant (even if one can see here and there a drop in fertility). The 'successes' of the informal societies are already threatened by this explosion in numbers. In many regions there are too many workshops, and price competition is leading to a drop in quality and in the qualifications of the producers. A kind of race is in progress, between the construction of a new society able to regulate population, and the continuation of current trends compromising this construction. The figures are enough to induce vertigo. Africa had 219 million inhabitants in 1950, 623 million in 1988, and will probably exceed a billion by the year 2000. Interestingly, however, in the new society of the shantytowns and rural settlements, there is often awareness of the problem. The Naams in Burkina Faso are busy with family planning, as are the women of the greater Yoff in Senegal. Here and there the rural exodus is slowing down, which would in time make more possible the construction of a better-balanced society, with control over demographic and economic dynamics. And when dealing with abstractions it is important to keep things in perspective: after all, what 200 million Americans currently consume would be enough to enable 14 billion Burkinaby people to survive![13]

The issues are weighty and complex. The West has been a civilisation of the *quantitative*. The cult of life without quality, the search for a mechanical and anonymous mode of social organisation, mass-production and consumption, all this indicates indifference to the *person* at the same time as tending to reinforce the production of numbers. On the other hand, the dramatic fall in reproduction rates in the West shows the indifference of the rank and file to the perpetuation and proliferation of the species, if these entail more costs than advantages.

The inverse paradox is observed in the Third World. Children are desired and welcomed as a wealth and a promise. They are constitutive elements of the person, and weave the links between generations. But at the same time, their abundance compromises the maintenance of personal relationships. Here one runs into a new contradiction: social solidarity is forged within large families, but the multiplication of prolific households destroys the very possibility of links of solidarity. A difficult balance has to be found. Nothing says that it necessarily will be. Nor can one assert confidently that the castaways will become conscious soon enough of their predicament and of the possibilities open to them. It is not unreasonable to hope so; equally, it is realistic to assume that the adaptations will not be made without pain.

Holism and individualism

The crisis of modernity and the titanic antagonism between modernity and tradition give rise to some real antinomies, which surface alongside the conflicts between rural and urban, and the opposition between quality and quantity as suggested by the population question. The castaways' societies are confronted in practical terms with these problems, which for them are so many challenges to overcome. The impossible synthesis of holism with individualism is no doubt one of the most formidable of these challenges. The fusion of technological society together with a society with a human face and the weaving together of dynamism with solidarity are hardly less difficult.

Almost everything possible has been said on holism and on individualism, and yet everything has to be said again, because we remain still at the same point. According to received wisdom, traditional communities are holistic. The autonomy of their members is limited by hierarchies and obligations to the group. Only outcasts are real individuals. But this vision is rejected by some proponents of individualism. According to the likes of Jean Baechler, even in the most primitive communities the individual is still there, with his or her strategies and calculations. There is an important grain of truth in this. Yet these 'individuals' think of themselves as *members* of a community whose language and myths provide the foundation stone. Conversely, individualistic society reposes on the collective fictions of natural man and the social contract. The mythical character of the first of these fictions has been demonstrated many times, and cultural anthropology has brought all possible and imaginable proofs of its inanity. We come into this world as members of a family – without having chosen it, we are born as French, English, German, Japanese, or whatever. A totally individualistic society is impossible. The Iks rather prove this.

The paradoxes of the idea of a social contract have been highlighted since the beginning. Hegel provided a decisive refutation of the three main formulations of the passage from the state of nature to the civilised state, those of Hobbes, Pufendorf and Rousseau.[14] As regards Hobbes, Hegel wrote:

> According to the fiction of the state of nature, this state is left behind because of the ills associated with it. This signals nothing more than that one presupposes what one wants to arrive at, namely that an accord between the elements in conflict with each other in the situation of primitive chaos is good and desirable, and is what one should reach.

Henri Denis adds:

> If the war of everyone against everyone must cease on account of the ills that it entails, it must be that primitive men are aware of the benefits to be gained from peace, thus that they are already civilised men.

Concerning Pufendorf's version, in which it is supposed that 'there exists in natural man an instinct of sociability', Hegel retorts that the problem is presupposed as solved from the outset. Finally Rousseau 'postulates that primitive man is an isolated individual', but he shows him immediately submitted to the consequences of a historical movement which implies that people are already in some relationship to each other.

In the end, though, the prettiest refutations in the world do not change much. The authors of the myth of natural man and the social contract were themselves fairly conscious of their fictional character. This fiction has real pedagogical value, and captures *some part* of reality. Since methodological individualism is interwoven with ontological individualism, the degree of truth becomes closer to the *heart* of things precisely to the extent that we are concerned with a self-fulfilling prophecy. Today, most people believe that the individual is an end in itself, and desire that this be so. And the emancipatory virtues of individualism are undeniable. No one who has become acquainted, up close or from afar, with the *benefits* of modern society wants to renounce them altogether. As empty, formal and abstract as individual liberty and human rights may be, their acquisition is none the less real and irreversible. The freedoms of thought and of expression, the right of personal initiative, have an almost universal significance. These notions are more or less inherent in the very conception of 'man' as a thinking, talking animal.

However, the dominant forms of these 'rights' have been the product exclusively of the modern West. One consequence of this has been the way in which, in many Third World countries, the dictator-ships more or less directly spawned by the West have been able to make this 'Westernness' a pretext for refusing such rights to their peoples – while none the less confiscating the more traditional forms of liberty and democracy. These traditional forms are less systematic, more fragile and more messy than those engendered by individualistic ideology. The freedoms valued in holistic communities show up typically in public domains that are out-of-bounds to certain categories of persons (women most often, and also dependants, non-caste indi-viduals, etc.). The respect for status which penetrates most intimately into the private sphere acts as a protection against the sort of annihi-lation of the person that has been brought about by modern totalitarianism, yet by definition it contradicts the ideal of a universal value. The exclusion of foreigners from any official recognition serves to guarantee the values of the group while downgrading the rights of people at large. But there is not a total absence of recognition of the other. The right of asylum, for example, which even criminals benefit from in traditional societies, indicates a respect of the *person* without taking account of the individual. Plants and animals are also included in a respect for life which is evidence of a larger universalism. The condemnation of individual excess by social fiat (e.g. penalty of ostracism or other withdrawal of privileges) is, unarguably, a means of protecting the rights of everyone. We can, indeed, understand this within our own way of thinking, as amounting to a version of the principle: 'Liberty exists only up to the point at which it does not interfere with another person.'

Argumention between these concrete liberties of non-Westerners and our abstract values is interminable and unfinished; correspond-ingly there is widespread complaint about the negation of rights on both sides.[15] 'Nationalistic' states, brought into being by imitation of the nation-states of the West, borrow Western techniques especially for the army and the police. In the name of modernity, they destroy the infra-national forms in which former concrete freedoms were expressed, and in the name of authenticity they suppress any form of grassroots democracy or elementary guarantees of respect for the human person.

One should not confound the current negations of respect of human rights in the Third World with holism. All the same, it is undeniable that traditional societies place a heavy collar and chain on individuals. Concrete freedoms are often obtained through the negation of abstract liberty. Hierarchies are very severe, and indeed become intolerable, unacceptable and unjust once the belief in their transcendental foundation – the belief that assures their legitimacy – breaks down. Syntheses of holism and individualism have sometimes ended up with hollow formulae inspiring misbegotten attempts at restoring community on the basis of an individualistic society. This totalitarian impasse seems assured of fair success *also* in the Westernised Third World.[16]

In the practical life of the informal society, on the other hand, the fusion sometimes happens naturally. The entrepreneurs of the informal sector are *individuals* in their own right *at the same time* as members of a community. It is not just traditional solidarities that are in play, but new ties are also woven in work relationships (with wage- and salary-earners, with work colleagues) which have an important communal dimension. The market is very much present, with its competitive aspects and its depersonalising logic, but it does not dominate social life as a whole. The economic is *re-embedded* within the social.

The rights of the individual are recognised *de facto*, but within families whose extent is around 300 members each. The *individualistic mentality* is strongly inhibited by the weight of the community. This achievement may be only a precarious and transitory equilibrium, unlikely to last or to extend to all aspects of social life and become institutionalised. It will probably continue to be fragile in many cases, especially if the pressures of the world system continue in the direction of individualism. None the less, the non-conflictual coexistence of the two principles in certain favourable situations is an indication of a possible fusion. It is probably not coincidental that these embryonic fusions have forms anticipated by such political thinkers as Hegel (with his *états* or corporations) and Alexis de Tocqueville (with his 'intermediate bodies'). It is premature to try to theorise these fusions, but their embryonic existence is a promising sign.

Technological society versus society with a human face

Not least amongst the paradoxes of modernity is the way it has engendered, out of the humanism of the Renaissance, the most inhuman society ever constructed by man. The technological society is a diabolical machine which reduces human beings to the status of cogs, and pursues its infernal course without any human volition being able to intervene and countermand its onward march. The human person with universal rights is on the mythical horizon of this progressive movement, and the well-being of humanity is the incantatory chorus that one hears in all the cogs of the machine. The technocrats dream only of improving the lot of people; and the bureaucrats think only of the good of the people. All this piety notwithstanding, this *better* towards which we keep on rushing faster and faster is the irreconcilable enemy of the *good*.

Submitted to customs that are often absurd and sometimes barbaric, yet that long practice has shown to be workable, traditional communities take care of their members and even perhaps of humanity. Dominated by forces which are beyond them, whose outlines are traced by their myths, these societies are infinitely more human. One never sees members of the group being casually abandoned in neglect and indifference, or left to rot in the jungle of an omnipresent and mindless administrative paperchase, as one sees each day in our affluent society. There is no risk that they will be overtaken by inventions and technological changes. The inhuman forces that dominate society have inspired a wisdom so profoundly human that technical instruments are limited to what is strictly necessary, objects are reduced to physiological and cultural *needs*, and curiosity about the unknown is absent if not proscribed.

The castaways of development still dream about the unattainable abundance of industrial societies, but they continue to maintain traditional values. They possess technical knowledge derived from the West, but do not have the right organisation, material means or adequate knowhow to construct the whole production machine. On the other hand, they have urgent *needs* to satisfy. To adapt technical knowledge and rechannel the available means to produce what is needed, demands an ingenuity of which informal artisans give ample proof. The 'appropriate technique' here finds, quite naturally, its meaning and domain of application. A return to the wisdom of the ancients is no longer possible. Traditional techniques are not geared-up to solve the problems of a new urban society: they are mostly archaic. Thus the idea of an optimal utilisation of available means remains present, but it is never abstracted away from the finite object held in view.

The risk of falling back into the technological society is, in fact, rather slight, because the superhuman project of dominating nature, which underpins modernity, is absent from the castaways' way of thinking. The Westernisation of the world has succeeded in many respects, and sometimes very deeply. But what remains most vibrant in decultured societies, and irreducible to the Western metaphysics, is the relationship with nature. People feel that they are the servants and children of nature, not the masters. An example is given by the views of a magician from the Tanna Bush Centre in Vanuatu: 'You Whites, you think you're the best, you possess great powers, but you are small beside the Blacks ...' When asked why, he responded: 'We have the rocks ... . Without them, neither the trees nor the plants would grow, life would be extinguished.' The researcher summarises the thought of his native interlocutor:

> What can the power of an airplane really represent next to that which makes a tree be born and grow? How do mechanical forces compare beside those of life? The magicians of Tanna possess the secrets of magic nature, and have long since ceased to be bedazzled by the Whites' power.

One can find similar views in all places where people have remained close to nature, in village Africa, in Amazonia, among the Inuit, and so on.

However advanced technology may be, however fascinating scientific prowess, when reinserted in the informal society these knowhows and techniques lose their *autonomies*, they turn back into a means and are no longer an end in themselves. People take back the controls, because technology no longer imposes its own interests on them. Disinterest in technology for the sake of technology reopens the way to the problem of constructing a human society. Technology, which, like the economic, had been 'disembedded' from the social by modernity's 'great transformation', finds itself encased in this new *sociality*.

Dynamism and solidarity

Is there not a risk that our islanders will enclose themselves in a frozen, static system, with neither innovation nor progress? Notwithstanding all its faults and despite its ecological catastrophes and risks of nuclear apocalypse, modern society cannot be considered to be negative on the plane of technological and material performance. The immense increase in human productive power opens up possibilities that it would be absurd to refuse. A synthesis between modern society's dynamism and the solidarity of traditional communities thus appears necessary and desirable.

It must not be forgotten that the dynamism of modernity relates to the *maximine* principle, and that the mobilisation of maximum individual energy is obtained only through savage competition. Development's survivors, battered by the desperate fight for life and owing their survival only to solidarity, are not much inclined to build a new society founded on the *maximine* principle. Efficiency remains for them an important value, and the principle of least effort is certainly the element of modernity most in resonance with the logic of traditional communities. But pursuit of the maximum for its own sake, by contrast, is not their imperative. Adaptation to concrete needs linked to contextual values is much more in accord with their logic of operation than are abstract performance principles. Real people have need of a *good* house, of a *good* item of clothing, of *good* food, *good* tools, not necessarily of the *best* house, the *best* clothing, the *best* food, the *best* tool.

The pursuit of the best has meaning only in a unidimensional society where everything is made uniform and standardised. How do you define the best house? The least expensive, if they are all the same; or the biggest or the best equipped for the same price if they are constructed of the same materials and on the same model? How do you compare a cob cottage with a thatched roof, with a villa made of unfired bricks, with a flat on the nth level of a concrete housing estate, with a prefabricated 'individualised' apartment? What common denominator can be found between these different *technical* parameters, not to mention the qualities of site, architecture, style, and so on? Genuinely human societies are not obsessed by absolute calculability. They are *reasonable* but not rational. They pursue *effectiveness* but not *efficiency*.[17] The 'good' house is one that protects you *well* from inclement weather, satisfies the needs of the family, and encourages *joie de vivre*, all while remaining affordable. It was relatively easy for everyone to find such a habitation in traditional societies. In modern society one can, thanks to specialist publications, purchase the cheapest square metre or the most comfortable. However, that does not guarantee a satisfactory living space for everyone.

In the castaways' society, pressures for change will be infinitely less strong, and this is a good thing. For, over and above the 'stress' that it engenders, the course of progress brings enormous dangers to hang over humanity. Knowledge of the abstract wealth of possibilities is in no danger of being forgotten. But the law of technological society – that whatever can be done, must be done – will not be the law of this *post-modern* society. It is no doubt impossible for a Western mind to get rid of a nostalgia for progress. To give up the mastery of nature, abandon the unremitting war to unveil all secrets, will appear unacceptable if not crazy.

Yet collaboration with nature, rather than aggression, does not imply giving up either the benefits progress can bring or the initiation of new researches in an *other* spirit and in *other* directions. For the generations of the future, remarks François Partant, 'most of our progress will appear to be without the least practical interest if they live otherwise than us (with another familial and social organisation, another pattern of time usage, and so on)'. He gives an eloquent comparison:

> The Egyptians made remarkable progress in matters of pyramid construction. They put to work techniques so elaborate that we still do not know their secrets. But the pyramid constitutes progress only to the extent that it was essential in Egyptian society (with its social structures, its slaves, its conception of the world, its culture and religion, etc.) to honour its gods and inter its kings.[18]

That said, it remains the case that human minds have been Westernised on this point. Important elements of the culture of technology will survive durably. How is one to bring about the synthesis? What will the needs of future generations be? I do not claim to be able to answer these questions. But, at any rate, a reduction in the intensity of competition ought not to be a source of fear.

Notes

1. In fact this is also true in the Centre, in the midst of the successes of industrialism and consumerism.

2. Joël Bonnemaison, *La Dernière Ile*, op. cit., p. 370.

3. Ibid., p. 291

4. On this movement, I refer the reader back to the discussions devoted to it in *L'Occidentalisation du monde*, especially pp. 122-8.

5. V.S. Naipaul, *India: a wounded civilisation*, Alfred A. Knopf, New York, 1977, p. 63.

6. Ibid., p. 65. Tahar Ben Jelloun, often so perceptive and moving, does not mince words in describing Naipaul as 'an intellectual who is flattered, more or less fabricated through the media, and who is put on stage at exactly the moment when it serves the West's interests to show that the Third World is definitively down the drain' (cited in 'Naipaul: un tiers monde sur mesure pour l'Occident', *L'Etat du monde 1982*, La Découverte, Paris, pp. 478-9). He credits him neither with good faith nor with talent.

7. Colin Turnbull, *The Mountain People*, op. cit.

8. The phrase is from the title of the book by Pierre Pradervand, *Une Afrique en marche*, op. cit. The connotations are of being on-the-move, going somewhere, or of a machine working, functioning.

9. The Six Ss: *Se servir de la saison sèche dans la savane et au Sahel* (Making use of the dry season in the savanna and Sahel). The dry season was, traditionally, the 'down time', a season of relative idleness. The movement's goal is to put to good use this time resource, in such fruitful works as irrigation and land conservation.

10. Cited by Pierre Pradervand in *Une Afrique en marche*, op. cit., p. 13.

11. Pradervand, while providing an excellent set of observations about African events, falls into this moralism despite himself. Emmanuel Ndione, cited earlier, makes an excellent critique of these 'projections'.

12. Bernard Kouchner, 'Lutter pour les "boat-people"', *Le Monde*, 16 March 1990.

13. The figures are taken from Charles Condamines & Jean-Yves Carfantan, *Qui a peur du tiers monde?*, Seuil, Paris, 1980.

14. This analysis draws from the very insightful exegesis made by Henri Denis in his book *Hegel, penseur politique*, in the Collection 'Raison Dialectique', L'Age d'Homme, Lausanne, 1989, p. 206. The citations from Hegel are translated into English from Henri Denis's French texts.

15. At the time of writing the original French edition of this book (December 1989), the British government had just expelled the Vietnamese boat-people from Hong Kong, sending them back to their home country. France, which refused to house 'the whole of the world's misery', had meantime been preparing itself, together with other European countries, to sweep out its illegal immigrants. Whatever might be the solid grounds for these measures at the level of political and economic realism, it can hardly be said that they do honour to the West's pretended universalism. Human rights are recognised only when they do not cause too much trouble. In view of these contradictions of modernity, the drift towards totalitarianism is a constant danger in contemporary society.

16. For further elaborations on this point, see Serge Latouche, 'L'anthropologie et la clef du paradis perdu', *L'Homme et la société*, no. 71-2, January-June 1984.

17. I borrow this opposition between *effectiveness* and *efficiency* from my friend Wolfgang Sachs (see his article, 'Le culte de l'effience absolue', in the *Revue du MAUSS*, no. 3, 1989). In spite of the closeness of meaning of the two terms, *efficiency* has a specific sense in thermodynamics meaning the rate of transformation of heat into an output of work. In an exchange of letters on this point, Sachs points out: 'The fact that none the less, in our times, the two expressions are utilised for one another, highlights the problem: efficiency, while being a special case, becomes the dominant model or paradigm for effectiveness.'

18. François Partant, *Que la crise s'aggrave*, op. cit., p. 142.

Conclusion

Paul Valéry's quip that 'an author keeps on writing the same book' surely applies even more to pamphleteers than to fiction writers. Once engaged in the analysis of social reality, a theoretician finds himself unceasingly confronted by the same objections to *his system*. Each book is an attempt to respond to the criticisms of the preceding ones, an effort to go beyond the *aporiae* of his premises, to patch up the holes in his analytical schema while preserving the impetus of his original intuitions. The present book falls squarely into this pattern. There is no need for a conclusion, as the last chapter has been consecrated to the discussion of objections to and difficulties of the planet of the castaways. However, since the possible objections rebound off to infinity, and some of them fit badly in the framework of the preceding chapters, we will conclude our voyage by the examination of three difficulties more or less left aside during the trip. These are the questions of where the new society is located, of the recurrent dangers which weigh on its destiny, and of a non-utilitarian purpose for a human society.

The location of the castaways' society

The first pages of Chapter 1 evoked the existence of this 'other planet' at the gateways of Ouagadougou, at the heart of darkest Africa. Yet it is in the towns themselves, in the urban belts of the Third World's great metropolises that the real crucible of novelty and the basis of the castaways' planet is found, here in the shadow of the most grotesque signs of modernity: buildings of mirror-glass and pre-stressed concrete, motorway exchanges, telecommunication towers, the outposts of banks and multinational firms, universities, parliaments, high courts and central hospitals.

Should one, then, not expect to find extensions of this planet in the neighbourhoods of the North itself, in the shadow of the central institutions of the modernity-world? Indeed there exists, *de facto*, a Fourth World International. We have our own disinherited, our own unclaimed baggage, our outcasts, our marginals. The wounded and the victims of development are before our doors; there is no need to go and search for them in the outer suburbs of the West, we run into them in our own backyards.

In an unpublished document, given to me after I had written the first draft of this book, François Partant also evoked the possibility of the reconstruction of an autonomous life by the unemployed and outcasts of the grand society, within the Centre itself. In doing this, he utilises the same metaphor of shipwreck:

> Imagine that a ferry goes down during a crossing. A few hundred people escape, and find themselves on a desert island where they know that no one will come looking for them. The castaways will have to organise themselves to survive. After making an inventory of the island's resources, they share out the jobs, some being in charge of providing food, others of the construction of shelters. If, having found a few ears of wild wheat, they decide to cultivate it, they will not ask whether their yields per hectare are comparable to those of the Beauce, nor if their cereal production will be competitive with that of the United States. The only question will be to know whether the wheat harvest will be enough to ensure bread for everybody. The same will go for every productive activity.[1]

He goes on to explain in detail the islanders' organisation. I will cite his tale at some length, because it illustrates better than anything I could say, my own vision of the planet of the castaways.

> Will they be poor? They won't be if, having enough resources, they manage to *diversify* their activities sufficiently. But they will not be able to satisfy their needs with the goods and services that we produce. Which does not mean that they will be less well satisfied. On the contrary, the castaways will in fact very quickly see that non-satisfaction is a key fact in the whirlwind system that they have just been dropped out of, that it is both a factor in and a consequence of that dynamic. They will see that it was a mistake to identify standard of living with purchasing power, that the quantity of market goods consumed has less importance than the conditions in which these goods are produced, that in fact the standard of living depends on the quality of social relationships. They will be a lot richer than the French, if they can organise themselves in such a way that these relations are harmonious, that each individual has the possibility (in the actual interests of the social group) of fully expressing himself, that in consequence all relations of dominance are excluded along with the contradic-

tions of *interests* which justify, in our society, most of the institutional relations of domination.

This hypothetical island, where a few hundred people have been obliged to get organised to survive, could easily be made a reality by a few thousand unemployed seeking to live from their own work. It would suffice for them to meet and agree on a programme of both social and economic character, starting from the ideas that they are more or less cut off from the rest of the world, that they can in fact produce everything that they need without worrying about the national or world norms of production (for example of wheat on lands which have been abandoned because they do not permit more than two tonnes/hectare), and finally that their standard of living ought not to be compared with the consumption level of the average Frenchman, but with the material and moral poverty of the average unemployed person.[2]

Turning to the possibility of achieving this utopia, Partant evokes the numerous obstacles of a technical nature, and also the difficulties inherent in recreating links of social solidarity. Much the same set of questions lies at the heart of my own analysis.

In the shipwreck of the grand society, will the barque of development be lost with all hands, or will there be a few life-saving planks left for the Westerners themselves? The universalist ideal of a fraternal humanity, produced by the West itself, would demand that the latter be the case. It is also tempting for Westerners to try to monopolise the interpretation of history even in defeat, and to seek to project themselves into the post-development world. Of course, there is nothing really to rule out such an attempt. After all, the informal economy is flourishing *also* in the North, and we find *there also* a degree of re-embedding of the economy within a larger sociality (above all when the outcasts are originally from the Third World).

Consider the 'Green' movements, which are in the vanguard of authentically Western alternative movements. One goal of many Green groups is to recreate a convivial society through deliberate construction of small-scale community and solidarity networks of all sorts. Yet the Greens are in a situation rather different from that of the neo-tribal networks in Black Africa. In Africa, insertion within the group is not the effect of a totally free choice and a contractual membership, rather it results from a prior *belonging*. The solidarity here is *vertical*, the obligations being embedded in values with roots anchored in long traditions. In the West, the new communities are really *voluntary associations* of free and equal individuals; they are always fragile because they are not held together by the entanglements of roots. The solidarity is *horizontal*. The values on which these groupings rest are actually those of the West and of modernity: freedom, equality, democracy. The right of the individual is still supreme over the right of the 'tribe'. The rule of the majority is at odds with conflictual consensus through palaver in a universe of negotiated hierarchy.

In Western communal life, advantage is always thought of in terms of utilitarian calculation, and competition is kept at bay only with constant effort. In Africa, by contrast, *relational* calculation wins out *naturally* over monetary profit, and the sense of solidarity works spontaneously to limit competition in the domain of material life. Even when reconstituted in shantytowns, the solidarities of the Third World are close to being communities fused together by passions and feelings which give them their *cohesion*, whereas those of the networks in the North remain founded on interests which assure their *coherence*. Of course this opposition is not totally hard and fast. Even leaving aside the penetration in the West of networks due to immigration, there are traditions predating modernity that remain alive and well: regional-isms, old Germanic and Celtic cultural wellsprings, nostalgias for lost communities. Yet it remains infinitely more difficult for those in the West, whether excluded in fact or voluntarily marginalised, to *de-Westernise* themselves, than for the Burkinaby people in the shantytowns of Ouagadougou. The obstacles and contradictions of the grand society push the North's outcasts more into a dead-end than towards the new planet. Activists run up against severe obstacles in coming to terms with their situation. They are often at risk of falling prey to bad faith, and of tumbling into self-flagellation rather than any serene lucidity. The ways are narrow and prone to ambush; the path towards invention of an authentic universalism founded on a negoti-ated reciprocity is long and tortuous.

The dangers threatening the new planet

The informal sphere offers a rough sketch of what could be a new and authentically *post-modern* society. Its existence and viability is in itself a refutation of the grand society's universalist pretensions. But there is no certainty that the new castaways' society will succeed. This is one more reason that it is misplaced to present the informal as a miracle solution. Serious dangers weigh on the future of this new planet. We have already considered some of the challenges that it must overcome: population threat, contradictions between holism and individualism, and so on.

So, while ideas for solutions are being plotted and syntheses sought, nothing is definite. The lasting and conflictual coexistence of the two societies puts the new one rudely to the test. The members of the informal networks live also in the grand society. The temptation to find an individual solution is always present, and sometimes legitimate. Those who have succeeded can at any time break with the community which has helped them and repudiate their obligations to it. Some, stifling any scruples, may even be tempted to disappear along with the group's cash-box, and dive off into the delights of the grand society; in the Third World stories of this sort are legion. From this point of view, the informal sector is condemned to being only the refuge of the poor and miserable. Any success brings the danger of fragmentation through the flight of the successful elements. The most *gifted* will quit the island-trashcan, leaving only the weak and lame.

The fascination for fraud which saps the grand society is also strongly at work on the castaways. The more burdensome the ties of support networks, the greater the temptation to take the money and run. Individual success is circumscribed within the informal networks, which tend to confiscate the opportunities of any aspiring candidate. The latter is condemned to poverty, without doubt convivial but galling when it is the result of constraint.

In fact, the informal society can retaliate when faced with the threat of flight of its *capital* and brains. But the counter-measures, while legitimate when it is a case of punishing rip-offs, can reach objectionable proportions if they end by stifling all individual success. Sanctions invoked can range from vengeance pure and simple to symbolic condemnation. The latter is no less effective than the former. In West Africa, one of the most widely felt forms of sanction is the fear of being *marabouté* (hexed by a priest or witchdoctor). As in any system of magic or sorcery, this has a formidable effectiveness for all the members of the group (and sometimes for others as well). Even those who are the most Westernised in appearance are not free from fear. The problem is that, although necessary as forms of social control, such practices can easily become excessive and sclerotic. Walking this tightrope poses one more recurrent danger in the construction of the castaways' planet.

Happiness without more

The castaways' society is authentically *post-modern* only by the fact of its rupture with utilitarian reason. The re-embedding of the economic within the social subsumes the *maximine* principle within a social functioning geared towards the objective of the common good. Does this mean that the objective of the greatest happiness of the largest number is repudiated? The question is difficult to answer, partly because it contains more than one pitfall. We have already seen what has to be said on the subject of numbers. The largest number is not a desirable nor even a meaningful objective. Moreover, a society ought to aim for the happiness of *all* its members. For reasons of social equilibrium (relations between generations, passing on of culture), for reasons of ecological balance (limited natural resources), and so as to maintain some sort of quality of life, undoubtedly it is not desirable that this number be too great. Even if a stationary state has its dangers, it is hardly preferable that world population growth should be too rapid.

All this may seem to contradict traditional economic logic, which proposes to resolve all such problems by a *fuite en avant*. According to this logic, an ever-more-numerous younger generation will provide the best basis for meeting all the needs of society. But if this dubious premise is rejected, it follows that the 'material' production of the castaways' society will *not* be maximal production. From this it follows, adapting Jean-Baptiste Say's famous syllogism, that if less is produced, fewer needs will be satisfied, and so happiness will be lessened. So the new society will not achieve *the greatest happiness* either.

But one still has to ask what this notion of happiness really means. It is interesting that Saint-Just coined his famous phrase 'happiness is a new idea in Europe' at the exact moment that utilitarianism was triumphing and defining happiness through the satisfaction of material needs. All the same, pre-modern societies certainly did not set their sights on ensuring the misfortune of their members! They aimed, we might say, for the common good and justice. These objectives sometimes went *against* having material abundance enjoyed by their subjects. Prince Shang, the Chinese Machiavelli, argued that to keep the subjects obedient, the people should have only what was needed to live.[3] This way, the nation would be a happy one. Cardinal Richelieu, in his maxims, put forward a very similar sentiment: 'All men of government agree that, if the people are too comfortable, it becomes impossible to keep them within the confines of their duty.'[4] The society of the Ancien Régime proposed a different type of well-being, the *beatitudo*, being simultaneously 'religious *well-being*' and 'social *welfare*', which went beyond material happiness and did not exclude comfort for everyone.[5] The misuse of salvation by a corrupt and degenerate society has made odious a notion of beatitude which often refused necessities to the masses while a small minority lived in luxury. But the result has been to throw the baby out with the bathwater: an artificial division on the question of well-being, accompanied by some questionable logic about how to achieve it.

Modernity has legitimated, irreversibly, the *individual* pursuit of happiness. In this new sense, the idea of happiness is clearly a decisive contribution of the West. The cynical meditations of ancient governments seem outrageous to us. However, the utilitarian reduction of happiness to pleasure, of pleasure to the satisfaction of needs, of need to a *quantum* of consumption, and thus finally of happiness to its money measure, has to be doubted. In postulating that greatest happiness equates with highest income, one is turning an objective into a means, so emptying the former of all content. The happiness of persons, if this is taken as an objective of a *society*, cannot be a simple addition of states of pleasure of all its members separately obtained, each to the detriment of the others. Even if happiness is no more than the mere symbolic enjoyment felt by the subjects as a consequence of that of the ruler, it still possesses an irreducible personal aspect. A society cannot be said to be perfectly happy if one of its members is in misery. If the happiness of a society has a personal dimension, then personal happiness also has a collective dimension. You don't get your happiness all alone; in this, happiness is distinguished from pleasure. Pleasure can result from individual consumption (to the detriment, in some cases, of others). The sensual pleasures of life (eating well, sexual enjoyment) are momentary. It is well known that pleasure is not always much fun. Pleasure not shared can lead rapidly to satiety, sometimes to disgust and to sadness.

Happiness is plural and complex. It relates less to having than to being. In speaking of well-being, the moderns had a sound intuition. But in reducing well-being to *well-having*, and above all to *having more*, they have miscued completely. John Stuart Mill tried hard to prevent this slide by distinguishing the *useful* from the *expedient*. The useful for him was whatever contributes to general happiness, whereas the expedient relates exclusively to personal goals. But in a utilitarian world such a distinction is inconsistent. It is simply an attempt to patch up in advance the problem encountered by economic welfare theory when it tries to give new life to nostalgia for the communal but on foundations that deny its pertinence.

To *be well* implies an absorption of pleasure into the tissue of interpersonal relations. The emotions, sympathy, friendship, love, are there to be enjoyed, and are themselves sources of joy. Sacrifices, even suffering, which are the inevitable *costs* of living together, are not calculable in either money or consumption terms. While some forms of pain are unsupportable and destroy happiness, there is no happiness without some discord.

In aiming for the happiness of its members, the *post-modern* society has acquired something important from modernity. The well-being of persons is recognised, and is not improperly confounded with the glory of the state or ruler. But on the other hand, in renouncing the idea of maximising a happiness reduced to an empty utility level, the *post-modern* society harks back to the ideal of balance from earlier wisdoms, and gives a full content to the old objective of the *common good*.

Notes

1. François Partant, *Lettre au CCSC (Comité Chrétien de Solidarité avec les Chômeurs)*, confidential document, pp. 6-7. Partant died shortly after this letter was written.

2. Ibid.

3. Shang Yang, *The Book of Lord Shang* (c. 300 BC), translated from the Chinese by J.J.L. Duyvendak, University of Chicago Press, 1963, see especially bk. I, section 4, 'The elimination of strength', pp. 196-205.

4. Richelieu, *Maximes*, Wittmann, Paris, 1944, p. 90.

5. Raimundo Panikkar, *Religion ou politique? Y a-t-il une solution au dilemme de l'Occident?*, *Religione e Politica*, Istituto di Studi Filosofici di Roma, 1978, p. 4.

Bibliography

Thanks are due to Mark Brooks for assistance with the Notes and Bibliography.

Albagli, Claude, *L'Economie des dieux céréaliers*, L'Harmattan, Paris, 1989.

Amin, Samir, Alain Lipietz & Serge Latouche, 'Trois auteurs en quête d'un tiers monde', *Cosmopolitiques*, June 1988.

Andreff, Wladimir, *La Diversité des pratiques sportives et la 'marchandisation' du sport*, photocopied document, UNESCO, 1988.

Arendt, Hannah, *The Human Condition*, University of Chicago Press, 1958.

Augé, Marc, 'La société, le sida et le diable', *Le Monde*, 20 December 1988.

Austruy, Jacques, *Le Prince et le patron*, Cujas, Paris, 1972.

Baechler, Jean, *Démocraties*, Calmann-Lévy, Paris, 1985.

Balzac, Honoré de, *Etude sur la Chartreuse de Parme de Monsieur Beyle*, Climats, 1989.

Bataille, Georges, *La Part maudite*, Gallimard, Paris, 1930.

Bateson, Gregory, 'Double bind', in *Steps to an Ecology of Mind: collected essays in anthropology, psychiatry, evolution, and epistemology*, Chandler, San Francisco, 1972, pp. 271-8.

Bateson, Gregory, 'Toward a theory of schizophrenia', in *Behavioural Sciences*, vol. 1, no. 4, 1956; reprinted in *Steps to an Ecology of Mind: collected essays in anthropology, psychiatry, evolution, and epistemology*, Chandler, San Francisco, 1972, pp. 201-27.

Baudrillard, Jean, *America*, Grasset, Paris, 1986.

Baudrillard, Jean, *Fatal Strategies*, Semiotext(e), Pluto, London, 1990. (French original: *Les Stratégies fatales*, Grasset, Paris, 1983.)

Belloncle, Guy, *La Question paysanne en Afrique noire*, Karthala, Paris, 1982.

Ben Jelloun, Tahar, 'Naipaul: un tiers monde sur mesure pour l'Occident', *L'Etat du monde 1982*, La Découverte, Paris.

Benda, Julien, *La Trahison des clercs*, Grasset, Paris, 1927.

Bentham, Jeremy, *The Collected Works of Jeremy Bentham: Deontology, A Table of the Springs of Action, Article on Utilitarianism*, edited by Amnon Goldworth, Clarendon Press, Oxford, 1983.

Bentham, Jeremy, 'Déontologie', *Revue du MAUSS*, no. 5, 1989, pp. 77-98. (A French translation of passages from John Bowring's rendering of Bentham's *Deontology*.)

Bentham, Jeremy, *Théorie des peines et des récompenses*, French version originally published as an Appendix in Elie Halévy, *La Formation du radicalisme philosophique*, Alcan, Paris, 1901. Republished in *Revue du MAUSS*, no. 5, 1989, pp. 70-6, Paris.

Berger, Peter, *Les Mystificateurs du progrès: du Brézil à la Chine*, Presses Universitaires de France, Paris, 1978.

Bergeret, Anne, *L'Arbre nourricier en pays sahélien*, Maison des Sciences de l'Homme, Paris, 1990.

Biguma, Napoleon Constantin, *L'Economie informelle ou la naissance d'une alternative: le cas de Rwanda*, doctoral thesis, University of Lille, June 1989.

Boff, Leonardo, 'Eo povo que se organiza para a libertação', *Jornal do Brazil*, 3 May 1981.

Bonnemaison, Joël, *La Dernière Ile,* Arlea/Orstom, Paris, 1986.

Bonnot, Gérard, *La Vie c'est autre chose*, Belfond, Paris, 1976.

Bouche, Jean-Louis, 'De l'utilité dans la pensée économique pendant la Révolution française', *Revue du MAUSS*, no. 8, 1990, pp. 142-62.

Bricas, Nicolas & José Muchnik, 'Indigenous technologies and urban cottage industry in the food sector', in Philippe Hugon (editor), *Nourrir les villes*, L'Harmattan, Paris, 1985.

Brinkmann, Carl, 'Standards of living', in *Encyclopedia of the Social Sciences,* London, 1934, pp. 322-4.

Brune, François, *Le Bonheur conforme*, Gallimard, Paris, 1985.

Bury, J.B., *The Idea of Progress*, Dover edition, New York, 1955.

Caillé, Alain, *Critique de la raison utilitaire*, La Découverte, Paris, 1989.

Carton, Michel, 'Les marginaux informels préhistoriques et post-modernes?', *Entwicklung/Development*, no. 24, 1987.

Castoriadis, Cornélius, *L'Institution imaginaire de la société*, Seuil, Paris, 1975.

Charmes, Jacques, 'Quelles politiques publiques face au secteur informel?', *Notes et études de Caisse centrale de coopération économique*, no. 23, April 1989, p. 5.

Chauvin, Michel, 'Déculturalisation et sous-développement', CDTM (Centre du Documentation Tiers Monde de Paris), no. 3, August 1990.

Chauvin, Michel, *Tiers monde: la fin des idées reçues*, Syros, Collection Alternatives, Paris, 1991.

Chesnais, Jean-Claude, *La Revanche du tiers monde*, Laffont, Paris, 1987.

Chesneaux, Jean, *Modernité-monde*, La Découverte, Paris, 1989.

Chesneaux, Jean, 'Tiers monde offshore ou tiers monde quart-mondisé et libération du troisième type', *Revue Tiers Monde*, no. 100, October-December 1984, pp. 817-26.

Cheysson, Claude, 'La paix des grands, l'espoir des pauvres', *Le Monde Diplomatique*, 24 February 1989.

Chombart de Lauwe, Paul-Henry, *La Culture et le pouvoir*, Stock, Paris, 1975.

Chuang-Tzu, *Chuang-Tzu: the inner chapters*, translated from the Chinese by A.C. Graham, Mandala, London, 1991.

Clark, Colin, 'The economics of housework', *Bulletin of the Oxford Institute of Statistics*, vol. XX, no. 2, May 1958.

Clastres, Pierre, *Society against the State: the leader as servant and the humane uses of power among the Indians of the Americas*, Urizen Books, New York, 1977. (French original: *La Société contre l'état*, Minuit, Paris, 1974.)

Condamines, Charles & Jean-Yves Carfantan, *Qui a peur du tiers monde?*, Seuil, Paris, 1980.

Constant, Benjamin, *De l'esprit de conquête*, Librairie de Medicis, Paris, 1947.

Courlet, Claude, 'Les industrialisations endogènes', *Revue Tiers Monde*, no. 118, April-June 1989, pp. 413-21

Courlet, Claude (editor), dossier on 'Industrialisation rampante et diffuse dans les pays en développement: quelques points de repère', *Revue Tiers Monde*, no. 118, April-June 1989, pp. 403-53.

Davis, J., 'Standards and contents of living', *American Economic Review*, vol. 35, no. 1 (March 1945), pp. 1-15.

De Romana, Alfredo L., 'L'Economie autonome, une alternative en gestion à la société industrielle', *Interculture*, no. 4, 1989, Centre Monchanin, Montreal.

Deble, Isabelle & Philippe Hugon, *Vivre et survivre dans les villes africaines*, Presses Universitaires de France, 1983.

Denis, Henri, *Hegel, penseur politique*, Collection 'Raison Dialectique', L'Age d'Homme, Lausanne, 1989.

Dockes, Pierre & Bernard Rosier, *L'Histoire ambiguë*, Presses Universitaires de France, Paris, 1988.

Drouin, Pierre, 'La "force terrifiante" de l'Occident. Les colères salutaires et parfois excessives de Serge Latouche', *Le Monde*, 24 February 1989.

Dufumier, Marc, *Les Politiques agraires*, Presses Universitaires de France, Series 'Que sais-je?', Paris 1986.

Dumouchel, Paul & Jean-Pierre Dupuy, *L'Enfer des choses*, Seuil, Paris, 1979.

Erler, Brigitte, *L'Aide qui tue*, Editions d'En-Bas, Lausanne, 1987.

Escobar, Arturo, *Celebration of Common Man*, photocopy, 1988.

Evans-Pritchard, Edward E., *The Nuer: a description of the modes of livelihood and political institutions of a Nilotic people*, Clarendon Press, Oxford, 1940.

FAO, *Rapport sur la situation mondiale de l'alimentation et de l'agriculture de 1984*, Geneva.

Fourastier, Jean, 'Niveau de vie', in Jean Romoeuf, *Dictionnaire des Sciences Economiques*, Presses Universitaires de France, Paris, 1958, p. 800.

Gandhi, M., *Tous les hommes sont frères*, Gallimard, in the Collection 'Idées', Paris, 1969.

Garnier, Jean-Pierre, *Le Capitalisme high tec*, Spartacus, Paris, 1988.

Gilbert, Daniel, *Barriada Haute Espérance: récit d'une coopération au Pérou*, Karthala, 1990.

Girard, René, *Violence and the Sacred*, English translation, Johns Hopkins University Press, Baltimore, 1977. (French original: *La Violence et le sacré*, Grasset, Paris, 1972.)

Godelier, Maurice, *The Making of Great Men: male domination and power among the New Guinea Baruya*, translated by Rupert Swyer, Cambridge University Press, 1986. (French original: *La Production des grands hommes*, Fayard, Paris, 1982.)

Godelier, Maurice & Marilyn Strathern (editors), *Big Men and Great Men: personification of power in Melanesia*, Cambridge University Press, 1991.

Gouguet, Jean-Jacques, 'Du quatrième ordre au quart monde, les plus pauvres dans la démocratie, hier, aujourd'hui et demain', presented at the colloquium of the Mouvement ATD Quart Monde, Caen, October 1989.

Gouldner, Alvin W., 'La classe moyenne et l'esprit utilitaire', *Revue du MAUSS*, no. 5, 1989, pp. 14-38. (French translation of ch. 6 of *The Coming Crisis of Western Sociology*, Heinemann, London, 1971.)

Gouldner, Alvin W., *The Coming Crisis of Western Sociology*, Heinemann, London, 1971.

Harrison, Paul, *Inside the Third World*, Penguin Books, 1979.

Hayek, Friedrich A., *Law, Legislation, and Liberty*, 3 vols, Routledge & Kegan Paul, London, 1973-79.

Hecht, Jacqueline, 'De la Révolution scientifique à la Révolution culturelle: l'enseignement de l'économie politique', in Michel Servet (editor), *Idées économiques sous la Révolution 1789-1794*, Presses Universitaires de Lyon, Lyon, 1989.

Hegel, G.W.F., *Lectures on the History of Philosophy* (original *c.* 1830), translated from the German by E.S. Haldane & F.H. Simson, Kegan Paul, London, 1896, 3 vols.

Hegel, G.W.F., *Phenomenology of Spirit* (original 1807), translated from the German by A.V. Miller, Clarendon Press, Oxford, 1977.

Hugon, Philippe, 'Les petites activités marchandes dans les espaces urbains', *Revue Tiers Monde*, no. 82, April-June 1980, pp. 406-27.

Hugon, Philippe, 'Secteur informel et petite production marchande dans les villes du tiers monde', *Revue Tiers Monde*, no. 82, April-June 1980.

Hugon, Philippe (editor), *Nourrir les villes*, L'Harmattan, Paris, 1985.

Hussein, Mahmoud, *Le Versant sud de la liberté*, La Découverte, Paris, 1989.

Illich, Ivan, *Shadow Work*, Marion Boyars, London, 1981.

Illich, Ivan, *Tools for Conviviality*, Calder & Boyars, London, 1973.

Jackson, Michael, 'Un nouvel agenda pour les promoteurs des droits humains: les droits collectifs des nations autochtones', *Interculture*, no. 103, Montreal, Spring 1989.

Jaulin, Robert, 'Ethnocide, tiers monde, et ethno-développement', *Revue Tiers Monde*, no. 100, October-December 1984, pp. 913-27.

Jouvenel, Bertrand de, *Arcadie: essai sur le mieux-vivre*, Sedeis, Paris, 1968.

Judet, Pierre, 'Quand la Rhur entre au musée', *Revue Tiers Monde*, no. 118, April-June 1989, pp. 407-11.

Kamps, Michel, *Ouvriers et robots*, Spartacus, Paris, 1983.

Kennedy, John F., 'Inaugural Address to Congress', 20 January 1961, in *To Turn the Tide: a selection from President Kennedy's public statements 1961*, edited by John Gardner, Harper, New York, 1962.

Kern, Francis, 'La dynamique du marché intérieur comme stratégie de développement autonome', presented to an Alsace-Third World Conference in Strasbourg, 12-13 December 1986.

Kouchner, Bernard, *Charité business*, Le Pré-au-Clerc, Paris, 1986.

Kouchner, Bernard, 'Lutter pour les "boat-people" ', *Le Monde*, 16 March 1990.

Koyré, Alexandre, *Newtonian Studies*, Chapman & Hall, London, 1965.

Labonne, Michel, 'L'autosuffisance alimentaire en question', in Philippe Hugon (editor), *Nourrir les villes*, L'Harmattan, Paris, 1985.

Latouche, Serge, 'Les ambiguïtés de l'autosuffisance alimentaire', in *Cahiers lillois d'économie et de sociologie (Clés)*, no. 16, Lille, 2nd semester 1990.

Latouche, Serge, 'L'anthropologie et la clef du paradis perdu', in *L'Homme et la société*, no. 71-2, January-June 1984.

Latouche, Serge, *Critique de l'impérialisme: une analyse marxiste non-léniniste de l'impérialisme*, Editions Anthropos, Paris, 1979.

Latouche, Serge, *Epistémologie et économie: essai sur une anthropologie sociale freudo-marxiste*, Editions Anthropos, Paris, 1973.

Latouche, Serge, *Faut-il refuser le développement?*, Presses Universitaires de France, Paris, 1986.

Latouche, Serge, *L'Occidentalisation du monde: essai sur la signification, la portée et les limites de l'uniformisation planétaire*, La Découverte, Paris, 1989.

Latouche, Serge, *Le Procès de la science sociale*, Editions Anthropos, Paris, 1984.

Latouche, Serge, *Le Projet marxiste: analyse économique et matérialisme historique*, Presses Universitaires de France, Paris, 1975.

Latouche, Serge, 'Si la misère n'existait pas, il faudrait l'inventer', in G. Rist & F. Sabelli (editors), *Il était une fois le développement*, Editions d'En-Bas, Lausanne, 1986.

Latouche, Serge, 'Standard of living', in Wolfgang Sachs (editor), *The Development Dictionary*, Zed Books, London, 1992, pp. 250-63.

Lazard, Francette, 'Les "gagneurs" en crise?', Institut de Recherches Marxistes, October 1988.

Lévy, Pierre, *La Machine univers*, La Découverte, Paris, 1987.

Lie-Tsu, Chuang-Tzu, Lao Tzu et al., *Philosophes taoïstes*, Gallimard, Bibliothèque de la Pléiade, Paris, 1980.

Lipietz, Alain, *Choisir l'audace: une alternative pour le XXIe siècle*, La Découverte, Paris, 1989.

Malthus, Thomas, *Principles of Political Economy*, 1st edition, London, 1820; 2nd edition (1836), reprinted by Augustus Kelly, New York, 1968.

Manceaux, Michèle, *Le Fils de mon fils*, Plon, Paris, 1989.

Marx, Karl, *Capital*, Penguin/New Left Review, paperback edition, 1976.

McNamara, Robert, 'Address to the Board of Governors', World Bank, Nairobi, 24 September 1973. In Report WBI 3/2: G14, 1973.

Merchant, Carolyn, *The Death of Nature: women, ecology and the scientific revolution*, Harper & Row, San Francisco, 1980.

Mettelin, Pierre, 'Les conflits d'interprétation', in Penouil & Lachaud (editors), *Le Développement spontané des activités informelles en Afrique*, Pedone, 1985, pp. 70-103.

Meyssonnier, Simone, *La Balance et l'horloge: la genèse de la pensée libérale en France au 18ème siècle*, Editions de la Passion, Montreuil, 1989.

Miller, Jacques-Alain, 'Le despotisme de l'utile: la machine panoptique de Jeremy Bentham', *Ornicar*, no. 3, May 1975.

Mongin, Philippe, 'Le libéralisme, l'utilitarisme et l'économie politique classique dans l'interprétation d'Elie Halévy', *Revue du MAUSS*, no. 10, 1990, pp. 135-69.

Montesquieu, Charles de, *The Spirit of the Laws*, translated and edited by Anne Cohler, B.C. Miller & H.S. Stone, Cambridge University Press, 1989. (French original: *De l'esprit des lois*, Paris, 1748; new edition Belles Lettres, Paris, 1950.)

Morishima, Michio, *Why has Japan 'Succeeded'?: Western technology and the Japanese ethos*, Cambridge University Press, 1982.

Naipaul, V.S., *India: a wounded civilisation*, Alfred A. Knopf, New York, 1977.

NBER, *Studies in Income and Wealth (Problems in the International Comparison of Economic Accounts*, vol. XX), US National Bureau of Economic Research, Washington DC.

Ndione, Emmanuel, *Dynamique urbaine d'une société en grappe*, Enda, Dakar, 1987.

Necker, Jacques, *Sur la législation et le commerce des graines*, in *Oeuvres complètes*, vol. 1, new impression in series 'Scientia Antiqua' by K. Schill, 1971.

Niedergang, Marcel, 'Un écrivain dans le Pérou de tous les dangers', *Le Monde*, 4 April 1990.

Pack, Spencer J., *Capitalism as a Moral System: Adam Smith's critique of the free market economy*, Edward Elgar, Aldershot, 1991.

Panikkar, Raimundo, *Religion ou politique? Y a-t-il une solution au dilemme de l'Occident?*, *Religione e Politica*, Istituto di Studi Filosofici di Roma, 1978.

Partant, François, *Lettre au CCSC (Comité Chrétien de Solidarité avec les Chômeurs)*, confidential document.

Partant, François, *Que la crise s'aggrave*, Solin, Paris, 1978.

Paul VI, Pope, *Populorum Progressio*, Editions du Centurian et Editions Ouvrières, Paris, 1967.

Penouil, Marc & Jean-Pierre Lachaud (editors), *Le Développement spontané des activités informelles en Afrique*, Pedone, 1985.

Pere, Madeleine, *Les Lobi, tradition et changement*, Editions Siloe, Laval, 1988.

Perrot, Dominique, 'La "dimension culturelle du développement": un nouveau gadget', in the series *Cahiers lillois d'économie et de sociologie (Clés)*, no. 14, Lille, 2nd semester 1989.

Perrot, Dominique, 'Transferts de concepts et développement', *Bulletin du MAUSS*, no. 20, December 1986, pp. 103-20.

Platteau, Jean-Philippe, *Les Economistes classiques et le sous-développement*, 2 vols, Presses Universitaires de France, Paris, 1978.

Polanyi, Karl, *The Great Transformation*, Beacon Press, Boston, 1944; paperback edition 1957.

Popper, Karl, 'Conversation on economics', *Revue française d'economie*, no. 2, Autumn 1986, Fayard, Paris, p. 63.

Popper, Karl, *The Open Society and its Enemies*, 2 vols, Routledge & Kegan Paul, London, 1945.

Pourquery, Didier, 'Le mensonge, une arme économique', *Le Monde*, 12-13 November 1989.

Pradervand, Pierre, *Une Afrique en marche*, Plon, Paris, 1989.

Prouteau, Fréderic, 'Le capitalisme intelligent de la SIDI', *CFDT Magazine*, no. 158, March 1991.

Puel, Hugues, 'Peut-on connaître les besoins?', *Economie et humanisme*, no. 210, March-April 1973.

Radkowski, Georges Hubert, *Métamorphoses de la valeur: essai d'anthropologie économique*, Presses Universitaires de Grenoble, Grenoble, 1987.

Ramaholimihaso, Madeleine, *Quand la route est longue, la réflexion s'enrichit*, Madagascar Publishing Society, 1989.

Ravignan, François de, 'Les mythes de l'autosuffisance alimentaire', *Le Monde Diplomatique*, June 1987.

Requier-Desjardins, Denis, *L'Alimentation en Afrique: manger ce qu'on peut produire*, Karthala, PUSAF, 1989.

Riboud, Antoine, *Modernisation, mode d'emploi: rapport au Premier ministre*, Editions 10/18, 1987.

Richelieu, Cardinal, *Maximes*, Wittmann, Paris, 1944.

Robinson, Ronald (editor), *Industrialisation in Developing Countries: Proceedings of Conference, September 1964*, Cambridge University Overseas Studies Committee, Cambridge, 1965.

Rothkrug, Lionel, 'La réforme laïque: les précurseurs de l'utilitarisme', *Revue du MAUSS*, no. 5, 1989, pp. 99-124.

Sachs, Wolfgang, 'Le culte de l'efficience absolue', *Revue du MAUSS*, no. 3, 1989, pp. 85-95.

Sahlins, Marshall, *Stone Age Economics*, Aldine Atherton, Chicago, 1972.

Servet, Michel (editor), *Idées économiques sous la Révolution 1789-1794*, Presses Universitaires de Lyon, Lyon, 1989.

Smith, Adam, *An Inquiry into the Nature and Causes of the Wealth of Nations* (The Glasgow Edition, edited by R.H. Campbell, A.S. Skinner & W.B. Todd), Clarendon Press, Oxford, 1976.

Sombart, Werner, *Le Bourgeois*, Seuil, Paris, 1928; new impression by Petite Bibliothèque Payot, 1966.

Sorman, Guy, *La Nouvelle Richesse des nations*, Fayard, Paris, 1987.

Soto, Hernando de, *El Otro Sendero: la revolucion informal*, Ojeva Negra, Bogota, 1987.

Staël, Germaine de, *De l'Allemagne*, Editions Charpentier, 1839.

Stankiewicz, François, *Les Stratégies d'entreprises face aux ressources humaines*, Economica, Paris, 1988.

Théry, Daniel, 'Le biais mimétique dans le choix des techniques: un facteur d'asphyxie du développement autocentré de Tanzania', *Revue Tiers Monde*, no. 100, October-December 1984, pp. 787-800.

Théry, Daniel, 'La brique en Tunisie: une occasion manquée d'embrayage technologique endogène', *Bulletin NEED*, no. 6, CIRED, Paris, December 1987.

Tocqueville, Alexis de, *Democracy in America*, the Henry Reeve text, edited by Phillips Bradley, 2 vols, Vintage Books, New York, 1960. (French original: *De la démocratie en Amérique*, Paris, c. 1865; new edition Gallimard, Paris, 1986.)

Tocqueville, Alexis de, *The Old Regime and the French Revolution*, translated by Stuart Gilbert, Doubleday, New York, 1955; reprinted by P. Smith, Gloucester, Mass., 1978. (French original: *L'Ancien Régime et la Révolution*, Paris, c. 1887.)

Tolstoi, Leon, 'L'enfer reconstruit', in *Inédits*, Bonard, Paris, 1925.

Touré, Abdou, *Les Petits Métiers d'Abidjan*, Karthala, Paris, 1985.

Truman, Harry S., 'Address on Point 4', 24 June 1949, in *Harry S. Truman: documents*, Government Printing Office, Washington DC, 1961.

Truman, Harry S., 'Inaugural Address on the state of the Union', 20 January 1949, in *Harry S. Truman: documents*, Government Printing Office, Washington DC, 1961.

Turnbull, Colin, *The Mountain People*, Cape, London, 1973.

UNICEF, *L'Ajustement à visage humain: protéger les groupes vulnérables et favoriser la croissance*, Economica, Paris, 1987.

United Nations, *Report on International Definition and Measurement of Standard Levels of Living,* Document E.CN 5/299, 1954.

Veblen, Thorstein, *The Theory of the Leisure Class,* Vanguard Press, New York, 1928.

Verhelst, Thierry, *No Life without Roots,* Zed Books, London. (French original: *Des Racines pour vivre,* Duculot, Brussels, 1987.)

Vianes, André, 'La pensée du 19ème siècle face au premier centenaire', in Michel Servet (editor), *Idées économiques sous la Révolution 1789-1794,* Presses Universitaires de Lyon, Lyon, 1989.

Weber, Max, *The Protestant Ethic and the Spirit of Capitalism,* translation from the German by Talcott Parsons, Allen & Unwin, London, 1930; 2nd impression 1948.

World Bank (International Bank for Reconstruction and Development), *Third Annual Report 1947-1948.*

Xenophon, *Memoirs of Socrates and The Symposium,* translated by Hugh Tredennick, Penguin, 1970.

Yang, Shang, *The Book of Lord Shang* (*c.* 300 BC), translated from the Chinese by J.J.L. Duyvendak, University of Chicago Press, 1963.

Index